CSET Mathematics
110 Teacher Certification Exam
111
112
By: Sharon Wynne, M.S.
Southern Connecticut State University

XAMonline, INC.
Boston

Copyright © 2008 XAMonline, Inc.
All rights reserved. No part of the material protected by this copyright notice may be reproduced or utilized in any form or by any means, electronic or mechanical, including photocopying, recording or by any information storage and retrievable system, without written permission from the copyright holder.

To obtain permission(s) to use the material from this work for any purpose including workshops or seminars, please submit a written request to:

XAMonline, Inc.
21 Orient Ave.
Melrose, MA 02176
Toll Free 1-800-509-4128
Email: info@xamonline.com
Web www.xamonline.com
Fax: 1-781-662-9268

Library of Congress Cataloging-in-Publication Data

Wynne, Sharon A.
  Mathematics 110, 111, 112: Teacher Certification / Sharon A. Wynne. -2nd ed.
  ISBN 978-1-58197-285-6
  1. Mathematics 110, 111, 112.   2. Study Guides.   3. CSET
  4. Teachers' Certification & Licensure.   5. Careers

Disclaimer:

The opinions expressed in this publication are the sole works of XAMonline and were created independently from the National Education Association, Educational Testing Service, or any State Department of Education, National Evaluation Systems or other testing affiliates.

Between the time of publication and printing, state specific standards as well as testing formats and website information may change that is not included in part or in whole within this product. Sample test questions are developed by XAMonline and reflect similar content as on real tests; however, they are not former tests. XAMonline assembles content that aligns with state standards but makes no claims nor guarantees teacher candidates a passing score. Numerical scores are determined by testing companies such as NES or ETS and then are compared with individual state standards. A passing score varies from state to state.

Printed in the United States of America   œ - 1, 07

CSET: Mathematics 110, 111, 112
ISBN: 978-1-58197-285-6

TEACHER CERTIFICATION STUDY GUIDE

About the Subject Assessments

CSET™: Subject Assessment in the Mathematics examination

Purpose: The assessments are designed to test the knowledge and competencies of prospective secondary level teachers. The question bank from which the assessment is drawn is undergoing constant revision. As a result, your test may include questions that will not count towards your score.

Test Version: There are three versions of subject assessment for Mathematics tests in California. The Mathematics Subtest I (110) emphasizes comprehension in Algebra and Number Theory; Mathematics Subtest II (111) in Geometry Probability and Statistics; Mathematics Subtest III (112) for Calculus and the History of Mathematics. The first three subtests taken together represent the Single Subject Teaching Credential in Mathematics authorizing the teaching of all mathematics coursework. The Mathematics examination guide is based on a typical knowledge level of persons who have completed a *bachelor's degree program* in Mathematics.

Time Allowance and Format: You will have 5 hours to finish the test. Part of the test will consist of multiple-choice questions; part of the test will consist of focused and extended constructed-response questions. There are 90 multiple-choice questions and 12 focused constructed-response questions in the three subtests. If you fail one part of the exam, but not the other, you only need to re-take the part you have failed.

Weighting: There are 24 multiple-choice questions and 3 focused constructed-response questions in Subtest I for Algebra; 6 multiple-choice questions and 1 focused constructed-response questions for Number Theory. There are 22 multiple-choice questions and 3 focused constructed-response questions in Subtest II for Geometry; 8 multiple-choice questions and 1 focused constructed-response questions for Probability and Statistics. There are 26 multiple-choice questions and 3 focused constructed-response question in Subtest III in Calculus; 4 multiple-choice questions and 1 focused constructed-response question in the history of mathematics.

Additional Information about the CSET Assessments: The CSET™ series subject assessments are developed *National Evaluation Systems.* They provide additional information on the CSET series assessments, including registration, preparation and testing procedures, study materials such as three topical guides, one for each subtest, that are all together about 107 pages of information including approximately 57 additional sample questions.

MATHEMATICS

TEACHER CERTIFICATION STUDY GUIDE

TABLE OF CONTENTS

COMPETENCY 1.0 ALGEBRA

SKILL 1.1 ALGEBRAIC STRUCTURES

1.1a. Know why the real and complex numbers are each a field, and that particular rings are not fields (e.g., integers, polynomial rings, matrix rings) 1

1.1b. Apply basic properties of real and complex numbers in constructing mathematical arguments (e.g., if a < b and c < 0, then ac > bc) 3

1.1c. Know that the rational numbers and real numbers can be ordered and that the complex numbers cannot be ordered, but that any polynomial equation with real coefficients can be solved in the complex field 6

SKILL 1.2 POLYNOMIAL EQUATIONS AND INEQUALITIES

1.2a. Know why graphs of linear inequalities are half planes and be able to apply this fact (e.g., linear programming) 8

1.2b. Prove and use the following: the Rational Root Theorem for polynomials with integer coefficients; the Factor Theorem; the Conjugate Roots Theorem for polynomial equations with real coefficients; the Quadratic Formula for real and complex quadratic polynomials; the Binomial Theorem 15

1.2c. Analyze and solve polynomial equations with real coefficients using the Fundamental Theorem of Algebra 22

MATHEMATICS

TEACHER CERTIFICATION STUDY GUIDE

SKILL 1.3 FUNCTIONS

1.3a. Analyze and prove general properties of functions (i.e., domain and range, one-to-one, onto, inverses, composition, and differences between relations and functions) 27

1.3b. Analyze properties of polynomial, rational, radical, and absolute value functions in a variety of ways (e.g., graphing, solving problems) 30

1.3c. Analyze properties of exponential and logarithmic functions in a variety of ways (e.g., graphing, solving problems) 41

SKILL 1.4 LINEAR ALGEBRA

1.4a. Understand and apply the geometric interpretation and basic operations of vectors in two and three dimensions, including their scalar multiples and scalar (dot) and cross products 46

1.4b. Prove the basic properties of vectors (e.g., perpendicular vectors have zero dot product) 51

1.4c. Understand and apply the basic properties and operations of matrices and determinants (e.g., to determine the solvability of linear systems of equations) 54

COMPETENCY 2.0 GEOMETRY

SKILL 2.1 Parallelism

2.1a. Know the Parallel Postulate and its implications, and justify its equivalents (e.g., the Alternate Interior Angle Theorem, the angle sum of every triangle is 180 degrees) 61

2.1b. Know that variants of the Parallel Postulate produce non-Euclidean geometries (e.g., spherical, hyperbolic) 65

SKILL 2.2 PLANE EUCLIDEAN GEOMETRY

2.2a. Prove theorems and solve problems involving similarity and congruence 67

2.2b. Understand, apply, and justify properties of triangles (e.g., the Exterior Angle Theorem, concurrence theorems, trigonometric ratios, Triangle Inequality, Law of Sines, Law of Cosines, the Pythagorean Theorem and its converse) 78

2.2c. Understand, apply, and justify properties of polygons and circles from an advanced standpoint (e.g., derive the area formulas for regular polygons and circles from the area of a triangle) 91

2.2d. Justify and perform the classical constructions (e.g., angle bisector, perpendicular bisector, replicating shapes, regular n-gons for n equal to 3, 4, 5, 6, and 8) 106

2.2e. Use techniques in coordinate geometry to prove geometric theorems 113

SKILL 2.3 THREE-DIMENSIONAL GEOMETRY

2.3a. Demonstrate an understanding of parallelism and perpendicularity of lines and planes in three dimensions 117

2.3b. Understand, apply, and justify properties of three-dimensional objects from an advanced standpoint (e.g., derive the volume and surface area formulas for prisms, pyramids, cones, cylinders, and spheres) 120

SKILL 2.4 TRANSFORMATIONAL GEOMETRY

2.4a. Demonstrate an understanding of the basic properties of isometries in two- and three-dimensional space (e.g., rotation, translation, reflection) 124

2.4b. Understand and prove the basic properties of dilations (e.g., similarity transformations or change of scale) 130

COMPETENCY 3.0 NUMBER THEORY

SKILL 3.1 NATURAL NUMBERS

3.1a. Prove and use basic properties of natural numbers (e.g., properties of divisibility) 133

3.1b. Use the Principle of Mathematical Induction to prove results in number theory 136

3.1c. Know and apply the Euclidean Algorithm 138

3.1d. Apply the Fundamental Theorem of Arithmetic (e.g., find the greatest common factor and the least common multiple, show that every fraction is equivalent to a unique fraction where the numerator and denominator are relatively prime, prove that the square root of any number, not a perfect square number, is irrational) 139

COMPETENCY 4.0 PROBABILITY AND STATISTICS

SKILL 4.1 PROBABILITY

4.1a. Prove and apply basic principles of permutations and combinations 142

4.1b. Illustrate finite probability using a variety of examples and models (e.g., the fundamental counting principles) 146

4.1c. Use and explain the concept of conditional probability 150

4.1d. Interpret the probability of an outcome 152

4.1e. Use normal, binomial, and exponential distributions to solve and interpret probability problems 153

TEACHER CERTIFICATION STUDY GUIDE

SKILL 4.2 STATISTICS

4.2a. Compute and interpret the mean, median, and mode of both discrete and continuous distributions 157

4.2b. Compute and interpret quartiles, range, variance, and standard deviation of both discrete and continuous distributions 162

4.2c. Select and evaluate sampling methods appropriate to a task (e.g., random, systematic, cluster, convenience sampling) and display the results 168

4.2d. Know the method of least squares and apply it to linear regression and correlation 173

4.2e. Know and apply the chi-square test 179

COMPETENCY 5.0 CALCULUS

SKILL 5.1 TRIGONOMETRY

5.1a. Prove that the Pythagorean Theorem is equivalent to the trigonometric identity $\sin^2 x + \cos^2 x = 1$ and that this identity leads to $1 + \tan^2 x = \sec^2 x$ and $1 + \cot^2 x = \csc^2 x$ 182

5.1b. Prove the sine, cosine, and tangent sum formulas for all real values, and derive special applications of the sum formulas (e.g., double angle, half angle) 184

5.1c. Analyze properties of trigonometric functions in a variety of ways (e.g., graphing and solving problems) 191

5.1d. Know and apply the definitions and properties of inverse trigonometric functions (i.e., arcsin, arccos, and arctan) 197

5.1e. Understand and apply polar representations of complex numbers (e.g., DeMoivre's Theorem) 201

TEACHER CERTIFICATION STUDY GUIDE

SKILL 5.2 LIMITS AND CONTINUITY

5.2a. Derive basic properties of limits and continuity, including the Sum, Difference, Product, Constant Multiple, and Quotient Rules, using the formal definition of a limit 205

5.2b. Show that a polynomial function is continuous at a point 211

5.2c. Know and apply the Intermediate Value Theorem, using the geometric implications of continuity 215

SKILL 5.3 DERIVATICES AND APPLICATIONS

5.3a. Derive the rules of differentiation for polynomial, trigonometric, and logarithmic functions using the formal definition of derivative 217

5.3b. Interpret the concept of derivative geometrically, numerically, and analytically (i.e., slope of the tangent, limit of difference quotients, extrema, Newton's method, and instantaneous rate of change) 225

5.3c. Interpret both continuous and differentiable functions geometrically and analytically and apply Rolle's Theorem, the Mean Value Theorem, and L'Hopital's rule 232

5.3d. Use the derivative to solve rectilinear motion, related rate, and optimization problems 238

5.3e. Use the derivative to analyze functions and planar curves (e.g., maxima, minima, inflection points, concavity) 242

5.3f. Solve separable first-order differential equations and apply them to growth and decay problems 249

MATHEMATICS   vii

SKILL 5.4 INTEGRALS AND APPLICATIONS

5.4a. Derive definite integrals of standard algebraic functions using the formal definition of integral 255

5.4b. Interpret the concept of a definite integral geometrically, numerically, and analytically (e.g., limit of Riemann sums) 261

5.4c. Prove the Fundamental Theorem of Calculus, and use it to interpret definite integrals as antiderivatives 263

5.4d. Apply the concept of integrals to compute the length of curves and the areas and volumes of geometric figures 266

SKILL 5.5 SEQUENCES AND SERIES

5.5a. Derive and apply the formulas for the sums of finite arithmetic series and finite and infinite geometric series (e.g., express repeating decimals as a rational number) 272

5.5b. Determine convergence of a given sequence or series using standard techniques (e.g., Ratio, Comparison, Integral Tests) ... 279

5.5c. Calculate Taylor series and Taylor polynomials of basic functions 283

COMPETENCY 6.0 HISTORY OF MATHEMATICS

SKILL 6.1 CHRONOLOGICAL AND TOPICAL DEVELOPMENT OF MATHEMATICS

6.1a. Demonstrate understanding of the development of mathematics, its cultural connections, and its contributions to society 286

6.1b. Demonstrate understanding of the historical development of mathematics, including the contributions of diverse populations as determined by race, ethnicity, culture, geography, and gender 287

CONSTRUCTED RESPONSE EXAMPLES 289

CURRICULUM AND INSTRUCTION 295

SAMPLE TEST 301

ANSWER KEY 314

RIGOR TABLE 315

RATIONALES WITH SAMPLE QUESTIONS 316

TEACHER CERTIFICATION STUDY GUIDE

Great Study and Testing Tips!

What to study in order to prepare for the subject assessments is the focus of this study guide but equally important is *how* you study.

You can increase your chances of truly mastering the information by taking some simple, but effective steps.

Study Tips:

1. Some foods aid the learning process. Foods such as milk, nuts, seeds, rice, and oats help your study efforts by releasing natural memory enhancers called CCKs (*cholecystokinin*) composed of *tryptophan*, *choline*, and *phenylalanine*. All of these chemicals enhance the neurotransmitters associated with memory. Before studying, try a light, protein-rich meal of eggs, turkey, and fish. All of these foods release the memory enhancing chemicals. The better the connections, the more you comprehend.

Likewise, before you take a test, stick to a light snack of energy boosting and relaxing foods. A glass of milk, a piece of fruit, or some peanuts all release various memory-boosting chemicals and help you to relax and focus on the subject at hand.

2. Learn to take great notes. A by-product of our modern culture is that we have grown accustomed to getting our information in short doses (i.e. TV news sound bites or USA Today style newspaper articles.)

Consequently, we've subconsciously trained ourselves to assimilate information better in neat little packages. If your notes are scrawled all over the paper, it fragments the flow of the information. Strive for clarity. Newspapers use a standard format to achieve clarity. Your notes can be much clearer through use of proper formatting. A very effective format is called the *"Cornell Method."*

> Take a sheet of loose-leaf lined notebook paper and draw a line all the way down the paper about 1-2" from the left-hand edge.
>
> Draw another line across the width of the paper about 1-2" up from the bottom. Repeat this process on the reverse side of the page.

Look at the highly effective result. You have ample room for notes, a left hand margin for special emphasis items or inserting supplementary data from the textbook, a large area at the bottom for a brief summary, and a little rectangular space for just about anything you want.

MATHEMATICS

TEACHER CERTIFICATION STUDY GUIDE

3. Get the concept then the details. Too often we focus on the details and don't gather an understanding of the concept. However, if you simply memorize only dates, places, or names, you may well miss the whole point of the subject.

A key way to understand things is to put them in your own words. If you are working from a textbook, automatically summarize each paragraph in your mind. If you are outlining text, don't simply copy the author's words.

Rephrase them in your own words. You remember your own thoughts and words much better than someone else's, and subconsciously tend to associate the important details to the core concepts.

4. Ask Why? Pull apart written material paragraph by paragraph and don't forget the captions under the illustrations.

Example: If the heading is "Stream Erosion", flip it around to read "Why do streams erode?" Then answer the questions.

If you train your mind to think in a series of questions and answers, not only will you learn more, but it also helps to lessen the test anxiety because you are used to answering questions.

5. Read for reinforcement and future needs. Even if you only have 10 minutes, put your notes or a book in your hand. Your mind is similar to a computer; you have to input data in order to have it processed. *By reading, you are creating the neural connections for future retrieval.* The more times you read something, the more you reinforce the learning of ideas.

Even if you don't fully understand something on the first pass, *your mind stores much of the material for later recall.*

6. Relax to learn so go into exile. Our bodies respond to an inner clock called biorhythms. Burning the midnight oil works well for some people, but not everyone.

If possible, set aside a particular place to study that is free of distractions. Shut off the television, cell phone, pager and exile your friends and family during your study period.

If you really are bothered by silence, try background music. Light classical music at a low volume has been shown to aid in concentration over other types. Music that evokes pleasant emotions without lyrics are highly suggested. Try just about anything by Mozart. It relaxes you.

MATHEMATICS

7. Use arrows not highlighters. At best, it's difficult to read a page full of yellow, pink, blue, and green streaks. Try staring at a neon sign for a while and you'll soon see that the horde of colors obscure the message.

A quick note, a brief dash of color, an underline, and an arrow pointing to a particular passage is much clearer than a horde of highlighted words.

8. Budget your study time. Although you shouldn't ignore any of the material, *allocate your available study time in the same ratio that topics may appear on the test.*

TEACHER CERTIFICATION STUDY GUIDE

Testing Tips:

1. Get smart, play dumb. **Don't read anything into the question.** Don't make an assumption that the test writer is looking for something else than what is asked. Stick to the question as written and don't read extra things into it.

2. Read the question and all the choices *twice* before answering the question. You may miss something by not carefully reading, and then re-reading both the question and the answers.

If you really don't have a clue as to the right answer, leave it blank on the first time through. Go on to the other questions, as they may provide a clue as to how to answer the skipped questions.

If later on, you still can't answer the skipped ones . . . *Guess.* The only penalty for guessing is that you *might* get it wrong. Only one thing is certain; if you don't put anything down, you will get it wrong!

3. Turn the question into a statement. Look at the way the questions are worded. The syntax of the question usually provides a clue. Does it seem more familiar as a statement rather than as a question? Does it sound strange?

By turning a question into a statement, you may be able to spot if an answer sounds right, and it may also trigger memories of material you have read.

4. Look for hidden clues. It's actually very difficult to compose multiple-foil (choice) questions without giving away part of the answer in the options presented.

In most multiple-choice questions you can often readily eliminate one or two of the potential answers. This leaves you with only two real possibilities and automatically your odds go to Fifty-Fifty for very little work.

5. Trust your instincts. For every fact that you have read, you subconsciously retain something of that knowledge. On questions that you aren't really certain about, go with your basic instincts. **Your first impression on how to answer a question is usually correct.**

6. Mark your answers directly on the test booklet. Don't bother trying to fill in the optical scan sheet on the first pass through the test.

Just be very careful not to miss-mark your answers when you eventually transcribe them to the scan sheet.

7. Watch the clock! You have a set amount of time to answer the questions. Don't get bogged down trying to answer a single question at the expense of 10 questions you can more readily answer.

MATHEMATICS

THIS PAGE BLANK

TEACHER CERTIFICATION STUDY GUIDE

COMPETENCY 1.0 ALGEBRA

SKILL 1.1 ALGEBRAIC STRUCTURES

1.1a. **Know why the real and complex numbers are each a field, and that particular rings are not fields (e.g., integers, polynomial rings, matrix rings)**

Algebra must be systematically organized in order to create the axioms for sets of numbers. The binary relation symbols +, −, · and ÷ are operators that require two inputs and obey the algebraic axioms of field theory. Any set that includes at least two nonzero elements that satisfies the field axioms for addition and multiplication is a **field**. The real numbers, $\mathbb{R}$, as well as the complex numbers, $\mathbb{C}$, are each a field, with the real numbers being a subset of the complex numbers. The field axioms are summarized below.

Addition:

Commutativity	$a + b = b + a$
Associativity	$a + (b + c) = (a + b) + c$
Identity	$a + 0 = a$
Inverse	$a + (-a) = 0$

Multiplication:

Commutativity	$ab = ba$
Associativity	$a(bc) = (ab)c$
Identity	$a \cdot 1 = a$
Inverse	$a \cdot \dfrac{1}{a} = 1 \quad (a \neq 0)$

Addition and multiplication:

Distributivity	$a(b+c) = (b+c)a = ab + ac$

Note that both the real numbers and the complex numbers satisfy the axioms summarized above.

MATHEMATICS 1

A **ring** is an integral domain with two binary operations (addition and multiplication) where, for every non-zero element a and b in the domain, the product ab is non-zero. A field is a ring where multiplication is commutative, or $a \cdot b = b \cdot a$, and all non-zero elements have a multiplicative inverse. The set $\mathbb{Z}$ (integers) is a ring that is not a field in that it does not have the multiplicative inverse; therefore, integers are not a field. A polynomial ring is also not a field, as it also has no multiplicative inverse. Furthermore, matrix rings do not constitute fields because matrix multiplication is not generally commutative.

Note: Multiplication is implied when there is no symbol between two variables. Thus, $a \times b$ can be written ab. Multiplication can also be indicated by a raised dot ($\cdot$).

TEACHER CERTIFICATION STUDY GUIDE

1.1b. Apply basic properties of real and complex numbers in constructing mathematical arguments (e.g., if a < b and c < 0, then ac > bc)

Basic Properties of Real and Imaginary/Complex Numbers

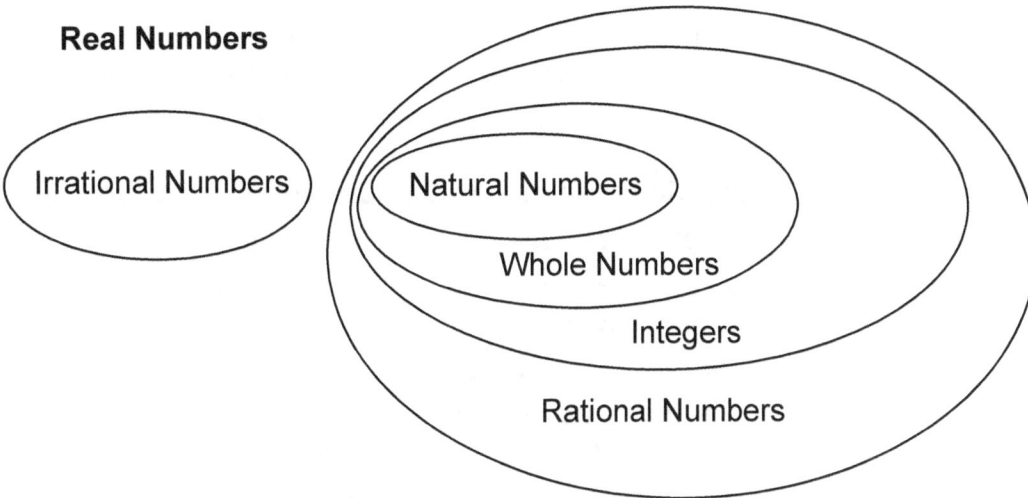

Real numbers are denoted by $\mathbb{R}$ and are numbers that can be shown by an infinite decimal representation such as 3.286275347.... Real numbers include rational numbers, such as 242 and −23/129, and irrational numbers, such as the $\sqrt{2}$ and π, can be represented as points along an infinite number line. Real numbers are also known as "the unique complete Archimedean *ordered field*." Real numbers are to be distinguished from imaginary numbers.

Real numbers are classified as follows:

A. **Natural numbers, denoted by** $\mathbb{N}$: the counting numbers, 1, 2, 3,....

B. **Whole numbers**: the counting numbers along with zero, 0, 1, 2, 3,....

C. **Integers, denoted by** $\mathbb{Z}$: the counting numbers, their negatives, and zero, ...,−2, −1, 0, 1, 2,....

D. Rationals, denoted by $\mathbb{Q}$: all of the fractions that can be formed using whole numbers. Zero cannot be the denominator. In decimal form, these numbers will either be terminating or repeating decimals. Simplify square roots to determine if the number can be written as a fraction.

E. Irrationals: Real numbers that cannot be written as a fraction. The decimal forms of these numbers are neither terminating nor repeating. Examples include π, e and $\sqrt{2}$.

Imaginary and complex numbers are denoted by $\mathbb{C}$. The set $\mathbb{C}$ is defined as $\{a+bi : a, b \in \mathbb{R}\}$ ($\in$ means "element of"). In other words, complex numbers are an extension of real numbers made by attaching an imaginary number i, which satisfies the equality $i^2 = -1$. Complex numbers are of the form **a + bi**, where a and b are *real* numbers and $i = \sqrt{-1}$. Thus, a is the real part of the number and b is the imaginary part of the number. When *i* appears in a fraction, the fraction is usually simplified so that *i* is not in the denominator. The set of complex numbers includes the set of real numbers, where any real number *n* can be written in its equivalent complex form as *n* + 0*i*. In other words, it can be said that $\mathbb{R} \subseteq \mathbb{C}$ (or $\mathbb{R}$ is a subset of $\mathbb{C}$).

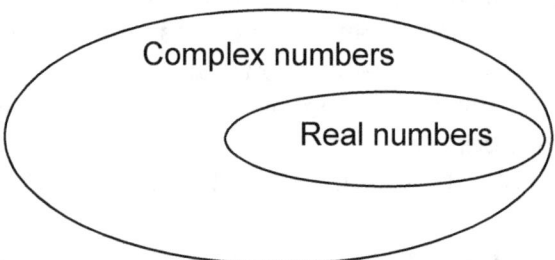

The number 3*i* has a real part 0 and imaginary part 3; the number 4 has a real part 4 and an imaginary part 0. As another way of writing complex numbers, we can express them as ordered pairs:

Complex number	Ordered pair
$3 + 2i$	$(3, 2)$
$\sqrt{3} + \sqrt{3}i$	$(\sqrt{3}, \sqrt{3})$
$7i$	$(0, 7)$
$\dfrac{6 + 2i}{7}$	$\left(\dfrac{6}{7}, \dfrac{2}{7}\right)$

These properties of real and complex numbers can be applied to the construction of various mathematical arguments. A **mathematical argument** proves that a proposition is true.

Example: Prove that for every integer y, if y is an even number, then y^2 is even.

The definition of even implies that for each integer y there is at least one integer x such that $y = 2x$.

$$y = 2x$$
$$y^2 = 4x^2$$

Since $4x^2$ is always evenly divisible by two ($2x^2$ is an integer), y^2 is even for all values of y.

Example: If a, b, and c are positive real numbers, prove that $c(a+b) = (b+a)c$.

Use the properties of the set of real numbers.

$$c(a+b) = c(b+a) \quad \text{Additive commutativity}$$
$$= cb + ca \quad \text{Distributivity}$$
$$= bc + ac \quad \text{Multiplicative commutativity}$$
$$= (b+a)c \quad \text{Distributivity}$$

Example: Given real numbers a, b, c and d where $ad = -bc$, prove that $(a + bi)(c + di)$ is real.

Expand the product of the complex numbers.

$$(a+bi)(c+di) = ac + bci + adi + bdi^2$$

Use the definition of i^2.

$$(a+bi)(c+di) = ac - bd + bci + adi$$

Apply the fact that $ad = -bc$.

$$(a+bi)(c+di) = ac - bd + bci - bci = ac - bd$$

Since a, b, c and d are all real, $ac - bd$ must also be real.

MATHEMATICS

1.1c. **Know that the rational numbers and real numbers can be ordered and that the complex numbers cannot be ordered, but that any polynomial equation with real coefficients can be solved in the complex field**

The previous skill section reviews the properties of both real and complex numbers. Based on these properties, it can be shown that real and rational numbers can be ordered but complex numbers cannot be ordered.

Real numbers are an ordered field and can be ordered. As such, an ordered field F must contain a subset P (such as the positive numbers) such that if a and b are elements of P, then both $a + b$ and ab are also elements of P. (In other words, the set P is closed under addition and multiplication.) Furthermore, it must be the case that for any element c contained in F, exactly one of the following conditions is true: c is an element of P, $-c$ is an element of P or
$c = 0$.

Likewise, **the rational numbers also constitute an ordered field**. The set P can be defined as the positive rational numbers. For each a and b that are elements of the set $\mathbb{Q}$ (the rational numbers), $a + b$ is also an element of P, as is ab. (The sum $a + b$ and the product ab are both rational if a and b are rational.) Since P is closed under addition and multiplication, $\mathbb{Q}$ constitutes an ordered field.

Complex numbers, unlike real numbers, cannot be ordered. Consider the number $i = \sqrt{-1}$ contained in the set $\mathbb{C}$ of complex numbers. Assume that $\mathbb{C}$ has a subset P (positive numbers) that is closed under both addition and multiplication. Assume that $i > 0$. A difficulty arises in that $i^2 = -1 < 0$, so i cannot be included in the set P. Likewise, assume $i < 0$. The problem once again arises that $i^4 = 1 > 0$, so i cannot be included in P. It is clearly the case that $i \neq 0$, so there is no place for i in an ordered field. Thus, the complex numbers cannot be ordered.

Polynomial equations with real coefficients cannot, in general, be solved using only real numbers. For instance, consider the quadratic function given below:

$$f(x) = x^2 + 1$$

There are no real roots for this equation, since

$$f(x) = 0 = x^2 + 1 \Rightarrow x^2 = -1$$

The Fundamental Theorem of Algebra, however, indicates that there must be two (possibly non-distinct) solutions to this equation. (See Skill 1.2c for more on the Fundamental Theorem of Algebra.) Not that if the complex numbers are permitted as solutions to this equation, then

$$x = \pm i$$

Thus, generally, solutions to any polynomial equation with real coefficients exist in the set of complex numbers.

SKILL 1.2 POLYNOMIAL EQUATIONS AND INEQUALITIES

1.2a. **Know why graphs of linear inequalities are half planes and be able to apply this fact (e.g., linear programming)**

Linear Inequalities

To graph **a linear inequality** expressed in terms of y, solve the inequality for y. This renders the inequality in **slope-intercept form** (for example: $y < mx + b$). The point $(0, b)$ is the y-intercept and m is the slope of the line. If the inequality is expressed only in terms of x, solve for x. When solving the inequality, remember that dividing or multiplying by a negative number will reverse the direction of the inequality sign.

An inequality that yields any of the following results in terms of y, where a is some real number, then the solution set of the inequality is bounded by a **horizontal line**:

$$y < a \qquad y \leq a \qquad y > a \qquad y \geq a$$

If the inequality yields any of the following results in terms of x, then the solution set of the inequality is bounded by a **vertical line**:

$$x < a \qquad x \leq a \qquad x > a \qquad x \geq a$$

When graphing the solution of a linear inequality, the boundary line is drawn in a dotted manner if the inequality sign is $<$ or $>$. This indicates that points on the line do not satisfy the inequality. If the inequality sign is either $\geq$ or $\leq$, then the line on the graph is drawn as a solid line to indicate that the points on the line satisfy the inequality.

The line drawn as directed above is only the boundary of the solution set for an inequality. The solutions actually include the half plane bounded by the line. Since, for any line, half of the values in the full plane (for either x or y) are greater than those defined by the line and half are less, the solution of the inequality must be graphed as a half plane. (In other words, a line divides the plane in half.) Which half plane satisfies the inequality can be found by testing a point on either side of the line. The solution set can be indicated on a graph by shading the appropriate half plane.

For inequalities expressed as a function of x, shade above the line when the inequality sign is $\geq$ or $>$. Shade below the line when the inequality sign is $<$ or $\leq$. For inequalities expressed as a function of y, shade to the right for $>$ or $\geq$. Shade to the left for $<$ or $\leq$.

The solution to a system of linear inequalities consists of the portion of the graph where the shaded half planes for all the inequalities in the system overlap. For instance, if the graph of one inequality was shaded with red, and the graph of another inequality was shaded with blue, then the overlapping area would be shaded purple. The points in the purple area would be the solution set of this system.

Example: Solve by graphing:

$$x + y \leq 6$$
$$x - 2y \leq 6$$

Solving the inequalities for y, they become the following:

$y \leq -x + 6$ (y-intercept of 6 and slope of –1)

$y \geq \frac{1}{2}x - 3$ (y-intercept of –3 and slope of 1/2)

A graph with the appropriate shading is shown below:

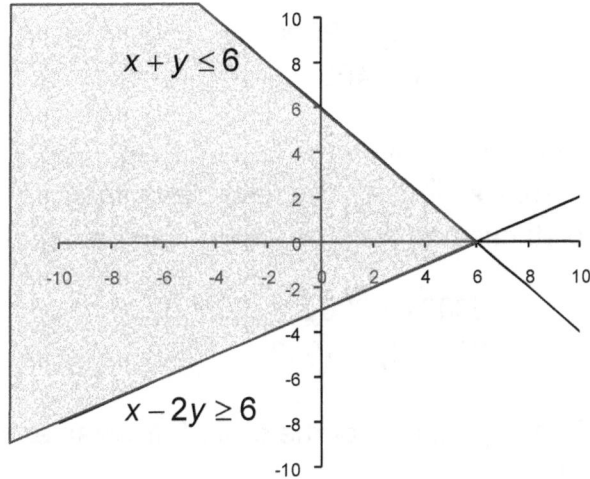

Linear programming, or linear optimization, involves finding a maximum or minimum value for a linear function subject to certain constraints (such as other linear functions or restrictions on the variables). Linear programming can be used to solve various types of practical, real-world word problems. It is often used in various industries, ecological sciences and governmental organizations to determine or project, for instance, production costs or the amount of pollutants dispersed into the air. The key to most linear programming problems is to organize the information in the word problem into a chart or graph of some type. By plotting the inequalities that define the problem, for instance, the range of possible solutions can be shown visually.

Example: A printing manufacturer makes two types of printers: a Printmaster and a Speedmaster printer. The Printmaster requires 10 cubic feet of space, weighs 5,000 pounds and the Speedmaster takes up 5 cubic feet of space and weighs 600 pounds. The total available space for storage before shipping is 2,000 cubic feet and the weight limit for the space is 300,000 pounds. The profit on the Printmaster is $125,000 and the profit on the Speedmaster is $30,000. How many of each machine should be stored to maximize profitability and what is the maximum possible profit?

First, let x represent the number of Printmaster units sold and let y represent the number of Speedmaster units sold. Then, the equation for the space required to store the units is the following.

$$10x + 5y \leq 2000$$
$$2x + y \leq 400$$

Since the number of units for both models must be no less than zero, also impose the restrictions that $x \geq 0$ and $y \geq 0$. The restriction on the total weight can be expressed as follows.

$$5000x + 600y \leq 300000$$
$$25x + 3y \leq 1500$$

The expression for the profit P from sales of the printer units is the following.

$$P = \$125,000x + \$30,000y$$

The solution to this problem, then, is found by maximizing P subject to the constraints given in the preceding inequalities, along with the constraints that $x \geq 0$ and $y \geq 0$. The equations are grouped below for clarity.

$$x \geq 0$$
$$y \geq 0$$
$$2x + y \leq 400$$
$$25x + 3y \leq 1500$$
$$P = \$125,000x + \$30,000y$$

The two inequalities in two variables are plotted in the graph below. The shaded region represents the set of solutions that obey both inequalities. (Note that the shaded region in fact only includes points where both x and y are whole numbers.)

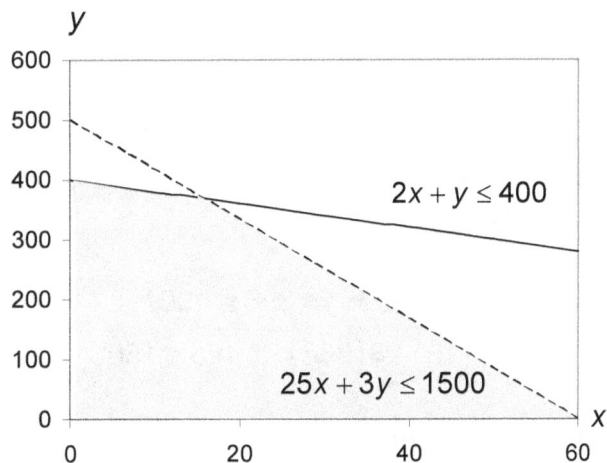

Note that the border of the shaded region that is formed by the two inequalities includes the solutions that constitute the maximum value of y for a given value of x. Note also that x cannot exceed 60 (since it would violate the second inequality). The solution to the problem, then, must lie on the border of the shaded region, since the border spans all the possible solutions that maximize the use of space and weight for a given number x.

To visualize the solution, plot the profit as a function of the solutions to the inequalities that lie along the border of the shaded area.

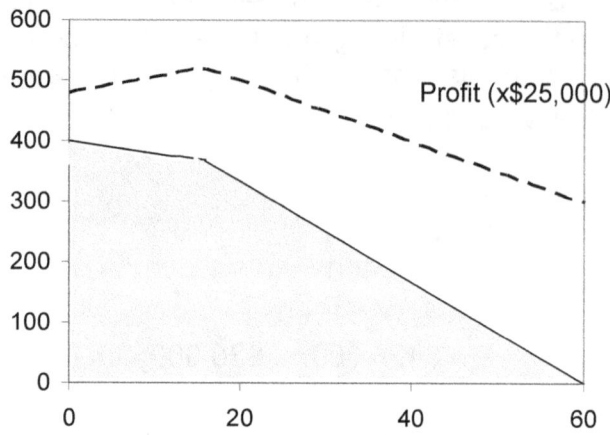

The profit curve shows a maximum at about $x = 16$. Test several values using a table to verify this result.

x	y	P (x$25,000)
15	370	519
16	366	519.2
17	358	514.6

Also double check to be sure that the result obeys the two inequalities.

$$2(16) + (366) = 398 \leq 400$$
$$25(16) + 3(366) = 1498 \leq 1500$$

Thus, the optimum result is storage of 16 Printmaster and 366 Speedmaster printer units.

Example: Sharon's Bike Shoppe can assemble a 3-speed bike in 30 minutes and a 10-speed bike in 60 minutes. The profit on each bike sold is $60 for a 3 speed or $75 for a 10-speed bike. How many of each type of bike should it assemble during an 8-hour day (480 minutes) to maximize the possible profit? Total daily profit must be at least $300.

Let x be the number of 3-speed bikes and y be the number of 10-speed bikes. Since there are only 480 minutes to use each day, the first inequality is the following.

$$30x + 60y \leq 480$$
$$x + 2y \leq 16$$

Since the total daily profit must be at least $300, then the second inequality can be written as follows, where P is the profit for the day.

$$P = \$60x + \$75y \geq \$300$$
$$4x + 5y \geq 20$$

To visualize the problem, plot the two inequalities and show the potential solutions as a shaded region.

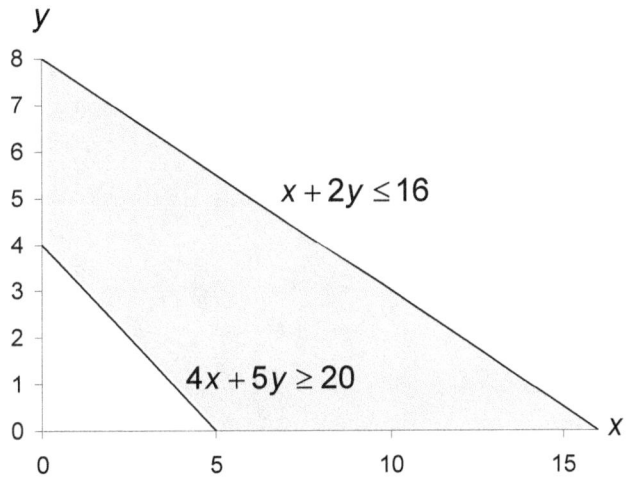

The solution to the problem is the ordered pair of whole numbers in the shaded area that maximizes the daily profit. The profit curve is added as shown below.

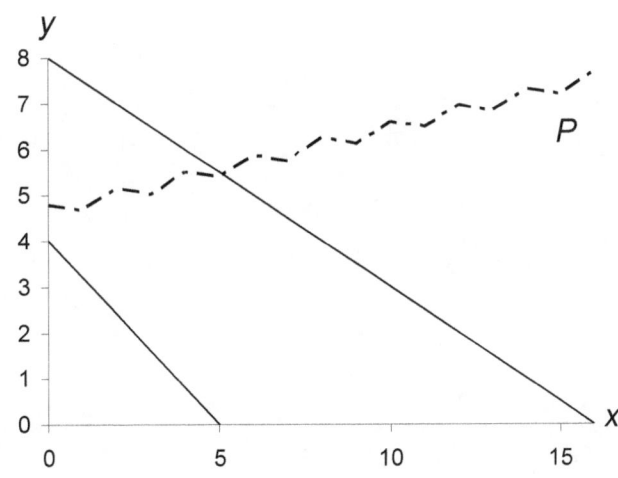

Based on the above plot, it is clear that the profit is maximized for the case where only 3-speed bikes (corresponding to x) are manufactured. Thus, the correct solution can be found by solving the first inequality for $y = 0$.

$$x + 2(0) \leq 16$$
$$x \leq 16$$

The manufacture of 16 3-speed bikes (and no 10-speed bikes) maximizes profit to $960 per day.

1.2b. Prove and use the following: the Rational Root Theorem for polynomials with integer coefficients; the Factor Theorem; the Conjugate Roots Theorem for polynomial equations with real coefficients; the Quadratic Formula for real and complex quadratic polynomials; the Binomial Theorem

A **polynomial** is a sum of terms where each term is a constant multiplied by a variable raised to a positive integer power. The general form of a polynomial $P(x)$ is

$$P(x) = a_n x^n + a_{n-1} x^{n-1} + \ldots + a_2 x^2 + a_1 x + a_0$$

Polynomials written in **standard form** have the terms written in decreasing exponent value, as shown above. The above example is a "degree n" polynomial (assuming $a_n \neq 0$) because the exponent of the first term is n. A particular case of a polynomial is the quadratic equation, which is degree two.

The Rational Root Theorem

The Rational Root Theorem, also known as the Rational Zero Theorem, allows determination of all possible rational roots (or zeroes) of a polynomial equation with integer coefficients. (A root is a value of x such that $P(x) = 0$.) Every rational root of $P(x)$ can be written as $x = \dfrac{p}{q}$, where p is an integer factor of the constant term a_0 and q is an integer factor of the leading coefficient a_n.

To prove the Rational Root Theorem, first assume that $x = \dfrac{p}{q}$ is a root of $P(x)$, where p and q are integers with a greatest common denominator (GCD) of 1. Then:

$$P\left(\frac{p}{q}\right) = a_n \left(\frac{p}{q}\right)^n + a_{n-1} \left(\frac{p}{q}\right)^{n-1} + \ldots + a_2 \left(\frac{p}{q}\right)^2 + a_1 \left(\frac{p}{q}\right) + a_0 = 0$$

Multiply the entire expression by q^n.

$$a_n p^n + a_{n-1} p^{n-1} q + \ldots + a_2 p^2 q^{n-2} + a_1 p q^{n-1} + a_0 q^n = 0$$

Since each coefficient a_i is an integer, as are p and q, each term in the above expression must also be an integer. Consequently, any partial sum of the terms is an integer as well. Rewrite the sum as follows.

$$a_n p^n = -a_{n-1} p^{n-1} q - \ldots - a_2 p^2 q^{n-2} - a_1 p q^{n-1} - a_0 q^n$$

$$a_n p^n = q\left(-a_{n-1} p^{n-1} q^0 - \ldots - a_2 p^2 q^{n-3} - a_1 p q^{n-2} - a_0 q^{n-1}\right)$$

$$\frac{a_n p^n}{q} = \left(-a_{n-1} p^{n-1} q^0 - \ldots - a_2 p^2 q^{n-3} - a_1 p q^{n-2} - a_0 q^{n-1}\right)$$

Since p is not divisible by q (the GCD of p and q is 1), a_n must be divisible by q since the sum in the parentheses is an integer. Likewise,

$$a_0 q^n = p\left(-a_n p^{n-1} - a_{n-1} p^{n-2} q - \ldots - a_2 p^1 q^{n-2} - a_1 q^{n-1}\right)$$

$$\frac{a_0 q^n}{p} = \left(-a_n p^{n-1} - a_{n-1} p^{n-2} q - \ldots - a_2 p^1 q^{n-2} - a_1 q^{n-1}\right)$$

By the same reasoning, a_0 must be divisible by p. The theorem has thus been proven, since p is a factor of a_0 and q is a factor of a_n.

<u>Example:</u> Find the rational roots of $P(x) = 3x^3 - 7x^2 + 3x - 2$.

By the Rational Root Theorem, the roots must be of the form

$$x = \mp \frac{1, 2}{1, 3}$$

The candidates are then

$$x = \pm 1, \pm \frac{1}{3}, \pm \frac{2}{3}, \pm 2$$

Test each possibility. The only result that works is $x = 2$. (Note that the Rational Root Theorem does not guarantee that each potential rational number that includes factors of the leading and constant terms is a root. The theorem only states that roots will include these factors.)

The Factor Theorem

The Factor Theorem establishes the relationship between the factors and the zeros or roots of a polynomial and is useful for finding the factors of higher-degree polynomials. The theorem states that a polynomial $P(x)$ has a factor $(x - a)$ if and only if $P(a) = 0$.

The simplest proof of the Factor Theorem uses a Taylor series expansion. (For more on Taylor series, see Skill 5.5c.) Since a polynomial can be differentiated an infinite number of times. Assum $x = c$ is a root of $P(x)$; write $P(x)$ as a Taylor series expansion.

$$P(x) = P(c) + P'(c)(x-c) + \frac{P''(c)(x-c)^2}{2!} + \frac{P'''(c)(x-c)^3}{3!} + \ldots$$

Since $x = c$ is a root, $P(c) = 0$. Then,

$$P(x) = P'(c)(x-c) + \frac{P''(c)(x-c)^2}{2!} + \frac{P'''(c)(x-c)^3}{3!} + \ldots$$

Note that $(x - c)$ is a factor of each term in the Taylor series. Thus, $(x - c)$ must be a factor of $P(x)$. To divide out a factor $(x - c)$ from a polynomial, synthetic division is one potential tool. See Skill 1.2c for more on synthetic division.

The Complex Conjugate Root Theorem

For a polynomial $P(x)$ with real coefficients, if $P(x)$ has a complex root z, then it must also have a complex root $\bar{z}$. (The bar notation indicates **complex conjugate**. Thus, if $z = a + bi$, then $\bar{z} = a - bi$.)

This theorem can be proven easily using the tenets of complex analysis. Of main interest is that the complex conjugate of any function can be found by taking the complex conjugate of each part (that is, each additive or multiplicative term). Assume z is a complex root of $P(x)$. Then,

$$P(z) = a_n z^n + a_{n-1} z^{n-1} + \ldots + a_2 z^2 + a_1 z + a_0 = 0$$

Take the complex conjugate of $P(z)$. Note that the complex conjugate of zero is zero.

$$\bar{P}(z) = a_n \bar{z}^n + a_{n-1} \bar{z}^{n-1} + \ldots + a_2 \bar{z}^2 + a_1 \bar{z} + a_0 = 0$$

But this is simply $P(\bar{z})$. Thus,

$$\bar{P}(z) = P(\bar{z}) = a_n\bar{z}^n + a_{n-1}\bar{z}^{n-1} + \ldots + a_2\bar{z}^2 + a_1\bar{z} + a_0 = 0$$

Then $\bar{z}$ is also a root of the polynomial. If one complex root of a polynomial is known, therefore, the corresponding conjugate root is also known.

The Quadratic Formula

A **quadratic equation** is written in the form $ax^2 + bx + c = 0$. One method of solving it is by **factoring** the quadratic expression and applying the condition that at least one of the factors must equal zero in order for the whole expression to be zero.

The proof of the quadratic formula uses the following approach.

$$ax^2 + bx + c = 0$$
$$x^2 + \frac{b}{a}x + \frac{c}{a} = 0$$
$$x^2 + \frac{b}{a}x = -\frac{c}{a}$$

Complete the square of the left-hand side of the equation.

$$x^2 + \frac{b}{a}x + \left(\frac{b}{2a}\right)^2 = -\frac{c}{a} + \left(\frac{b}{2a}\right)^2$$

Factor and take the square root while simultaneously simplifying the right-hand side of the equation.

$$\left(x + \frac{b}{2a}\right)^2 = -\frac{(4a)c}{(4a)a} + \frac{b^2}{4a^2}$$

$$x + \frac{b}{2a} = \pm\sqrt{\frac{b^2 - 4ac}{4a^2}}$$

Note that both signs (positive and negative) for the square root must be accounted for.

$$x = -\frac{b}{2a} \pm \frac{\sqrt{b^2 - 4ac}}{2a}$$

$$x = \frac{-b \pm \sqrt{b^2 - 4ac}}{2a}$$

This is the familiar quadratic formula. Note that no assumptions were made about a, b and c: these numbers can be either real or complex. In addition, the roots of the quadratic function can be either real or complex, depending on a, b and c, as well as the value of the expression under the square root. (Even if all the coefficients are real, the root can be complex if $b^2 - 4ac < 0$.

Example: Solve the equation $3x^2 = 6x + 6$.

First, rewrite the equation as a quadratic equation in standard form.

$$x^2 = 2x + 2$$
$$x^2 - 2x - 2 = 0$$

There is no obvious way to factor this quadratic expression, so use the quadratic formula.

$$x = \frac{-(-2) \pm \sqrt{(-2)^2 - 4(1)(-2)}}{2(1)}$$
$$x = \frac{2 \pm \sqrt{4+8}}{2} = \frac{2 \pm \sqrt{12}}{2}$$
$$x = \frac{2 \pm 2\sqrt{3}}{2} = 1 \pm \sqrt{3}$$

In this case, the roots are real and are approximately equal to -0.732 and 2.732.

The Binomial Theorem

The Binomial Theorem expresses a binomial to some power (that is, $(x+y)^n$) as a polynomial. For small values of n, such as 2 or 3, the binomial can be expanded easily. For instance,

$$(x+y)^2 = x^2 + 2xy + y^2$$
$$(x+y)^3 = (x^2 + 2xy + y^2)(x+y) = x^3 + 3x^2y + 3xy^2 + y^3$$

For slightly larger values of n, **Pascal's triangle** can be used to determine the coefficients of the terms, where

$$(x+y)^n = a_n x^n + a_{n-1} x^{n-1} y + a_{n-2} x^{n-2} y^1 + \ldots + a_1 x^1 y^{n-1} + a_0 y^n$$

Pascal's triangle starts with 1 (or two parallel 1's), and each successive row is the sum of adjacent numbers in the previous row.

$$\begin{array}{c} 1 \\ 1\ 1 \\ 1\ 2\ 1 \\ 1\ 3\ 3\ 1 \\ 1\ 4\ 6\ 4\ 1 \\ \text{etc.} \end{array}$$

Notice the pattern in the expansions below.

$$(x+y)^2 = x^2 + 2xy + y^2$$
$$(x+y)^3 = x^3 + 3x^2 y + 3xy^2 + y^3$$
$$(x+y)^4 = x^4 + 4x^3 y + 6x^2 y^2 + 4xy^3 + y^4$$
$$(x+y)^5 = x^5 + 5x^4 y + 10x^3 y^2 + 10x^2 y^3 + 5xy^4 + y^5$$

For a general closed-form expression, however, the Binomial Theorem is needed. To prove the theorem, note that the expansion is in fact composed of terms where x or y is chosen from the binomial n different times.

$$(x+y)^n = (x+y)(x+y)(x+y)\ldots(x+y)$$

There are a total of 2^n terms (some terms combine) that must be added. Each term has a number k of x factors and a number n − k of y factors. Since the order in which they are chosen is irrelevant, the total number of like terms is the number of combinations of n taken k at a time. Then,

$$(x+y)^n = \sum_{k=0}^{n} \binom{n}{k} x^{n-k} y^k$$

If this summation is expanded, the result is

$$(x+y)^n = x^n + \binom{n}{1}x^{n-1}y + \binom{n}{2}x^{n-2}y^2 + \ldots + \binom{n}{n-1}xy^{n-1} + y^n$$

Note that the notation $\binom{n}{k}$ is the same as $\dfrac{n!}{k!(n-k)!}$. The Binomial Theorem can also be proven using mathematical induction. (For more on mathematical induction, see Skill 3.1b.)

Example: Expand $(3x+y)^5$.

Use the Binomial Theorem.

$$(3x+y)^5 = (3x)^5 + 5(3x)^4 y + 10(3x)^3 y^2 + 10(3x)^2 y^3 + 5(3x)y^4 + y^5$$
$$(3x+y)^5 = 243x^5 + 405x^4y + 270x^3y^2 + 90x^2y^3 + 15xy^4 + y^5$$

1.2c. **Analyze and solve polynomial equations with real coefficients using the Fundamental Theorem of Algebra**

The Fundamental Theorem of Algebra states that a polynomial expression of degree n must have n roots (which may be real or complex and which may not be distinct). It follows from the theorem that if the degree of a polynomial is odd, then it must have at least one real root.

Polynomial equations are in the form of $P(x)$ given below, where n is the degree of the polynomial and the constant a_n is non-zero.

$$P(x) = a_n x^n + a_{n-1} x^{n-1} + \ldots + a_2 x^2 + a_1 x + a_0$$

If $P(c) = 0$ for some number c, then c is said to be a **zero** (or **root**) of the function. A zero is also called a **solution** to the equation.

The existence of n solutions can be seen by looking at a factorization of $P(x)$. For instance, consider $P(x) = x^2 - x - 6$. This second-degree polynomial can be factored into

$$P(x) = (x+2)(x-3)$$

Note that $P(x)$ has two roots in this case: $x = -2$ and $x = 3$. This corresponds to the degree of the polynomial, $n = 2$. In some cases, however, there may be non-distinct roots. Consider $P(x) = x^2$.

$$P(x) = (x)(x)$$

Note that the polynomial is factored in the same way as the previous example, but, in this case, the roots are identical: $x = 0$. Thus, although there are two roots for this second-degree polynomial, the roots are not distinct.

Likewise, roots of a polynomial may be complex. Consider $P(x) = x^2 + 1$. The range of this function is $P(x) \geq 1$, so there is no root in the sense that the function crosses the real x-axis. Nevertheless, if complex values of x are permitted, there are cases where $P(x)$ is zero. Factor $P(x)$ as before, but this time use complex numbers.

$$P(x) = (x+i)(x-i)$$

MATHEMATICS

The solutions are $x = i$ and $x = -i$. Thus, this second-degree polynomial still has two roots.

For a general n^{th} degree polynomial, the function $P(x)$ can be factored in a similar manner.

$$P(x) = (x - c_n)(x - c_{n-1})\ldots(x - c_2)(x - c_1)$$

As with the second-degree polynomial examples examined above, a general n^{th} degree polynomial can have roots c_i that are distinct or non-distinct, and real or complex.

Since this is the case, if all of the roots of a polynomial are known, then a function $P(x)$ is determined based on the factoring approach shown above.

In addition, if a single root c is known, then the polynomial can be simplified (that is, it can be reduced by one degree) using division.

$$Q(x) = \frac{P(x)}{x - c}$$

Here, if $P(x)$ has degree n, then $Q(x)$ has degree $n - 1$. If some number of roots are known, the task of finding the remainder of the roots can be simplified by performing the division represented above. As each successive root is found, the degree of the polynomial can be reduced to further simplify finding the remainder of the roots.

Finding a root can sometimes be done analytically, but other times it may require either a graphical approach, whereby the behavior of the function is examined on a visual plot, or it may require a numerical approach, such as Newton's method (see Skill 5.3b for more on Newton's method).

In some cases, dividing a polynomial by $(x - c)$ is simple, but generally speaking it is a complicated process. The process can be simplified using **synthetic division**, however.

Synthetic Division

To perform synthetic division of a polynomial $P(x)$ by $(x - c)$ to get a new polynomial $Q(x)$, first draw an upside-down division symbol as shown below, using the coefficients of $P(x)$ and the root c.

$$P(x) = a_n x^n + a_{n-1} x^{n-1} + \ldots + a_2 x^2 + a_1 x + a_0$$

$$Q(x) = \frac{P(x)}{x - c}$$

$$c \,\big|\, a_n \quad a_{n-1} \quad a_{n-2} \quad \ldots$$

The first step of synthetic division is to carry the first term, a_{n-1}.

$$c \,\big|\, a_n \quad a_{n-1} \quad a_{n-2} \quad \ldots$$
$$\underline{}$$
$$a_n$$

Each successive step involves multiplying c by the previously carried term and then placing the result under the next term. Then add the two results to get the next carry value.

$$c \,\big|\, a_n \quad a_{n-1} \quad a_{n-2} \quad \ldots$$
$$ ca_n$$
$$\underline{}$$
$$a_n$$

$$c \,\big|\, a_n \quad a_{n-1} \quad a_{n-2} \quad \ldots$$
$$ ca_n$$
$$\underline{}$$
$$a_n \quad (a_{n-1} - ca_n)$$

The process should be repeated until the last carry term is found. The result should be zero. (If the final carry value is non-zero, then c is not a root. This can be a useful test of whether a particular value is a root, especially for polynomials of high degrees.) The result of the division is the set of new coefficients for the quotient.

$$Q(x) = a_n x^{n-1} + (a_{n-1} - ca_n) x^{n-2} + \ldots$$

<u>Example:</u> Divide $x^4 - 7x^2 - 6x$ by $(x + 2)$. Find the roots of the polynomial.

Use synthetic division. Notice that even the terms with coefficient zero must be included. (In other words, first write the polynomial as $x^4 + 0x^3 - 7x^2 - 6x + 0$.

```
-2 | 1   0  -7  -6   0
   |
   |_____
```

Perform the division.

```
-2 | 1   0  -7  -6   0
   |
   |_____
     1
```

```
-2 | 1   0  -7  -6   0
   |    -2
   |_____
     1  -2
```

```
-2 | 1   0  -7  -6   0
   |    -2   4
   |_____
     1  -2  -3
```

```
-2 | 1   0  -7  -6   0
   |    -2   4   6
   |_____
     1  -2  -3   0
```

```
-2 | 1   0  -7  -6   0
   |    -2   4   6   0
   |_____
     1  -2  -3   0   0
```

Thus, –2 is indeed a root of the polynomial. The result is then

$$\frac{x^4 - 7x^2 - 6x}{x+2} = x^3 - 2x^2 - 3x$$

Note that the remainder of the roots of this polynomial can be found much more easily than if the original polynomial was analyzed as is. Factor the result further.

$$x^3 - 2x^2 - 3x = x(x^2 - 2x - 3) = x(x-3)(x+1)$$

Thus, the roots are –2, –1, 0 and 3.

SKILL 1.3 FUNCTIONS

1.3a. **Analyze and prove general properties of functions (i.e., domain and range, one-to-one, onto, inverses, composition, and differences between relations and functions)**

A **relation** is any set of ordered pairs. The **domain** of a relation is the set containing all the first coordinates of the ordered pairs, and the **range** of a relation is the set containing all the second coordinates of the ordered pairs.

A **function** is a relation in which each value in the domain corresponds to only one value in the range. It is notable, however, that a value in the range may correspond to any number of values in the domain. Thus, although a function is necessarily a relation, not all relations are functions, since a relation is not bound by this rule.

On a graph, use the **vertical line test** to check whether a relation is a function. If any vertical line intersects the graph of a relation in more than one point, then the relation is not a function.

A relation is considered **one-to-one** if each value in the domain corresponds to only one value in the range and if each value in the range corresponds to only one value in the domain. Thus, a one-to-one relation is also a function, but it adds an additional condition.

In the same way that the graph of a relation can be examined using the vertical line test to determine whether it is a function, the **horizontal line test** can be used to determine if a function is a one-to-one relation. If no horizontal lines superimposed on the plot intersect the graph of the relation in more than one place, then the relation is one-to-one (assuming it also passes the vertical line test and, therefore, is a function).

A **mapping** is essentially the same as a function. Mappings (or maps) can be depicted using diagrams with arrows drawn from each element of the domain to the corresponding element (or elements) of the range. If two arrows originate from any single element in the domain, then the mapping is not a function. Likewise, for a function, if each arrow is drawn to a unique value in the range (that is, there are no cases where more than one arrow is drawn to a given value in the range), then the relation is one-to-one.

Example: Determine the domain and range of this mapping.

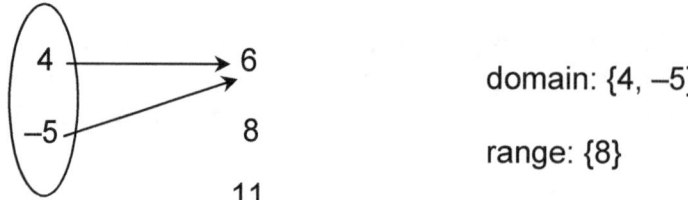

domain: {4, −5}

range: {8}

In some cases, a function (or mapping) may relate one set to another such that the range of the function consists of all the elements of a given set S. Thus, if the range of the function is S, then the function maps **onto** S.

Example: Determine if the function $f(x) = 2x$ maps onto $\mathbb{R}$.

The range of f includes all the values on the real number line (note that the graph of the line 2x extends to both positive and negative infinity, both along the x- and y-axes). Thus, the range of f is $\mathbb{R}$, so f maps onto $\mathbb{R}$.

The properties of functions:
As mentioned above, a function is a relation where each value in the domain corresponds to only one value in the range. Functions can be expressed discretely, as sets of ordered pairs, or they can be expressed more generally as formulas. For instance, the function y = x is a function that represents an infinite set of ordered pairs (x, y) where each value in the domain (x) corresponds to the same value in the range (y).

If two parameters vary directly, then, as one gets larger, the other also gets larger. If one gets smaller, then the other gets smaller as well. If x and y vary directly, there should be a constant, c, such that $y = cx$. The parameters are not necessarily limited to linear values such as x and y, but can include such expressions as x^2, $\ln x$ and $\sin x$. For instance, the statement "y varies directly with the natural logarithm of x" leads to the equation $y = c \ln x$, where c is an unspecified multiplicative constant that determines the magnitude of variation.

If two parameters vary inversely, then, as one gets larger, the other one gets smaller instead. If x and y vary inversely, there should be a constant, c, such that $xy = c$ or $y = c/x$. As with direct variation, inverse variation can involve any number of expressions involving x or y.

Example: If $30 were paid for 5 hours work, how much would be paid for 19 hours work?

This is direct variation and $30 = 5c, so the constant is 6 ($6/hour). So $y = 6(19)$ or $y = \$114$.

This could also be done as a proportion:
$$\frac{\$30}{5} = \frac{y}{19}$$
$$5y = 570$$
$$y = 114$$

Composition of functions is way of combining functions such that the range of one function is the domain of another. For instance, the composition of functions f and g can be either $f \circ g$ (the composite of f with g) or $g \circ f$ (the composite of g with f). Another way of writing these compositions is $f(g(x))$ and $g(f(x))$. The domain of $f(g(x))$ includes all values x such that $g(x)$ is in the domain of $f(x)$.

Example: What is the composition $f \circ g$ for functions $f(x) = ax$ and $g(x) = bx^2$?

The correct answer can be found by substituting the function $g(x)$ into $f(x)$.

$$f(g(x)) = ag(x) = abx^2$$

On the other hand, the composition $g \circ f$ would yield a different answer.

$$g(f(x)) = b(f(x))^2 = b(ax)^2 = a^2bx^2$$

MATHEMATICS

1.3b. **Analyze properties of polynomial, rational, radical, and absolute value functions in a variety of ways (e.g., graphing, solving problems)**

Polynomial Functions

Polynomial functions in a single variable (x, for instance), can be expressed as follows.

$$f(x) = a_n x^n + a_{n-1} x^{n-1} + \ldots + a_2 x^2 + a_1 x + a_0$$

The **degree of a polynomial function** in one variable is the value of the largest exponent to which the variable is raised. The above expression is a polynomial of degree n (assuming that $a_n \neq 0$). Any function that represents a line, for instance, is a polynomial function of degree one.

Graphing a polynomial function involves plotting representative points and graphing the results. For polynomials with few terms, the number of representative points may be small. For polynomials with many terms, however, the number of points needed to create an accurate graph may be large.

Solving problems that involve polynomial equations can involve a range of potential methods. For instance, in cases where a polynomial is highly complicated or involves constants that do not permit methods such as factoring, a numerical approach may be appropriate. Newton's method is one possible approach to solving a polynomial equation numerically. (See Skill 5.3b for more information on Newton's method.) When using Newton's method, graphing the function can be helpful for estimating the locations of the roots (if any).

Rational Functions

A rational function $r(x)$ can be written as the ratio of two polynomial expressions $p(x)$ and $q(x)$, where $q(x)$ is nonzero.

$$r(x) = \frac{p(x)}{q(x)}$$

Examples of rational functions (and their associated expressions) are

$$r(x) = \frac{x^2 + 2x + 4}{x - 3} \quad \text{and} \quad r(x) = \frac{x}{x^2 + 1}$$

Each of these examples is clearly the ratio of two polynomials. The following, however, is also a rational expression.

$$f(x) = \frac{1}{x + \frac{2}{x}}$$

This function can be shown to be a rational expression by converting it to standard form.

$$f(x) = \frac{1}{x + \frac{2}{x}} \cdot \frac{x}{x} = \frac{x}{x^2 + 2}$$

Since rational functions involve a denominator that is polynomial expression (and not simply a constant), complicated division may be required to evaluate the function. Rational expressions are just like fractions and can be changed into other equivalent fractions through similar methods.

To reduce a rational expression with more than one term in the denominator, the expression must be factored first. Factors that are the same will cancel. Addition or subtraction of rational expressions may first require finding a common denominator. The first step to this end is to factor the denominators of both expressions to find the common factors. Then, proceed to rewrite the expressions with the common denominator by using the same methods as are used for numerical fractions.

Example: Re-write the following fraction with a denominator of $(x + 3)(x - 5)(x + 4)$.

$$\frac{x + 2}{x^2 + 7x + 12}$$

First, factor the denominator.

$$\frac{x+2}{x^2+7x+12} = \frac{x+2}{(x+3)(x+4)}$$

Multiply both the numerator and denominator by $(x - 5)$.

$$\frac{x+2}{x^2+7x+12} = \frac{x+2}{(x+3)(x+4)} \cdot \frac{x-5}{x-5} = \frac{(x+2)(x-5)}{(x+3)(x-5)(x+4)}$$

Although it is not necessary, the numerator and denominator can be multiplied out to represent the result as a rational expression in terms of polynomials.

$$\frac{x+2}{x^2+7x+12} = \frac{x^2-3x-10}{x^3+2x^2-19x-60}$$

The use of common denominators is helpful for **addition and subtraction of rational expressions**. Multiplication and division of rational expressions follows the standard rules of these operations.

Example: Evaluate the following expression.

$$\frac{5}{x^2-9} - \frac{2}{x^2+4x+3}$$

Let the expression above be labeled $f(x)$. First, find the common denominator, then subtract appropriately.

$$f(x) = \frac{5}{(x-3)(x+3)} - \frac{2}{(x+3)(x+1)}$$

$$f(x) = \frac{5(x+1)}{(x-3)(x+3)(x+1)} - \frac{2(x-3)}{(x-3)(x+3)(x+1)}$$

$$f(x) = \frac{5(x+1)-2(x-3)}{(x-3)(x+3)(x+1)} = \frac{5x+5-2x+6}{(x-3)(x+3)(x+1)}$$

$$f(x) = \frac{3x+11}{(x-3)(x+3)(x+1)} = \frac{3x+11}{x^3+x^2-9x-9}$$

The above expression is the result, both in factored form and in standard form.

Example: Evaluate the following expression.

$$\left(\frac{x^2-2x-24}{x^2+6x+8}\right)\left(\frac{x^2+3x+2}{x^2-13x+42}\right)$$

Label the expression as f(x). First, factor each polynomial, simplifying as appropriate, then multiply.

$$f(x) = \left(\frac{(x-6)(x+4)}{(x+2)(x+4)}\right)\left(\frac{(x+1)(x+2)}{(x-6)(x-7)}\right)$$

$$f(x) = \left(\frac{x-6}{x+2}\right)\left(\frac{(x+1)(x+2)}{(x-6)(x-7)}\right)$$

$$f(x) = \frac{x+1}{x-7}$$

To solve an **equation with rational expressions**, set the expression equal to zero (which leads to the elimination of the denominator) and solve, as with simple polynomials.

$$r(x) = 0 = \frac{p(x)}{q(x)}$$

$$p(x) = 0$$

Note, however, that solutions to $p(x)=0$ may lead to undefined values for r(x) (that is, values for which q(x) = 0), and must be checked prior to acceptance. This difficulty can be alleviated to some extent by factoring p(x) and q(x) and eliminating common factors.

Example: Find the solutions for $\dfrac{12}{2x^2-4x} + \dfrac{13}{5} = \dfrac{9}{x-2}$

Factor and rearrange the equation as follows, then solve for x.

$$\frac{12}{2x(x-2)} - \frac{9}{x-2} = -\frac{13}{5}$$

$$\frac{12}{2x(x-2)} - \frac{9(2x)}{2x(x-2)} = \frac{-18x+12}{2x(x-2)} = -\frac{13}{5}$$

$$-18x + 12 = -\frac{13}{5}2x(x-2) = -\frac{26}{5}x^2 + \frac{52}{5}x$$

$$\frac{26}{5}x^2 - \frac{52}{5}x - 18x + 12 = 0$$

$$0 = \frac{26}{5}x^2 - \frac{142}{5}x + 12 = 26x^2 - 142x + 60 = 13x^2 - 71x + 30$$

The solutions for x can be found by factoring the above expression.

$$13x^2 - 71x + 30 = (x-5)(13x-6) = 0$$

Thus, $x = 5$ or $x = \frac{6}{13}$. These solutions can be confirmed by substitution into the original equation.

Rational functions can be graphed with the aid of **asymptotes**. Rational functions approach asymptotes for large magnitudes of the variable. Setting the denominator equal to zero and solving will give the value(s) of the vertical asymptote(s), since the function will be undefined at such points. If the value of the function approaches b as the absolute value of x increases, the equation $y = b$ is a horizontal asymptote. Horizontal asymptotes can be found using limits (for more on limits, see Skill 5.2). If either

$$\lim_{x \to \infty} f(x) = b \quad \text{or} \quad \lim_{x \to -\infty} f(x) = b$$

then b is a horizontal asymptote.

If there is more than one vertical asymptote, remember to choose numbers to the right and left of each asymptote to find the horizontal asymptotes. Also, use a sufficient number of points to graph the function.

<u>Example</u>: Graph the function $f(x) = \frac{3x+1}{x-2}$.

To find the vertical asymptote, set the denominator equal to zero.

$$x - 2 = 0$$
$$x = 2$$

The horizontal asymptote is (using L'Hopital's rule—see Skill 5.3c)

$$\lim_{x \to \infty} \frac{3x+1}{x-2} = \lim_{x \to -\infty} \frac{3x+1}{x-2} = 3$$

Next, make a table of values to find the values of appropriate points for the function.

x	f(x)
−4	1.83
−2	1.25
0	−0.5
1	−4
1.5	−11
1.75	−25
2.25	31
2.5	17
3	10
5	5.33
7	4.4

Using this information, sketch the graph. The horizontal and vertical asymptotes are plotted as dashed lines.

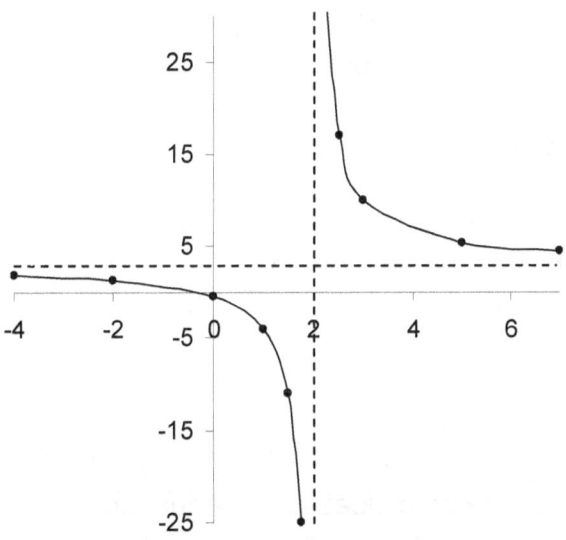

Radical Functions

When dealing with radical functions, first simplify as much as possible. If any factors can reasonably be brought outside the radical, this can aid in solving problems or graphing functions. Once simplified, treat each radical expression as its own factor. In some instances, such as when dealing with various types of roots (square roots, cube roots or other roots), it is helpful to express roots as fractional exponents. Thus, for instance,

$$\sqrt[n]{x} = x^{\frac{1}{n}}$$

Solving equations with radicals can be a complicated process, and some equations may be impossible or impractical to solve analytically. In such cases, a numerical approach, such as Newton's method, may be required. Solving a radical equation analytically typically involves either the use of logarithms or exponents. When the function is expressed in terms of exponents, simply follow the rules of exponents. (For instance, if two factors in a product have the same base, simply add the exponents to find the product.) A simple solution process for a radical equation is as follows.

1. Isolate the radical term on one side of the equation.
2. Raise both **sides** of the equation to the inverse of the exponent for the radical term. Combine any like terms.
3. If there is another radical still in the equation, repeat steps 1 and 2. Repeat as necessary to eliminate all radicals.
4. Solve the resulting equation.
5. Check all solutions in the original equation and discard any extraneous solutions.

Example: Find the roots of the equation $f(x) = 3\sqrt{x} - x$

Set $f(x)$ equal to zero and rearrange the results. Also, express each term using exponents instead of radicals.

$$f(x) = 0 = 3x^{\frac{1}{2}} - x$$
$$3x^{\frac{1}{2}} = x$$

Square both sides of the equation.

$$\left[3x^{\frac{1}{2}}\right]^2 = x^2 = 9x$$

Rearrange and factor the result.

$$x^2 - 9x = x(x-9) = 0$$

Thus, the roots of f(x) are at $x = 0$ and $x = 9$. Test each result to be sure:

$$f(0) = 3\sqrt{0} - 0 = 0 \qquad f(9) = 3\sqrt{9} - 9 = 3(3) - 9 = 0$$

Example: Solve the equation $\sqrt{2x+1} + 7 = x$.

First, isolate the radical, then square both sides of the equation.

$$\sqrt{2x+1} = x - 7$$
$$2x + 1 = (x-7)^2 = x^2 - 14x + 49$$

Simplify and solve by factoring.

$$x^2 - 14x - 2x + 49 - 1 = 0$$
$$x^2 - 16x + 48 = 0$$
$$(x - 12)(x - 4) = 0$$

The solutions are $x = 12$ and $x = 4$. Check both solutions in the original expression.

$$\sqrt{2(12)+1} + 7 = \sqrt{25} + 7 = 5 + 7 = 12$$
$$\sqrt{2(4)+1} + 7 = \sqrt{9} + 7 = 3 + 7 = 10 \neq 4$$

Only $x = 12$ satisfies the original expression. This is therefore the only solution to the equation.

Plotting a radical function follows a process similar to that of plotting virtually any other function. A set of representative points is needed, and prior knowledge of the domain of the function is helpful (for instance, if only real numbers are considered, the function in the previous example has only non-negative numbers in its domain). Typically, a calculator is needed to find the values of the function for specific variable values.

Absolute Value Equations

Absolute value equations are, essentially, two functions that can be expressed as a single piecewise continuous function using absolute value notation. To **solve an absolute value equation,** follow these steps:

MATHEMATICS

1. Isolate the absolute value expression on one side of the equation.
2. Split the absolute value equation into two separate standard equations. For one equation, set the expression in the absolute value equal to the expression on the other side of the original equality. For the second equation, set the expression in the absolute value equal to the negation of the expression on the other side of the original equality.
3. Solve each new equation.
4. Check each answer by substituting them into the original equation. Discard any extraneous solutions.

Example: Solve the following equation for x: $|2x-5|+1=12$.

Isolate the absolute value and then split the result into two equivalent equations.

$|2x-5|=11$

$2x-5=11 \qquad 2x-5=-11$

Solve each equation.

$2x=16 \qquad\qquad 2x=-6$
$x=8 \qquad\qquad\quad x=-3$

Check both solutions in the original expression.

$|2(8)-5|+1=11+1=12 \qquad |2(-3)-5|+1=11+1=12$

Both solutions are valid in this case.

Graphing an absolute value function is, in many ways, similar to graphing any other function. A set of representative points is needed to sketch the graph of the function. Due to the absolute value, however, the curve may demonstrate one or more slope discontinuities (a sharp change in direction of the curve), and it is helpful to find the locations of these points. Once the absolute value expression is isolated, the slope discontinuities can be found by determining the boundaries of the domains over which each of the two separate equations that result from the absolute value apply. Consider the following example function, $h(x)$:

$$h(x)=|f(x)|+g(x)$$

Then,

$$h(x) = f(x) + g(x) \quad \text{for} \quad f(x) \geq 0$$
$$h(x) = -f(x) + g(x) \quad \text{for} \quad f(x) < 0$$

Thus, the solutions of the equation $f(x) = 0$ are the x values of the slope discontinuities. Using this information, an arbitrary absolute value equation (assuming only one instance of an absolute value) can be graphed.

Example: Sketch the graph of the following expression:
$f(x) = |x^2 - 1| - 1$.

The function can be written as

$$f(x) = x^2 - 1 - 1 = x^2 - 2 \quad \text{for} \quad x^2 - 1 \geq 0$$
$$f(x) = -x^2 + 1 - 1 = -x^2 \quad \text{for} \quad x^2 - 1 < 0$$

The slope discontinuities are located at the solutions of the following equation:

$$x^2 - 1 = 0$$

Then:

$$x^2 = 1$$
$$x = \pm 1$$

Note that $x^2 - 1 < 0$ between $x = 1$ and $x = 2$, and $x^2 - 1 \geq 0$ everywhere else. The plot of the function is then the following.

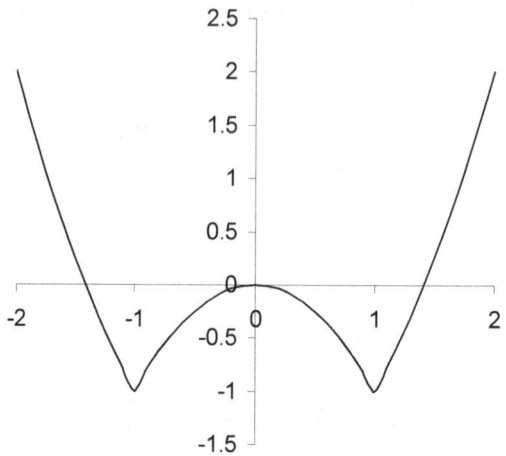

Notice the slope discontinuities at $x = 1$ and $x = -1$.

1.3c. Analyze properties of exponential and logarithmic functions in a variety of ways (e.g., graphing, solving problems)

Exponentials and logarithms are complementary. The general relationship for logarithmic and exponential functions is as follows.

$$y = \log_b x \quad \text{if and only if} \quad x = b^y$$

The relationship is as follows for the exponential base e and the natural logarithm (ln).

$$y = \ln x \quad \text{if and only if} \quad e^y = x$$

The following properties of logarithms are helpful in solving equations.

Multiplication Property $\quad \log_b mn = \log_b m + \log_b n$

Quotient Property $\quad \log_b \dfrac{m}{n} = \log_b m - \log_b n$

Powers Property $\quad \log_b n^r = r \log_b n$

Equality Property $\quad \log_b n = \log_b m$ if and only if $n = m$.

Change of Base Formula $\quad \log_b n = \dfrac{\log n}{\log b}$

$$\log_b b^x = x \quad \text{and} \quad b^{\log_b x} = x$$

Solving problems involving exponentials or logarithms typically involves isolating the terms with the exponential or logarithmic function and using the inverse operation to "extract" the argument. For instance, given the following equation,

$$\ln f(x) = c$$

the function $f(x)$ can be determined by raising e to each side of the equation.

$$e^{\ln f(x)} = f(x) = e^c$$

Alternatively, if the function is in terms of an exponent e,

$$e^{f(x)} = c$$

solve by taking the natural logarithm of both sides.

$$\ln e^{f(x)} = f(x) = \ln c$$

Although these examples are in terms of e and the natural logarithm, the same logic applies to exponentials and logarithms involving different bases as well.

<u>Example</u>: Find the roots of $f(x) = \ln(x^2 + 2) - 3$.

Set $f(x)$ equal to zero and simplify.

$$f(x) = 0 = \ln(x^2 + 2) - 3$$
$$\ln(x^2 + 2) = 3$$

Raise e to both sides of the equation and solve for x.

$$e^{\ln(x^2+2)} = x^2 + 2 = e^3$$
$$x^2 = e^3 - 2$$
$$x = \pm\sqrt{e^3 - 2} \approx \pm 4.252$$

<u>Example</u>: Find the roots of $f(x) = e^{-2x^2} - 1$.

Set $f(x)$ equal to zero and simplify.

$$f(x) = 0 = e^{-2x^2} - 1$$
$$e^{-2x^2} = 1$$

Solve for x by taking the natural logarithm of both sides of the equation.

$$\ln e^{-2x^2} = -2x^2 = \ln 1 = 0$$

The solution is then $x = 0$.

Graphing exponential and logarithmic functions involves finding a set of representative points, plotting these points on a graph and then connecting the points with appropriate curves. The domain of an exponential function includes all real numbers, but the domain of a logarithmic functions includes only the positive real numbers. The basic shapes of the exponential and logarithmic functions are illustrated below.

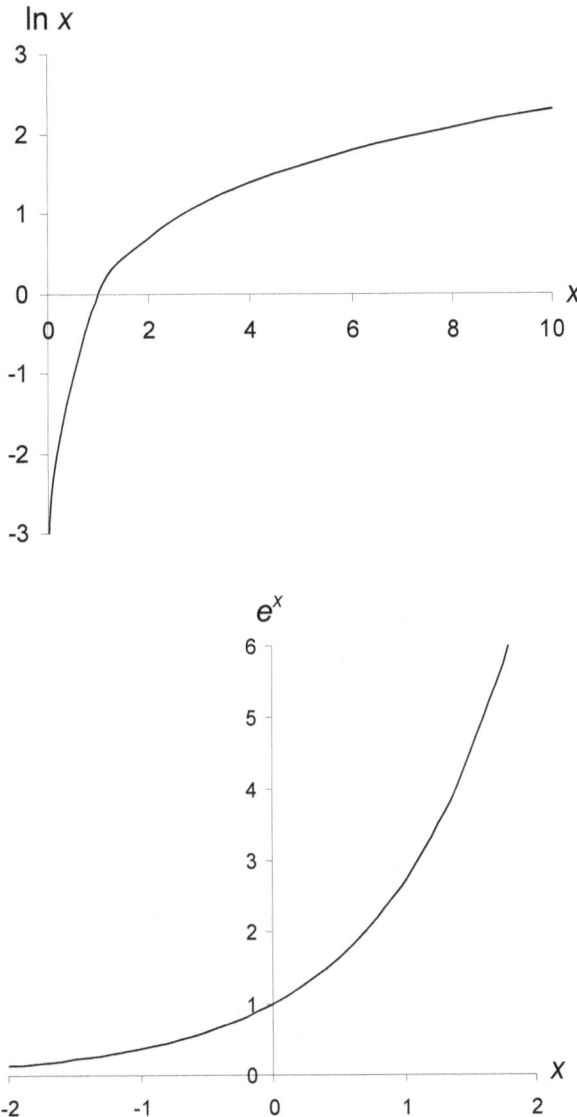

Note that the function e^x has an asymptote at $y = 0$ (the limit of the exponential function as x goes to negative infinity is zero), and the function $\ln x$ has an asymptote at $x = 0$ (the limit of the natural logarithmic function as x goes to zero from the right is negative infinity). The asymptotes of these functions can be helpful in sketching accurate graphs.

Example: Sketch the graph of the function $f(x) = \ln(x^2 - 2)$.

In this case, the domain of the function is the set of values for which $x^2 - 2 > 0$, which requires that $x > \sqrt{2}$ or $x < -\sqrt{2}$. Note that the asymptotes are located at the x value for which the arguments of the natural logarithm is zero.

$$x^2 - 2 = 0$$
$$x^2 = 2$$
$$x = \pm\sqrt{2}$$

Also note that the function is symmetric about the y-axis. Some values for the function for $x > \sqrt{2}$ are shown in the table below.

x	f(x)
1.5	−1.39
1.75	0.06
2	0.69
3	1.95
4	2.64
5	3.14
6	3.53

The plot of the function is shown below, with the asymptotes displayed as dashed lines.

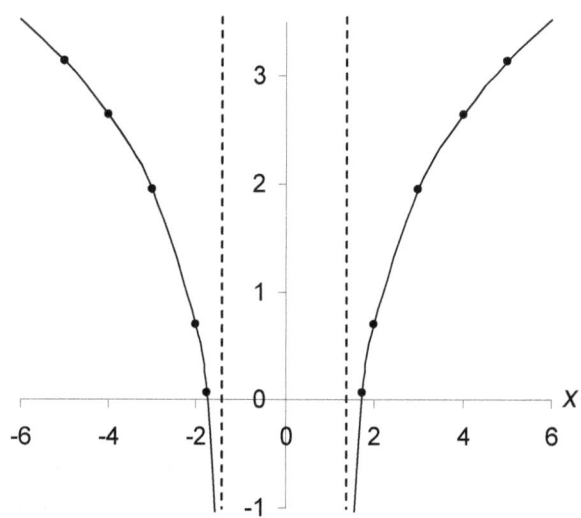

Example: Sketch the graph of the function $f(x) = e^{2x-1} + 1$.

The function f(x) has an asymptote at y = 1, since

$$\lim_{x \to -\infty} e^{2x-1} + 1 = e^{-2\infty - 1} + 1 = 0 + 1 = 1$$

The y-intercept of the function is

$$f(0) = e^{2(0)-1} + 1 = e^{-1} + 1 = \frac{1}{e} + 1 \approx 1.368$$

The following table of values can be used to plot the function.

x	f(x)
−5	1.00
−4	1.00
−3	1.00
−2	1.01
−1	1.05
0	1.37
1	3.72
2	21.1

The graph of the function is shown below with the asymptote displayed as a dashed line.

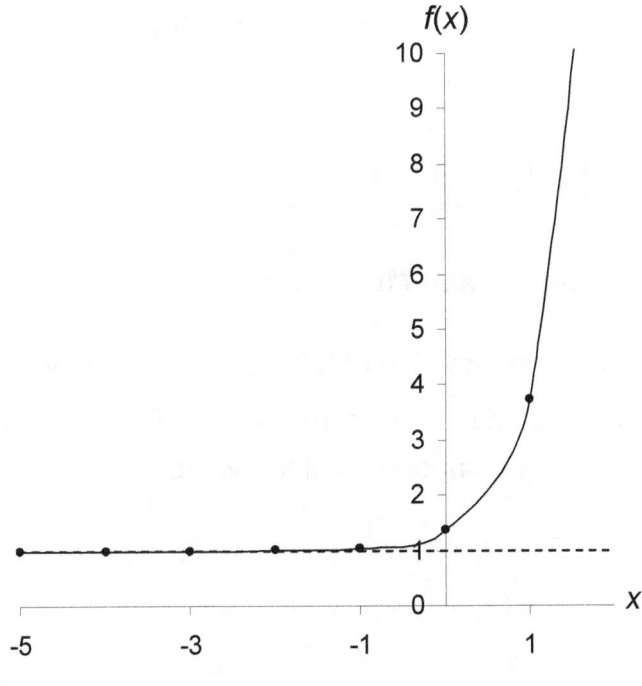

SKILL 1.4 LINEAR ALGEBRA

1.4a. **Understand and apply the geometric interpretation and basic operations of vectors in two and three dimensions, including their scalar multiples and scalar (dot) and cross products**

Vectors

A vector is any quantity that has a **magnitude** (or length) and a **direction**. Vectors do not have specified locations, so they can be translated as long as their direction and magnitude are the same. A vector is often written in the same form as a point; for instance, a vector can be written as (x_1, y_1, z_1). In this case, the direction and magnitude of the vector are defined by a ray that starts at the origin and terminates at the point (x_1, y_1, z_1).

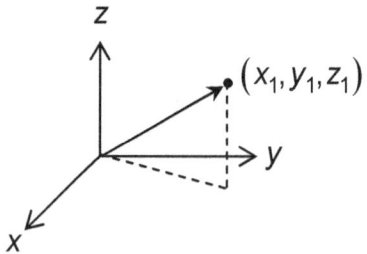

As noted before, however, the vector is not confined to the location shown above. The magnitude of a vector is simply the distance from the origin to the point (x_1, y_1, z_1). If $\vec{A} = (x_1, y_1, z_1)$, then the magnitude is written as $|\vec{A}|$.

$$|\vec{A}| = \sqrt{x_1^2 + y_1^2 + z_1^2}$$

Addition and Scalar Multiplication

Addition and subtraction of two vectors $\vec{A} = (x_1, y_1, z_1)$ and $\vec{B} = (x_2, y_2, z_2)$ can be performed by adding or subtracting corresponding components of the vectors.

$$\vec{A} + \vec{B} = (x_1 + x_2, y_1 + y_2, z_1 + z_2)$$
$$\vec{A} - \vec{B} = (x_1 - x_2, y_1 - y_2, z_1 - z_2)$$

Geometrically, addition involves placing the tail of $\vec{B}$ on the head of $\vec{A}$, as shown below. The result is a vector that starts from the tail of $\vec{A}$ and ends at the head of $\vec{B}$.

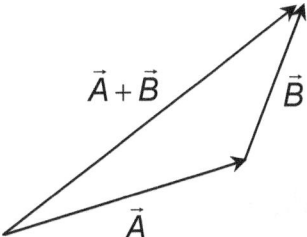

Subtraction of two vectors involves the same process, except that the direction of $\vec{B}$ must be reversed.

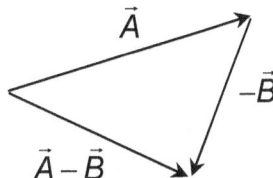

Multiplication of a vector by a scalar simply involves multiplying each component by the scalar.

$$c\vec{A} = (cx_1, cy_1, cz_1)$$

Geometrically, this operation extends the length of the vector by a factor c.

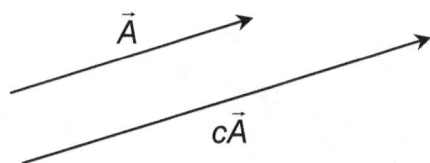

Note that the direction of a vector can be written as a unit vector $\vec{u}$ of length 1, such that

$$\vec{A} = \vec{u}|\vec{A}|$$

Vectors obey the laws of associativity, commutativity, identity and additive inverses:

$$\vec{A} + (\vec{B} + \vec{C}) = (\vec{A} + \vec{B}) + \vec{C}$$
$$\vec{A} + \vec{B} = \vec{B} + \vec{A}$$
$$\vec{A} + 0 = \vec{A}$$
$$\vec{A} + (-\vec{A}) = 0$$

Multiplication of Vectors

Vector multiplication takes two forms: the **dot product** (or scalar product) and the **cross product** (or vector product). The dot product is calculated by multiplying corresponding components of two vectors. The operator for this product is typically a small dot (·).

$$\vec{A} \cdot \vec{B} = x_1 x_2 + y_1 y_2 + z_1 z_2$$

Notice that the dot product yields a single scalar value. Also note that the magnitude of a vector can be written in terms of the dot product.

$$|\vec{A}| = \sqrt{\vec{A} \cdot \vec{A}}$$

Geometrically, the dot product is a **projection** of one vector onto another.

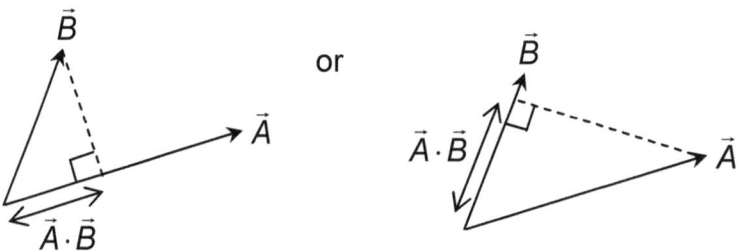

It can be shown that the dot product of two vectors is equivalent to the following:

$$\vec{A} \cdot \vec{B} = |\vec{A}||\vec{B}| \cos \theta$$

The cross product of two vectors, typically symbolized by a ×
operator, yields a third vector. The cross product is defined as
follows.

$$\vec{A} \times \vec{B} = (y_1 z_2 - y_2 z_1, z_1 x_2 - z_2 x_1, x_1 y_2 - x_2 y_1)$$

Geometrically, the cross product of $\vec{A}$ and $\vec{B}$ is a third vector that is
perpendicular to both $\vec{A}$ and $\vec{B}$ (that is, to the plane formed by $\vec{A}$
and $\vec{B}$), with the direction defined by the so-called right-hand screw
rule. If a right-hand screw is turned in the direction from $\vec{A}$ to $\vec{B}$,
the result is the direction of the cross product.

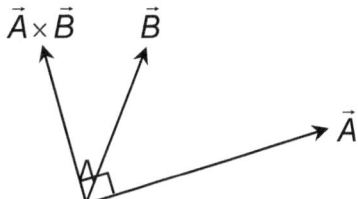

The magnitude of $\vec{A} \times \vec{B}$ is the area of the parallelogram defined by
$\vec{A}$ and $\vec{B}$.

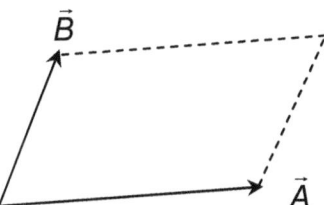

The magnitude of the cross product can also be written as follows.

$$\left| \vec{A} \times \vec{B} \right| = \left| \vec{A} \right| \left| \vec{B} \right| \sin \theta$$

Multiplication of vectors, either by the dot product or cross product,
obeys the rule of distibutivity, where ∗ symbolizes either · or ×.

$$\vec{A} * (\vec{B} + \vec{C}) = \vec{A} * \vec{B} + \vec{A} * \vec{C}$$

Only the dot product obeys commutativity, however. There is a
similar rule for cross products, though.

$$\vec{A} \cdot \vec{B} = \vec{B} \cdot \vec{A}$$
$$\vec{A} \times \vec{B} = -\vec{B} \times \vec{A}$$

Example: Find the cross product $\vec{a} \times \vec{b}$, where $\vec{a} = (-1, 4, 2)$ and $\vec{b} = (3, -1, 4)$.

Use the expression given to calculate the cross product.

$$\vec{a} \times \vec{b} = (4 \cdot 4 - (-1) \cdot 2, 2 \cdot 3 - 4 \cdot (-1), (-1) \cdot (-1) - 3 \cdot 4)$$
$$\vec{a} \times \vec{b} = (16 + 2, 6 + 4, 1 - 12) = (18, 10, -11)$$

Example: Find the following for $\vec{a} = (1, 2, 3)$, $\vec{b} = (2, 3, 1)$ and $c = 2$: $c(\vec{a} \cdot \vec{b})$.

First, find the dot product, then multiply. Note that the result must be a scalar.

$$c(\vec{a} \cdot \vec{b}) = 2[1(2) + 2(3) + 3(1)] = 2[11] = 22$$

TEACHER CERTIFICATION STUDY GUIDE

1.4b. **Prove the basic properties of vectors (e.g., perpendicular vectors have zero dot product)**

Using the fundamental understanding of vectors and the types of products of vectors (vector and scalar products, or, equivalently, cross and dot products) presented in the preceding section, certain basic properties of vectors can be proven.

For instance, the dot product of two perpendicular vectors can be proven to be zero by using the following approach. Let two vectors $\vec{a}$ and $\vec{b}$ with angle α between them. Although the vectors may be expressed in terms of three coordinate dimensions, they still form a plane, so the coordinate system can be adjusted so that the vectors need only be expressed in terms of two dimensions. Let vector $\vec{a}$ form an angle θ_1 with the x-axis and let vector $\vec{b}$ form an angle θ_2 with the x-axis, as shown below.

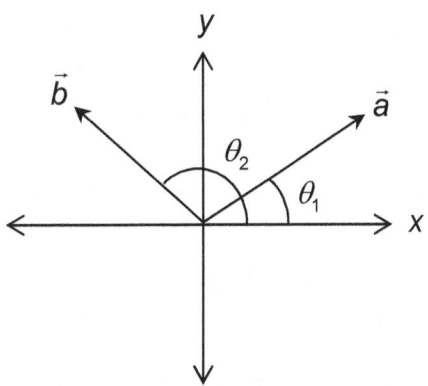

Note that the angle α is equal to $\theta_2 - \theta_1$. Write each vector in terms of its components, where $\hat{x}$ and $\hat{y}$ are unit vectors in the x and y directions, respectively.

$$\vec{a} = \hat{x} a \cos\theta_1 + \hat{y} a \sin\theta_1$$
$$\vec{b} = \hat{x} b \cos\theta_2 + \hat{y} b \sin\theta_2$$

Find the dot product of the $\vec{a}$ and $\vec{b}$.

$$\vec{a} \cdot \vec{b} = ab \cos\theta_1 \cos\theta_2 + ab \sin\theta_1 \sin\theta_2$$

Simplify the result.

$$\vec{a} \cdot \vec{b} = ab(\cos\theta_1 \cos\theta_2 + \sin\theta_1 \sin\theta_2)$$
$$\vec{a} \cdot \vec{b} = ab\cos(\theta_1 - \theta_2)$$

As mentioned, $\theta_2 - \theta_1$ is α. The sign of the argument of the cosine function does not affect the result, however.

$$\vec{a} \cdot \vec{b} = ab\cos(-\alpha) = ab\cos(\alpha)$$

If α is 90°, then the dot product is zero.

$$ab\cos(90°) = 0$$

Thus, if two vectors are perpendicular, their dot product is zero.

It can also be shown that if the dot product of a vector with itself is zero, then the vector must be equal to zero. Use the above result, substituting the values associated with $\vec{a}$ in place of those of $\vec{b}$.

$$\vec{a} \cdot \vec{a} = a^2 \cos(\theta_1 - \theta_1) = a^2 \cos 0 = a^2$$

Thus, if the dot product is zero, a^2 is zero, which means that the length of the vector is zero as well. The vector must then be zero.

Another property of vectors is that the cross product of two parallel vectors is zero.

Proof: Let vectors $\vec{a}$ and $\vec{b}$ be parallel (that is, let the angle between them be zero degrees). There is then a unit vector $\vec{u}$ of length one such that $\vec{a} = a\vec{u}$ and $\vec{b} = b\vec{u}$. Then, since a and b are scalars:

$$\vec{a} \times \vec{b} = (a\vec{u}) \times (b\vec{u}) = ab(\vec{u} \times \vec{u})$$

But the cross product of any vector with itself can be shown to be zero. Let $\vec{u} = (x, y, z)$. Then (using $\hat{x}$, $\hat{y}$ and $\hat{z}$ as the unit vectors along the three mutually perpendicular axes):

$$\vec{u} \times \vec{u} = \hat{x}(yz - zy) + \hat{y}(zx - xz) + \hat{z}(xy - yx) = 0$$

So, the cross product of any two parallel vectors is zero. Since a vector is parallel with itself, the cross product of a vector with itself must also be zero.

Other vector properties can be proven in a similar manner. For a given property, use general expressions for vectors and perform the necessary operations, in accordance with the assumptions of the problem, to arrive at the desired conclusion.

1.4c. **Understand and apply the basic properties and operations of matrices and determinants (e.g., to determine the solvability of linear systems of equations)**

Properties of Matrices

A **matrix** is an ordered set of numbers in rectangular form. An example matrix is shown below.

$$\begin{pmatrix} 0 & 3 & 1 \\ 4 & 2 & 3 \\ 1 & 0 & 2 \end{pmatrix}$$

Since this matrix has 3 rows and 3 columns, it is called a 3 × 3 matrix. The element in the second row of the third column would be denoted as $3_{2,3}$. In general, a matrix with r rows and c columns is an $r \times c$ matrix.

Matrices can be **added or subtracted** only if their dimensions are the same. To add (subtract) compatible matrices, simply add (subtract) the corresponding elements, as with the example below for 2×2 matrices.

$$\begin{pmatrix} a_{11} & a_{12} \\ a_{21} & a_{22} \end{pmatrix} + \begin{pmatrix} a_{11} & a_{12} \\ a_{21} & a_{22} \end{pmatrix} = \begin{pmatrix} a_{11}+b_{11} & a_{12}+b_{12} \\ a_{21}+b_{21} & a_{22}+b_{22} \end{pmatrix}$$

Matrix addition and subtraction obey the rules of associativity, commutativity, identity and additive inverse.

$$\overline{A} + (\overline{B} + \overline{C}) = (\overline{A} + \overline{B}) + \overline{C}$$
$$\overline{A} + \overline{B} = \overline{B} + \overline{A}$$
$$\overline{A} + 0 = \overline{A}$$
$$\overline{A} + (-\overline{A}) = 0$$

Multiplication for matrices is more complicated, except for the case of multiplication by a scalar. The product of a matrix and a scalar is found by multiplying each element of the matrix by the scalar.

$$c \begin{pmatrix} a_{11} & a_{12} \\ a_{21} & a_{22} \end{pmatrix} = \begin{pmatrix} ca_{11} & ca_{12} \\ ca_{21} & ca_{22} \end{pmatrix}$$

Multiplication of two matrices is only defined if the number of columns in the first matrix is equal to the number of rows in the second matrix. Matrix multiplication is not necessarily commutative. Given an $n \times m$ matrix ($\overline{A}$) multiplied by an $m \times p$ matrix ($\overline{B}$) (multiplied in that order), the product is an $n \times p$ matrix. Each element C_{ij} in the product matrix is equal to the sum of the elements in the ith row of the $n \times m$ matrix multiplied by the elements in the jth column of the $m \times p$ matrix. Thus, each element C_{ij} of the product matrix $\overline{AB}$ is equal to the following, where $\overline{AB} = \overline{C}$:

$$C_{ij} = \sum_{k=1}^{m} A_{ik} B_{kj}$$

Consider the following example.

$$\begin{pmatrix} 1 & 2 & 3 \\ 4 & 5 & 6 \end{pmatrix} \begin{pmatrix} 7 \\ 8 \\ 9 \end{pmatrix}$$

The solution is found as follows.

$$\begin{pmatrix} 1 & 2 & 3 \\ 4 & 5 & 6 \end{pmatrix} \begin{pmatrix} 7 \\ 8 \\ 9 \end{pmatrix} = \begin{pmatrix} (1)(7)+(2)(8)+(3)(9) \\ (4)(7)+(5)(8)+(6)(9) \end{pmatrix} = \begin{pmatrix} 50 \\ 122 \end{pmatrix}$$

Matrix multiplication obeys the rules of associativity and distributivity, but not commutativity.

$$\overline{A}(\overline{B}\overline{C}) = (\overline{A}\overline{B})\overline{C}$$
$$\overline{A}(\overline{B}+\overline{C}) = \overline{A}\overline{B} + \overline{A}\overline{C}$$
$$(\overline{B}+\overline{C})\overline{A} = \overline{B}\overline{A} + \overline{C}\overline{A}$$

Example: Determine the product AB of the following matrices.

$$A = \begin{pmatrix} -1 & 2 & 8 \\ 4 & -3 & 7 \\ 0 & 1 & 4 \end{pmatrix}, \quad B = \begin{pmatrix} 0 & 5 & 0 \\ 7 & -2 & -1 \\ -8 & 0 & 3 \end{pmatrix}$$

The product AB is a 3 × 3 matrix. The first column of AB is the dot product of the first column in B with each row of A.

$$AB = \begin{pmatrix} -1 & 2 & 8 \\ 4 & -3 & 7 \\ 0 & 1 & 4 \end{pmatrix} \begin{pmatrix} 0 & 5 & 0 \\ 7 & -2 & -1 \\ -8 & 0 & 3 \end{pmatrix} = \begin{pmatrix} 0+14-64 & \cdot & \cdot \\ -21-56 & \cdot & \cdot \\ 7-32 & \cdot & \cdot \end{pmatrix}$$

The other columns of AB are found using the same approach for the other columns of B.

$$AB = \begin{pmatrix} -50 & -9 & 22 \\ -77 & 26 & 24 \\ -25 & -2 & 11 \end{pmatrix}$$

Associated with every square matrix is a number called the determinant. The determinant of a matrix is typically denoted using straight brackets; thus, the determinant of matrix A is $|A|$. Use these formulas to calculate determinants.

$$\begin{vmatrix} a & b \\ c & d \end{vmatrix} = ad - bc$$

$$\begin{vmatrix} a_1 & b_1 & c_1 \\ a_2 & b_2 & c_2 \\ a_3 & b_3 & c_3 \end{vmatrix} = (a_1 b_2 c_3 + b_1 c_2 a_3 + c_1 a_2 b_3) - (a_3 b_2 c_1 + b_3 c_2 a_1 + c_3 a_2 b_1)$$

This is found by repeating the first two columns and then using the diagonal lines to find the value of each expression as shown below:

$$\begin{vmatrix} a_1^* & b_1^\circ & c_1^\bullet \\ a_2 & b_2^* & c_2^\circ \\ a_3 & b_3 & c_3^* \end{vmatrix} \begin{matrix} a_1 & b_1 \\ a_2^\bullet & b_2 \\ a_3^\circ & b_3^\bullet \end{matrix}$$

$$= (a_1 b_2 c_3 + b_1 c_2 a_3 + c_1 a_2 b_3) - (a_3 b_2 c_1 + b_3 c_2 a_1 + c_3 a_2 b_1)$$

Example: Find the value of the determinant of $\begin{pmatrix} 4 & -8 \\ 7 & 3 \end{pmatrix}$.

Use the formula for calculating the determinant.

$$\begin{vmatrix} 4 & -8 \\ 7 & 3 \end{vmatrix} = (4)(3) - (-8)(7) = 12 + 56 = 68$$

Matrices are often used to solve systems of equations. They are also used by physicists, mathematicians and biologists to organize and study data such as population growth, and they are used in finance for such purposes as investment growth and portfolio analysis. Matrices are easily translated into computer code in high-level programming languages and can be easily expressed in electronic spreadsheets.

The following is a simple financial example of using a matrix to solve a problem. A company has two stores. The income and expenses (in dollars) for the two stores, for three months, are shown in the matrices.

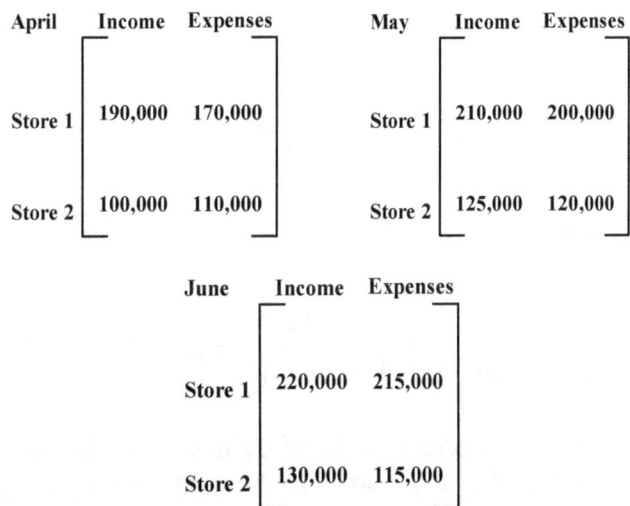

The owner wants to know what his first-quarter income and expenses were, so he adds the three matrices.

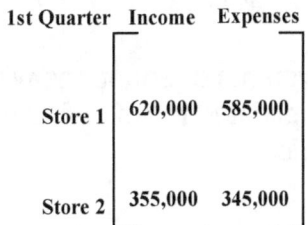

Then, to find the profit for each store:

Profit for Store 1 = $620,000 - $585,000 = $35,000
Profit for Store 2 = $355,000 - $345,000 = $10,000

Solving Systems of Equations

When given a system of equations, such as

$$ax + by = e$$
$$cx + dy = f$$

the matrix equation is written in the following form.

$$\begin{pmatrix} a & b \\ c & d \end{pmatrix} \begin{pmatrix} x \\ y \end{pmatrix} = \begin{pmatrix} e \\ f \end{pmatrix}$$

The same general pattern follows for n equations in n variables. (The result is an $n \times n$ matrix with a variable vector and a constant vector each with n entries.) The solution is found using the inverse of the matrix of coefficients. The inverse of a 2×2 matrix can be written as follows:

$$A^{-1} = \frac{1}{|A|} \begin{pmatrix} d & -b \\ -c & a \end{pmatrix}$$

Then,

$$\begin{pmatrix} a & b \\ c & d \end{pmatrix}^{-1} \begin{pmatrix} a & b \\ c & d \end{pmatrix} \begin{pmatrix} x \\ y \end{pmatrix} = \begin{pmatrix} x \\ y \end{pmatrix} = \begin{pmatrix} a & b \\ c & d \end{pmatrix}^{-1} \begin{pmatrix} e \\ f \end{pmatrix}$$

The solution set defined by the variable vector can then be found by performing the matrix multiplication on the right of the above equation.

$$\begin{pmatrix} x \\ y \end{pmatrix} = \frac{1}{|A|} \begin{pmatrix} d & -b \\ -c & a \end{pmatrix} \begin{pmatrix} e \\ f \end{pmatrix} = \frac{1}{|A|} \begin{pmatrix} ed - bf \\ af - ce \end{pmatrix}$$

Solving systems of equations with many variables can involve the more complicated tasks of finding the determinant and inverse of large matrices.

Note that if the determinant of a matrix is zero, then the matrix is called **singular**. In such cases, a unique solution does not exist.

If a matrix larger than 2 × 2 must be inverted, then **Gauss elimination** can be used to find the solution. The approach for this technique first involves augmenting the matrix with the constant vector. Using the above example, the augmented matrix is

$$\left(\begin{array}{cc|c} a & b & e \\ c & d & f \end{array} \right)$$

The goal of Gauss elimination is to perform row operations such that the coefficient matrix becomes the identity matrix:

$$\left(\begin{array}{ccc} 1 & 0 & \cdots \\ 0 & 1 & \cdots \\ \vdots & \vdots & \ddots \end{array} \right)$$

For the example matrix above, first divide the first row by a.

$$\left(\begin{array}{cc|c} 1 & \frac{b}{a} & \frac{e}{a} \\ c & d & f \end{array} \right)$$

Next, add c times the first row to the second row.

$$\left(\begin{array}{cc|c} 1 & \frac{b}{a} & \frac{e}{a} \\ 0 & d + \frac{cb}{a} & f + \frac{ec}{a} \end{array} \right)$$

The process can be continued until the result is found, which is

$$\left(\begin{array}{cc|c} 1 & 0 & \frac{ed - bf}{|A|} \\ 0 & 1 & \frac{af - ce}{|A|} \end{array} \right)$$

Example: Write the matrix equation of the following system of equations and solve for x and y.

$$3x - 4y = 2$$
$$2x + y = 5$$

$$\begin{pmatrix} 3 & -4 \\ 2 & 1 \end{pmatrix} \begin{pmatrix} x \\ y \end{pmatrix} = \begin{pmatrix} 2 \\ 5 \end{pmatrix}$$ Definition of matrix equation

$$\begin{pmatrix} x \\ y \end{pmatrix} = \frac{1}{11} \begin{pmatrix} 1 & 4 \\ -2 & 1 \end{pmatrix} \begin{pmatrix} 2 \\ 5 \end{pmatrix}$$ Multiply by the inverse of the coefficient matrix.

$$\begin{pmatrix} x \\ y \end{pmatrix} = \frac{1}{11} \begin{pmatrix} 22 \\ 11 \end{pmatrix}$$ Matrix multiplication.

$$\begin{pmatrix} x \\ y \end{pmatrix} = \begin{pmatrix} 2 \\ 1 \end{pmatrix}$$ Scalar multiplication.

The solution is then $x = 2$ and $y = 1$.

COMPETENCY 2.0 GEOMETRY

SKILL 2.1 Parallelism

2.1a. **Know the Parallel Postulate and its implications, and justify its equivalents (e.g., the Alternate Interior Angle Theorem, the angle sum of every triangle is 180 degrees)**

The Parallel Postulate

The **Parallel Postulate** in Euclidean planar geometry states that if a line *l* is crossed by two other lines *m* and *n* (where the crossings are not at the same point on *l*), then *m* and *n* intersect on the side of *l* where the sum of the interior angles α and β is less than 180°. This scenario is illustrated below.

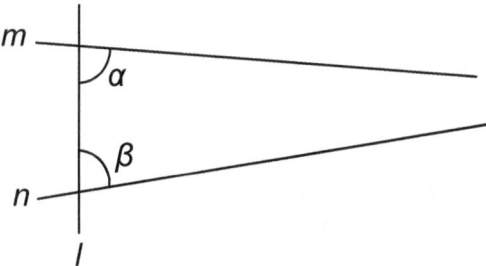

Based on this definition, a number of implications and equivalent formulations can be derived. First, note that the lines *m* and *n* intersect on the right-hand side of *l* above only if $\alpha + \beta < 180°$. This implies that if α and β are both 90° and, therefore, $\alpha + \beta = 180°$, then the lines do not intersect on either side. This is illustrated below.

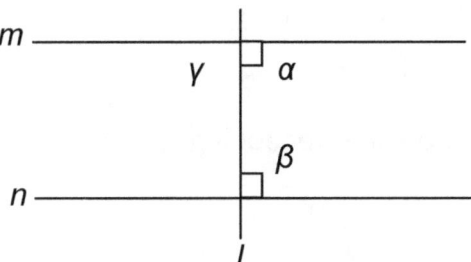

The supplementary angles formed by the intersection of *l* and *m* (and the intersection of *l* and *n*) must sum to 180°:

$\alpha + \gamma = 180°$ $\qquad\qquad \beta + \delta = 180°$

Since these sums are both equal to 180°, the lines *m* and *n* do not intersect on either side of *l*. That is to say, these lines are **parallel**.

The Alternate Interior Angle Theorem

Let the non-intersecting lines *m* and *n* used in the above discussion remain parallel, but adjust *l* such that the interior angles are no longer right angles.

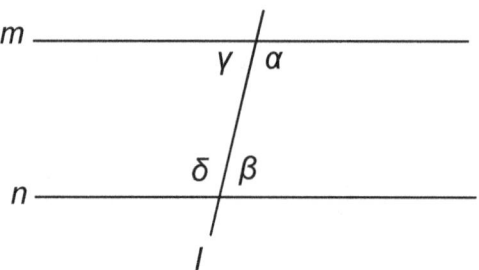

The Parallel Postulate still applies, and it is therefore still the case that $\alpha + \beta = 180°$ and $\gamma + \delta = 180°$. Combined with the fact that $\alpha + \gamma = 180°$ and $\beta + \delta = 180°$, the **Alternate Interior Angle Theorem** can be justified. This theorem states that if two parallel lines are cut by a transversal, the alternate interior angles are congruent.

By manipulating the four relations based on the above diagram, the relationships between alternate interior angles (γ and β form one set of alternate interior angles, and α and δ form the other) can be established.

$$\alpha = 180° - \beta$$
$$\alpha + \gamma = 180° = 180° - \beta + \gamma$$
$$-\beta + \gamma = 0$$
$$\gamma = \beta$$

By the same reasoning,

$$\gamma = 180° - \delta$$
$$\beta + \delta = 180° = \beta + 180° - \delta$$
$$\beta = \delta$$

Corresponding angles

One of the consequences of the Parallel Postulate, in addition the Alternate Interior Angle Theorem, is that **corresponding angles** are equal. If two parallel lines are cut by a transversal line, then the corresponding angles are equal. The diagram below illustrates one set of corresponding angles (α and β) for the parallel lines m and n cut by l.

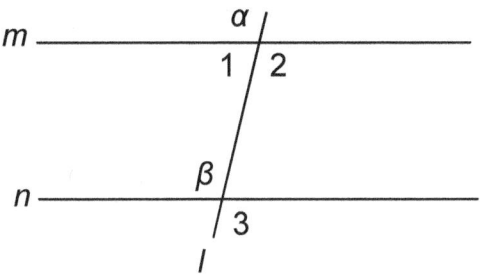

That α and β are equal can be proven as follows.

$\angle \beta = \angle 2$ Alternate Interior Angle Theorem
$\angle 1 + \angle 2 = 180°$ Supplementary angles
$\angle 2 = 180° - \angle 1$
$\angle 1 + \angle \alpha = 180°$ Supplementary angles
$\angle \alpha = 180° - \angle 1$
$\angle 2 = 180° - \angle 1 = \angle \alpha$
$\angle 2 = \angle \alpha$
$\angle \beta = \angle 2 = \angle \alpha$
$\angle \beta = \angle \alpha$

Thus, it has been proven that corresponding angles are equal.

Note, also, that the above proof also demonstrates that vertical angles are equal ($\angle 2 = \angle \alpha$). Thus, opposite angles formed by the intersection of two lines (called **vertical angles**) are equal. Furthermore, **alternate exterior angles** (angles α and 1 in the diagram above) are also equal.

$\angle \beta = \angle 3$ Vertical angles
$\angle \alpha = \angle 2$ Vertical angles
$\angle \beta = \angle 2$ Alternate Interior Angle Theorem
$\angle \alpha = \angle 2 = \angle \beta = \angle 3$
$\angle \alpha = \angle 3$

Sum of angles in a triangle

The sum of the measures of the angles of a **triangle** is 180°. This property can be justified as follows. Consider a triangle with angles α, β and γ. Draw two parallel lines such that one parallel line coincides with any side of the triangle, and the other parallel line intersects the vertex opposite that side.

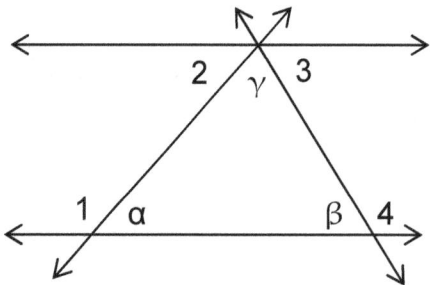

Proof: ∠α = ∠2   Alternate interior angles
∠β = ∠3   Alternate interior angles
∠2 + ∠3 + ∠γ = 180°   Supplementary angles
∠α + ∠β + ∠γ = 180°   Substitution

Thus, the sum of all the interior angles of a triangle is always 180°.

Example: Can a triangle have two right angles?

No. A right angle measures 90°; therefore, the sum of two right angles would be 180°, and there could not be a third angle.

Example: Can a right triangle have two obtuse angles?

No. Since an obtuse angle measures more than 90°, the sum of two obtuse angles would be greater than 180°.

Example: Can a right triangle be obtuse?

No. Once again, the sum of the angles would be more than 180°.

2.1b. Know that variants of the Parallel Postulate produce non-Euclidean geometries (e.g., spherical, hyperbolic)

Euclid wrote a set of 13 books around 330 B.C. called the Elements. He outlined 10 axioms and then deduced 465 theorems. Euclidean geometry is based on the undefined concept of the point, line and plane.

The fifth of Euclid's axioms (referred to as the parallel postulate) was not as readily accepted as the other nine axioms. Many mathematicians throughout the years have attempted to prove that this axiom is not necessary because it could be proved by the other nine. Among the many who attempted to prove this was Carl Friedrich Gauss; his work led to the development of hyperbolic geometry. Elliptical, spherical or Riemannian geometry were hypothesized by G.F. Berhard Riemann, who based his work on the theory of surfaces and used models as physical interpretations of the undefined terms that satisfy the axioms.

The variants of the Parallel Postulate that lead to non-Euclidean geometries are based on the number of possible unique lines that can be parallel to a line l, where the potential parallel lines must pass through a specific point not on l.

The chart below lists the fifth axiom (the Parallel Postulate) as it is given in each of the three geometries:

Euclidean Geometry	Spherical or Riemannian Geometry	Hyperbolic or Saddle Geometry
Through a point not on a line, there is no more than one line parallel to that line.	If l is any line and P is any point not on l, then there are no lines through P that are parallel to l.	If l is any line and P is any point not on l, then there exists at least two lines through P that are parallel to l.

Euclidean geometry is the study of flat, two-dimensional space. Non-Euclidean geometries involve **curved surfaces**, such as that of a sphere. These geometries have a direct connection to our experiences: for instant, the surface of the Earth is (roughly) spherical. Note the results of the parallel postulate for spherical geometry. (A line on a sphere is a so-called great circle, which is a circle of the same radius as the sphere.)

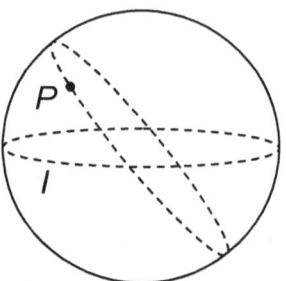

The line through point P is not parallel to line l. Furthermore, it is clear through observation of the figure that, since there is only one great circle through any given point, there are non-collinear parallel lines in spherical geometry. Thus, as is demonstrated by this example, varying the details of the Parallel Postulate leads to various types of non-Euclidean geometries.

Non-Euclidean geometries have application beyond just abstract mathematical theory. For instance, hyperbolic geometry is a central concept in Einstein's theory of relativity.

TEACHER CERTIFICATION STUDY GUIDE

SKILL 2.2 PLANE EUCLIDEAN GEOMETRY

2.2a. Prove theorems and solve problems involving similarity and congruence

About Euclidean Geometry Proofs

A proof of a geometrical proposition is typically presented in a format with two columns side by side. In a **two-column proof**, the left side of the proof should be the given information, or statements that could be proved by deductive reasoning. The right column of the proof consists of the reasons used to demonstrate that each statement to the left is true. The right side should identify given information or state the theorems, postulates, definitions or algebraic properties used to show that particular step is true.

A proof may directly demonstrate a proposition by beginning with the given information and showing that it leads to the proposition through logical steps. Alternatively, an indirect proof of a proposition may be used by demonstrating that the opposite of the proposition is untenable. In order to develop an **indirect proof**, assume the opposite of the proposition and develop the corresponding proof using the given information by finding a statement that contradicts either the original assumption or some other known fact. This contradiction indicates that the assumption made at the beginning of the proof is incorrect; therefore, the original proposition must be true.

The following **algebraic postulates** are frequently used as justifications for statements in two-column geometric proofs:

Addition Property:	If $a = b$ and $c = d$, then $a + c = b + d$.
Subtraction Property:	If $a = b$ and $c = d$, then $a - c = b - d$.
Multiplication Property:	If $a = b$ and $c \neq 0$, then $ac = bc$.
Division Property:	If $a = b$ and $c \neq 0$, then $a/c = b/c$.
Reflexive Property:	$a = a$
Symmetric Property:	If $a = b$, then $b = a$.
Transitive Property:	If $a = b$ and $b = c$, then $a = c$.
Distributive Property:	$a(b + c) = ab + ac$
Substitution Property:	If $a = b$, then b may be substituted for a in any other expression (a may also be substituted for b).

MATHEMATICS

Congruence

Congruent figures have the same size and shape; i.e., if one of the figures is superimposed on the other, the boundaries coincide exactly. Congruent line segments have the same length; congruent angles have equal measures. The symbol $\cong$ is used to indicate that two figures, line segments or angles are congruent.

The **reflexive, symmetric** and **transitive** properties described above for equality relationships may also be applied to congruence. For instance, if $\angle A \cong \angle B$ and $\angle A \cong \angle D$, then $\angle B \cong \angle D$ (transitive property).

The polygons (pentagons) *ABCDE* and *VWXYZ* shown below are congruent since they are exactly the same size and shape.

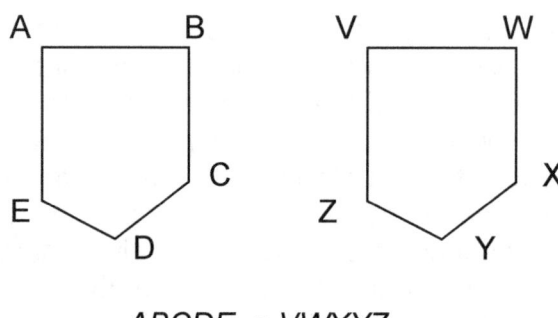

$ABCDE \cong VWXYZ$

Corresponding parts are congruent angles and congruent sides. For the polygons shown above:

corresponding angles	corresponding sides
$\angle A \leftrightarrow \angle V$	$AB \leftrightarrow VW$
$\angle B \leftrightarrow \angle W$	$BC \leftrightarrow WX$
$\angle C \leftrightarrow \angle X$	$CD \leftrightarrow XY$
$\angle D \leftrightarrow \angle Y$	$DE \leftrightarrow YZ$
$\angle E \leftrightarrow \angle Z$	$AE \leftrightarrow VZ$

Two triangles are congruent if each of the three angles and three sides of one triangle match up in a one-to-one fashion with congruent angles and sides of the second triangle. To see how the sides and angles match up, it is sometimes necessary to imagine rotating or reflecting one of the triangles so the two figures are oriented in the same position.

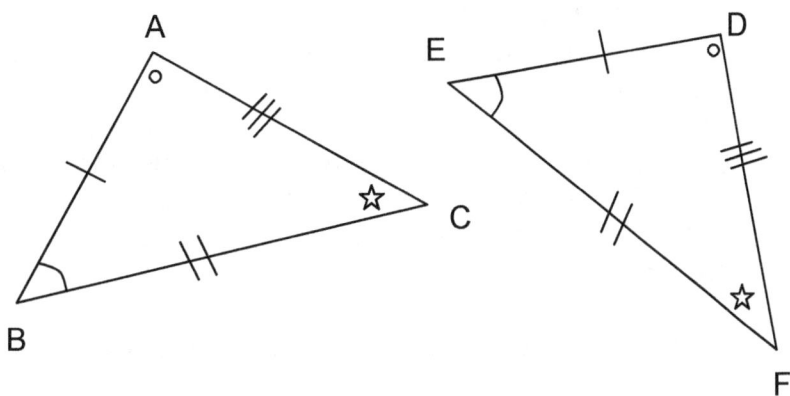

In the example above, the two triangles ABC and DEF are congruent if these 6 conditions are met:

1. $\angle A \cong \angle D$
2. $\angle B \cong \angle E$
3. $\angle C \cong \angle F$
4. $\overline{AB} \cong \overline{DE}$
5. $\overline{BC} \cong \overline{EF}$
6. $\overline{AC} \cong \overline{DF}$

The congruent angles and segments "correspond" to each other.

It is not always necessary to demonstrate all of the above six conditions to prove that two triangles are congruent. There are several "shortcut" methods described below.

The **SAS Postulate** (side-angle-side) states that if two sides and the included angle of one triangle are congruent to two sides and the included angle of another triangle, then the two triangles are congruent.

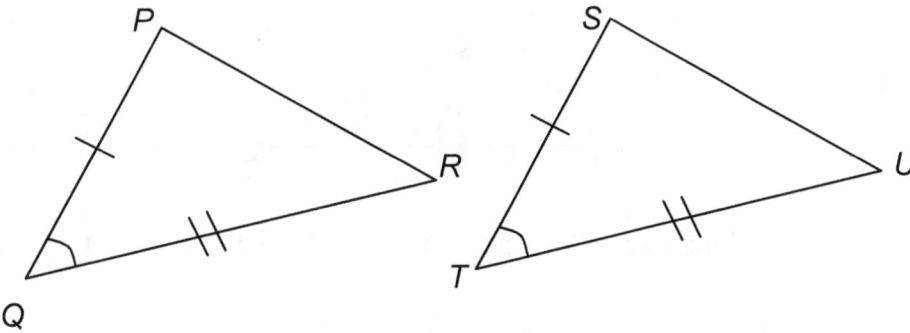

To see why this is true, imagine moving the triangle PQR (shown above) in such a way that the point P coincides with the point S, and line segment PQ coincides with line segment ST. Point Q will then coincide with T since PQ ≅ ST. Also, segment QR will coincide with TU, because ∠Q ≅ ∠T. Point R will coincide with U, because QR ≅ TU. Since P and S coincide and R and U coincide, line PR will coincide with SU because two lines cannot enclose a space. Thus the two triangles match perfectly point for point and are congruent.

Example: Are the following triangles congruent?

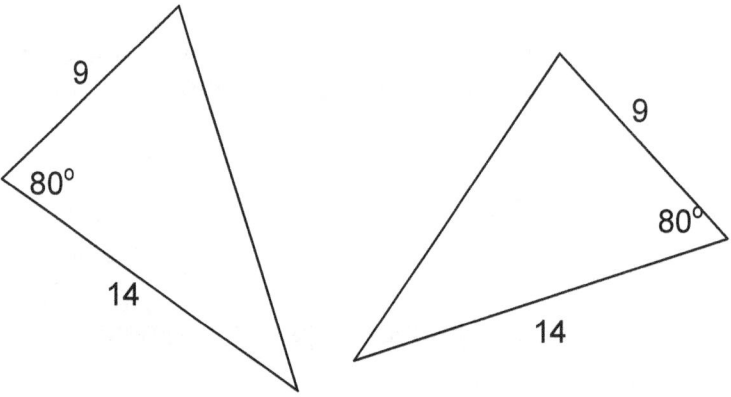

Each of the two triangles has a side that is 14 units and another that is 9 units. The angle included in the sides is 80° in both triangles. Therefore, the triangles are congruent by SAS.

The **SSS Postulate** (side-side-side) states that if three sides of one triangle are congruent to three sides of another triangle, then the two triangles are congruent.

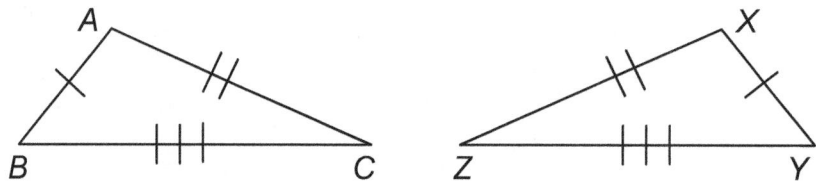

Since AB ≅ XY, BC ≅ YZ and AC ≅ XZ, then △ABC ≅ △XYZ.

Example: Given isosceles triangle ABC with D being the midpoint of base AC, prove that the two triangles ABD and ADC are congruent.

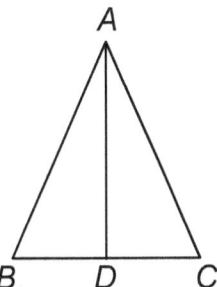

Proof:
1. Isosceles triangle ABC, D midpoint of base AC — Given
2. $AB \cong AC$ — An isosceles triangle has two congruent sides
3. $BD \cong DC$ — Midpoint divides a line into two equal parts
4. $AD \cong AD$ — Reflexive property
5. $\triangle ABD \cong \triangle BCD$ — SSS

The **ASA Postulate** (angle-side-angle) states that if two angles and the included side of one triangle are congruent to two angles and the included side of another triangle, the triangles are congruent.

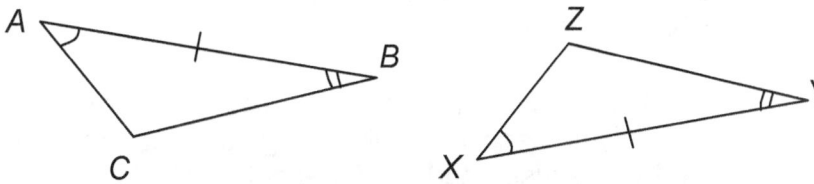

$\angle A \cong \angle X$, $\angle B \cong \angle Y$, $AB \cong XY$ then $\triangle ABC \cong \triangle XYZ$ by ASA

Example: Given two right triangles with one leg (AB and KL) of each measuring 6 cm and the adjacent angle 37°, prove the triangles are congruent.

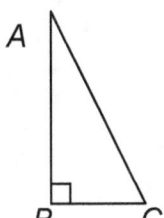 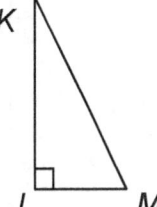

MATHEMATICS 71

Proof:

1. Right △ABC and △KLM
   AB = KL = 6 cm
   ∠A = ∠K = 37°
   Given

2. AB ≅ KL
   ∠A ≅ ∠K
   Figures with the same measure are congruent

3. ∠B ≅ ∠L
   All right angles are congruent.

4. △ABC ≅ △KLM
   ASA

Example: What method could be used to prove that triangles ABC and ADE are congruent?

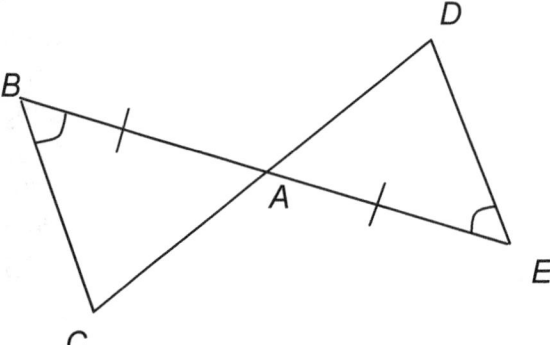

The sides AB and AE are given as congruent, as are ∠BAC and ∠DAE. ∠BAC and ∠DAE are vertical angles and are therefore congruent. Thus triangles △ABC and △ADE are congruent by the ASA postulate.

The **HL Theorem** (hypotenuse-leg) is a congruence shortcut that can only be used with right triangles. According to this theorem, if the hypotenuse and leg of one right triangle are congruent to the hypotenuse and leg of the other right triangle, then the two triangles are congruent.

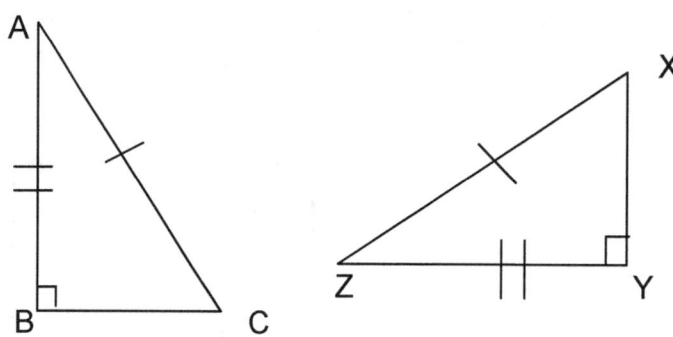

If ∠B and ∠Y are right angles and AC ≅ XZ (hypotenuse of each triangle), AB ≅ YZ (corresponding leg of each triangle), then △ABC ≅ △XYZ by HL.

Proof:

1. ∠B ≅ ∠Y
    AB ≅ YZ
    AC ≅ XZ   Given

2. $BC = \sqrt{AC^2 - AB^2}$ Pythagorean theorem
3. $XY = \sqrt{XZ^2 - YZ^2}$ Pythagorean theorem
4. $XY = \sqrt{AC^2 - AB^2} = BC$ Substitution (XZ ≅ AC, YZ ≅ AB)
5. △ABC ≅ △XYZ   SAS (AB ≅ YZ, ∠B ≅ ∠Y, BC ≅ XY)

Similarity

Two figures that have the same shape are **similar**. To be the same shape, corresponding angles must be equal. Therefore, polygons are similar if and only if there is a one-to-one correspondence between their vertices such that the corresponding angles are congruent. For similar figures, the lengths of corresponding sides are proportional. The symbol ~ is used to indicate that two figures are similar.

The polygons ABCDE and VWXYZ shown below are similar.

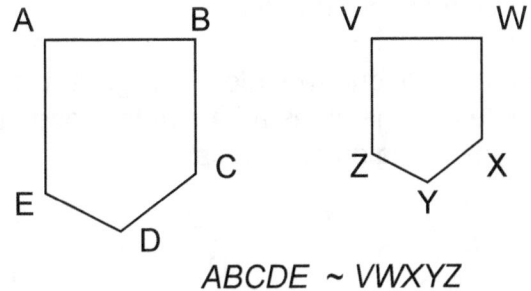

ABCDE ~ VWXYZ

Corresponding angles: ∠A = ∠V, ∠B = ∠W, ∠C = ∠X, ∠D = ∠Y, ∠E = ∠Z

Corresponding sides: $\dfrac{AB}{VW} = \dfrac{BC}{WX} = \dfrac{CD}{XY} = \dfrac{DE}{YZ} = \dfrac{AE}{VZ}$

Example: Given two similar quadrilaterals, find the lengths of sides x, y, and z.

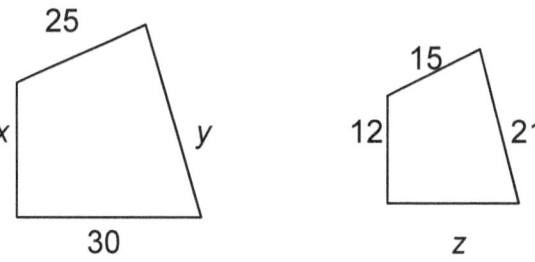

Since corresponding sides are proportional, 15/25 = 3/5, so the scale factor is 3/5.

$$\frac{12}{x} = \frac{3}{5} \qquad \frac{21}{y} = \frac{3}{5} \qquad \frac{z}{30} = \frac{3}{5}$$
$$3x = 60 \qquad 3y = 105 \qquad 5z = 90$$
$$x = 20 \qquad y = 35 \qquad z = 18$$

Just as for congruence, there are shortcut methods that can be used to prove similarity.

AA Similarity Postulate

If two angles of one triangle are congruent to two angles of another triangle, then the triangles are similar. It is obvious that if two of the corresponding angles are congruent, the third set of corresponding angles must be congruent as well. Hence, showing AA is sufficient to prove that two triangles are similar.

SAS Similarity Theorem

If an angle of one triangle is congruent to an angle of another triangle and the sides adjacent to those angles are in proportion, then the triangles are similar.

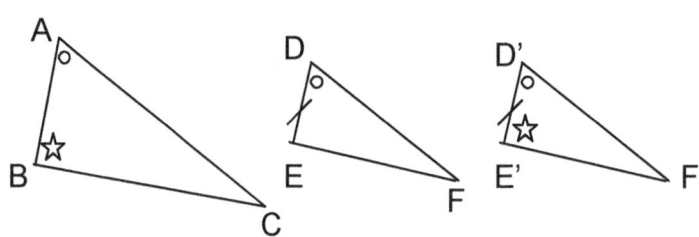

If $\angle A = \angle D$ and $\frac{AB}{DE} = \frac{AC}{DF}$, $\triangle ABC \sim \triangle DEF$.

Proof:

Let $\dfrac{AB}{DE} = \dfrac{AC}{DF} = k$. Draw another triangle D'E'F' such that ∠D' = ∠A=∠D, D'E'=DE, and ∠E' = ∠B.

By the AA postulate, △ABC ~ △D'E'F'.
Therefore, their sides are proportional $\dfrac{AB}{D'E'} = \dfrac{AC}{D'F'}$.

Since, D'E'=DE, $\dfrac{AB}{D'E'} = \dfrac{AB}{DE} = k$ (i.e., the scale factor between ABC and DEF is the same as the scale factor between AB and DE).

Hence, $\dfrac{AC}{D'F'} = k = \dfrac{AC}{DF} \Rightarrow D'F' = DF$.

Thus, △DEF ≅ △D'E'F' (SAS: D'E'=DE, ∠D' = ∠D, D'F'=DF). Since DEF and D'E'F' are congruent and D'E'F' is similar to ABC, triangle DEF must also be congruent to ABC.

Example: A graphic artist is designing a logo containing two triangles. The artist wants the triangles to be similar. Determine whether the artist has created similar triangles.

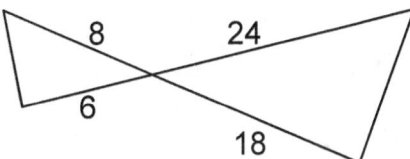

The sides are proportional $\left(\dfrac{8}{24} = \dfrac{6}{18} = \dfrac{1}{3}\right)$ and vertical angles are congruent. The two triangles are therefore similar by the SAS similarity theorem.

SSS Similarity Theorem

If the sides of two triangles are in proportion, then the triangles are similar.

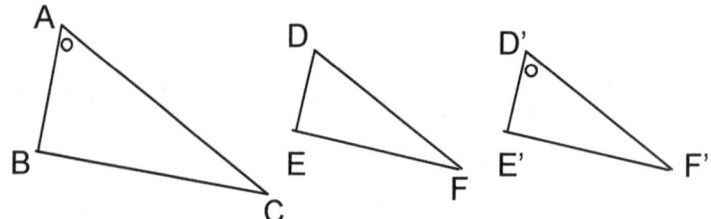

If $\dfrac{AB}{DE} = \dfrac{AC}{DF} = \dfrac{BC}{EF}$, $\triangle ABC \sim \triangle DEF$

Proof:

Let $\dfrac{AB}{DE} = \dfrac{AC}{DF} = \dfrac{BC}{EF} = k$. Draw another triangle D'E'F' such that $\angle D' = \angle A$, D'E'=DE, and D'F'=DF.

Substituting D'E' for DE and D'F' for DF in the above proportionality relationship yields $\dfrac{AB}{D'E'} = \dfrac{AC}{D'F'} = k$.

Thus triangles ABC and D'E'F' are similar by the SAS similarity theorem.

Hence all three sides of the triangles ABC and D'E'F' are proportional ($\dfrac{AB}{D'E'} = \dfrac{AC}{D'F'} = \dfrac{BC}{E'F'}$) by the same factor k.

Since DE=D'E' and DF=D'F', the proportionality relationships indicates that EF=E'F'.

Hence, $\triangle DEF \cong \triangle D'E'F'$ (SSS).

Since DEF and D'E'F' are congruent and D'E'F' is similar to ABC, triangle DEF must also be congruent to ABC.

Example: Tommy draws and cuts out 2 triangles for a school project. One of them has sides of 3, 6, and 9 inches. The other triangle has sides of 2, 4, and 6. Is there a relationship between the two triangles?

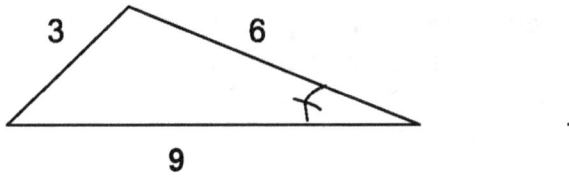
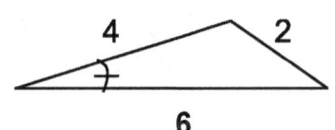

Determine the proportions of the corresponding sides.

$$\frac{2}{3} \qquad \frac{4}{6} = \frac{2}{3} \qquad \frac{6}{9} = \frac{2}{3}$$

The smaller triangle is 2/3 the size of the large triangle, therefore they are similar triangles by the SSS similarity theorem.

2.2b. **Understand, apply, and justify properties of triangles (e.g., the Exterior Angle Theorem, concurrence theorems, trigonometric ratios, Triangle Inequality, Law of Sines, Law of Cosines, the Pythagorean Theorem and its converse)**

Interior and exterior angles

The three angles within a triangle are known as the **interior angles**. In any triangle, the sum of the interior angles equals 180°.

Two adjacent angles form a linear pair when they have a common side and their remaining sides form a straight angle. Angles in a linear pair are supplementary. An **exterior angle** of a triangle forms a linear pair with an angle of the triangle.

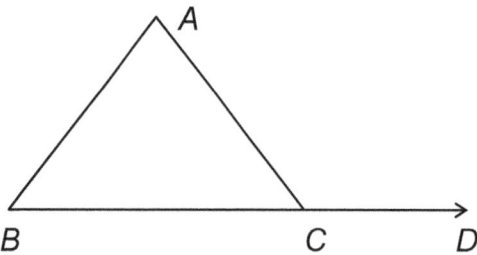

$\angle ACD$ is an exterior angle of triangle ABC, forming a linear pair with $\angle ACB$.

According to the **Exterior Angle Theorem**, the measure of an exterior angle of a triangle is equal to the sum of the measures of the two non-adjacent interior angles. We can easily demonstrate this by taking the above triangle ABC as an example. In this triangle, $\angle ABC + \angle BAC + \angle ACB = 180°$ (the sum of interior angles of a triangle). Also, $\angle ACD + \angle ACB = 180°$ (exterior angle and adjacent interior angle are supplementary). Therefore, $\angle ACD = \angle ABC + \angle BAC$.

Example: In triangle ABC, the measure of $\angle A$ is twice the measure of $\angle B$. $\angle C$ is 30° more than their sum. Find the measure of the exterior angle formed at $\angle C$.

Let x = the measure of $\angle B$
$2x$ = the measure of $\angle A$
$x + 2x + 30$ = the measure of $\angle C$
$x + 2x + x + 2x + 30 = 180$
$6x + 30 = 180$
$6x = 150$
$x = 25$
$2x = 50$

It is not necessary to find the measure of the third angle, since the exterior angle equals the sum of the opposite interior angles. Thus, the exterior angle at $\angle C$ measures 75°.

Concurrence theorems

If three or more segments intersect in a single point, the point is called a **point of concurrency**. The concurrence theorems, given below, make statements about the concurrence of the following sets of special segments associated with triangles:

1. **Angle bisectors**: An angle bisector is a line segment that bisects one of the angles of a triangle. **The three angle bisectors of a triangle intersect in a single point equidistant from all three sides of the triangle.** (Recall that the distance from a point to a side is measured along the perpendicular from the point to the side.) This point is known as the **incenter** and is the center of the **incircle** inscribed within the triangle tangent to each of the three sides.

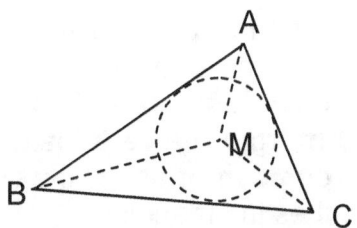

2. **Medians**: A median is a segment that connects a vertex to the midpoint of the side opposite from that vertex. **The three medians of a triangle are concurrent and intersect each other in a ratio 2:1 at the centroid of the triangle.**

The medians of the triangle ABC shown below intersect in the centroid G such that $\dfrac{AG}{GF} = \dfrac{BG}{GE} = \dfrac{CG}{GD} = \dfrac{2}{1}$.

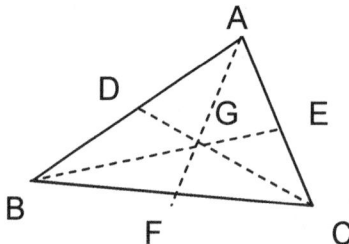

3. **Altitudes**: An altitude is a segment that extends from one vertex and is perpendicular to the side opposite that vertex. In some cases, the side opposite from the vertex used will need to be extended for the altitude to form a perpendicular to the opposite side. The length of the altitude is used when referring to the height of the triangle. **The altitudes of a triangle are concurrent** and meet at the orthocenter of the triangle.

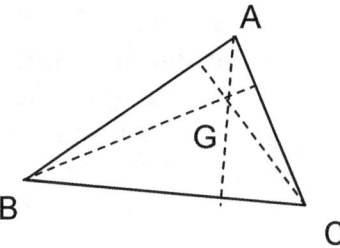

4. **Perpendicular Bisectors**: A perpendicular bisector of a triangle bisects one of the sides and is perpendicular to it. **The three perpendicular bisectors of a triangle meet in a point equidistant from the vertices of the triangle.** This point is known as the **circumcenter** and is the center of the **circumcircle** that circumscribes the triangles.

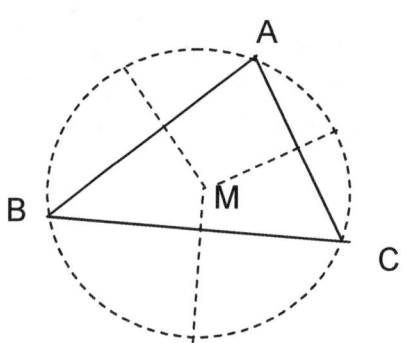

The points of concurrency can lie inside the triangle, outside the triangle, or on one of the sides of the triangle. The following table summarizes this information.

Possible Location(s) of the Points of Concurrency

	Inside the Triangle	Outside the Triangle	On the Triangle
Angle Bisectors	X		
Medians	X		
Altitudes	X	X	X
Perpendicular Bisectors	X	X	X

Example: BE and CD are altitudes of equilateral triangle ABC and intersect at the point G. What is the ratio of the area of triangle BDG to the area of triangle ABC?

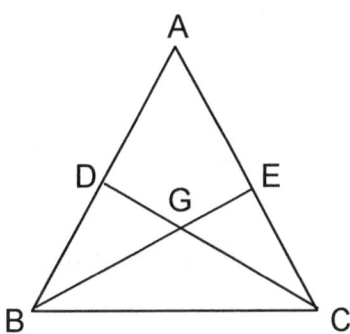

The area of triangle ABC = $\frac{1}{2}AB \times CD$. The area of triangle BDG = $\frac{1}{2}BD \times DG$. Since ABC is an equilateral triangle, the altitudes of the triangles are also medians. Therefore $BD = \frac{1}{2}AB$ and $GD = \frac{1}{3}CD$.

Thus, The area of triangle BDG = $\frac{1}{2}(\frac{1}{2}AB) \times (\frac{1}{3}CD) = \frac{1}{12}AB \times CD$.

Hence the area of triangle BDG is one-sixth the area of triangle ABC.

Triangle Inequality

The **Triangle Inequality Theorem** states that the sum of the lengths of any two sides of a triangle is greater than the length of the remaining side. In the triangle below,

$a + b > c$
$a + c > b$
$b + c > a$

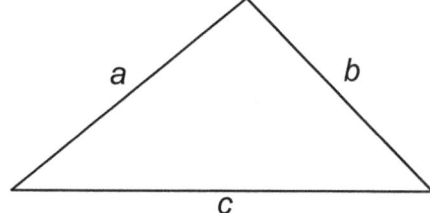

If a triangle has an unknown side, the Triangle Inequality Theorem can be applied to determine a reasonable range of possible values for the unknown side.

Example: Determine the range of possible values for the unknown side, *p*.

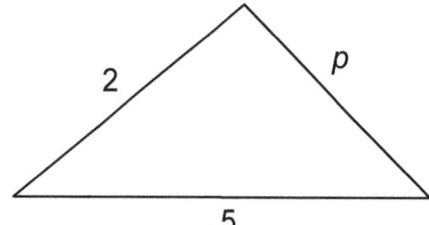

$2 + p > 5$
$2 + 5 > p$
$p + 5 > 2$

The expressions could be arranged to show: $p > 5–2$ or $p > 3$
$7 > p$
$p > –3$.

Thus *p* is a value between 3 and 7.

An angle-side relationship exists between angles and the sides opposite them. The side of the triangle that is opposite the largest angle is the longest side. The side opposite the smallest angle is the smallest. This rule can be used to determine a reasonable range of measurement for an unknown angle.

Example: Order the sides of the following triangle by length.

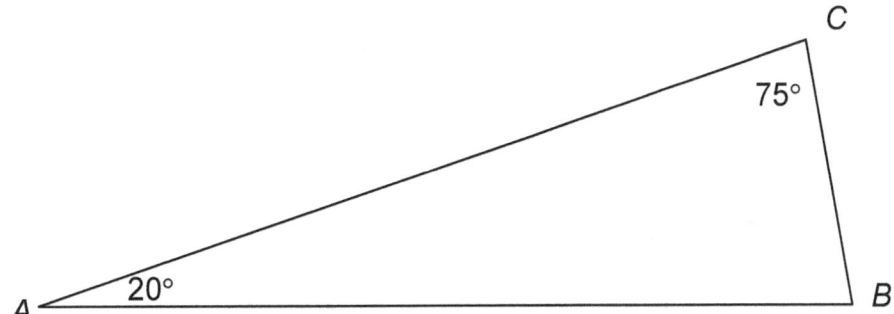

Because the sum of all angles in a triangle is equal to 180°, ∠B can be calculated.

$$\angle A + \angle B + \angle C = 180°$$
$$20° + \angle B + 75° = 180°$$
$$\angle B = 180° - 20° - 75°$$
$$\angle B = 85°$$

To order the sides according to size, the angle-side relationship can be applied: $\overline{BC} < \overline{AB} < \overline{AC}$

Trigonometric ratios

A **right triangle** is a triangle with one right angle. The side opposite the right angle is called the **hypotenuse**. The other two sides are the **legs**.

Given right triangle ABC, the adjacent side and opposite side can be identified for each angle A and B.

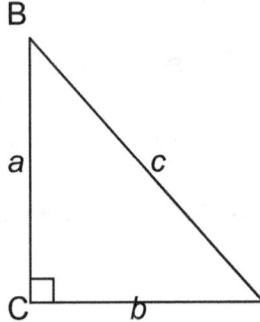

Looking at angle A, it can be determined that side *b* is adjacent to angle A and side *a* is opposite angle A.

If we now look at angle B, we see that side *a* is adjacent to angle B and side *b* is opposite angle B.

The longest side (opposite the 90 degree angle) is always called the hypotenuse.

The basic trigonometric ratios are listed below:

Sine = opposite/hypotenuse   Cosine = adjacent/hypotenuse   Tangent = opposite/adjacent

Example2:

1. Use triangle ABC to find the sine, cosine and tangent for angle A.

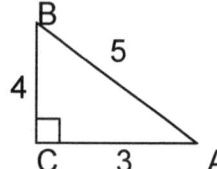

Sin A = 4/5
Cos A = 3/5
Tan A = 4/3

2. Use the basic trigonometric ratios of sine, cosine and tangent to solve for the missing sides of right triangles when given at least one of the acute angles.

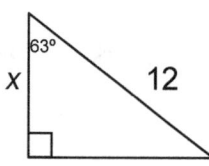

In the triangle ABC, an acute angle of 63 degrees and the length of the hypotenuse (12). The missing side is the one adjacent to the given angle.

The appropriate trigonometric ratio to use would be cosine since we are looking for the adjacent side and we have the length of the hypotenuse.

Cos x = adjacent/hypotenuse   1. Write formula.

Cos 63 = x/12   2. Substitute known values.

x = 5.448   3. Solve.

Law of sines

For any triangle ABC, the law of sines states that the following relationship holds:

$$\frac{\sin A}{BC} = \frac{\sin B}{AC} = \frac{\sin C}{AB}$$

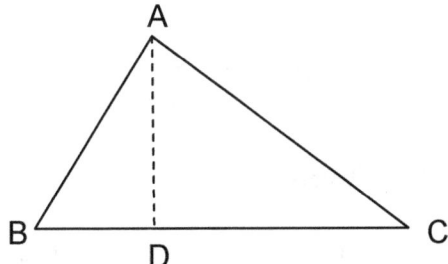

The law of sines may be derived by drawing an altitude AD from point A to side BC.

Considering the right triangle ABD,

$$\sin B = \frac{AD}{AB} \Rightarrow AD = AB \sin B$$

Considering the right triangle ADC,

$$\sin C = \frac{AD}{AC} \Rightarrow AD = AC \sin C$$

Thus,

$$AB \sin B = AC \sin C \Rightarrow \frac{\sin B}{AC} = \frac{\sin C}{AB}$$

The equality with the third ratio $\frac{\sin A}{BC}$ can be derived by drawing another altitude and going through the same exercise as above.

Example: Find side AB for the triangle shown below.

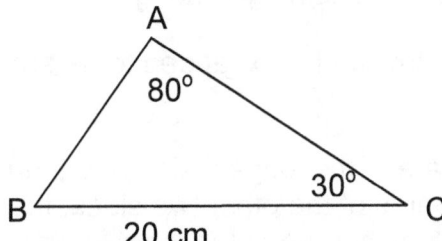

Using the law of sines, we have

$$\frac{\sin 30}{AB} = \frac{\sin 80}{20} \Rightarrow AB = 20 \times \frac{\sin 30}{\sin 80} = 20 \times \frac{0.5}{0.98} = 10.2 \, cm$$

Pythagorean theorem

The Pythagorean theorem states that the square of the length of the hypotenuse is equal to the sum of the squares of the lengths of the legs. Symbolically, this is stated as:

$$c^2 = a^2 + b^2$$

Example: Given the right triangle below, find the missing side.

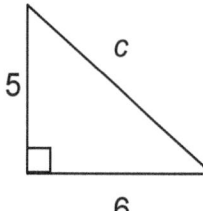

$c^2 = a^2 + b^2$ 1. write formula
$c^2 = 5^2 + 6^2$ 2. substitute known values
$c^2 = 61$ 3. take square root
$c = \sqrt{61}$ or 7.81   4. solve

The Converse of the Pythagorean Theorem states that if the square of one side of a triangle is equal to the sum of the squares of the other two sides, then the triangle is a right triangle.

Example: Given $\triangle XYZ$, with sides measuring 12, 16 and 20 cm. Is this a right triangle?

$c^2 = a^2 + b^2$
$20^2 \underline{\;?\;} 12^2 + 16^2$
$400 \underline{\;?\;} 144 + 256$
$400 = 400$

Yes, the triangle is a right triangle.

This theorem can be expanded to determine if triangles are obtuse or acute.

If the square of the longest side of a triangle is greater than the sum of the squares of the other two sides, then the triangle is an obtuse triangle. If the square of the longest side of a triangle is less than the sum of the squares of the other two sides, then the triangle is an acute triangle.

Example: Given △LMN with sides measuring 7, 12, and 14 inches. Is the triangle right, acute, or obtuse?

$$14^2 \; ? \; 7^2 + 12^2$$
$$196 \; ? \; 49 + 144$$
$$196 > 193$$

Therefore, the triangle is obtuse.

Law of cosines

The Pythagorean theorem is applicable only to right triangles. A general relationship between the sides of a triangle, valid for all triangles, is given by the law of cosines. According to this law, for a triangle ABC,

$$AB^2 = AC^2 + BC^2 - 2AC \cdot BC \cos C$$

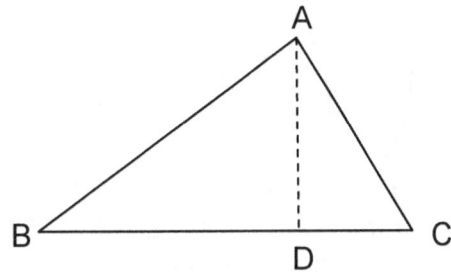

We can see that this law reduces to the Pythagorean theorem when C is a right angle and cos C = 0.

The law of cosines may be derived as follows:

Draw the altitude AD from point A to side BC.

$$\begin{aligned}
AB^2 &= AD^2 + BD^2 & \text{(Pythagorean theorem)} \\
&= (AC - DC)^2 + BD^2 \\
&= (AC - DC)^2 + BC^2 - DC^2 & \text{(Pythagorean theorem)} \\
&= AC^2 + DC^2 - 2AC \cdot DC + BC^2 - DC^2 \\
&= AC^2 + BC^2 - 2AC \cdot DC
\end{aligned}$$

Considering the right triangle BDC,

$$\cos C = \frac{DC}{BC} \Rightarrow DC = BC \cos C$$

Making this substitution for DC in the above equation we get,

$$AB^2 = AC^2 + BC^2 - 2AC \cdot BC \cos C \qquad \text{(Law of Cosines)}$$

Example: A triangle ABC has sides of measure BC = 9, AC = 8 and AB = 7. What is the measure of angle C?

Using the law of cosines we can write,

$$7^2 = 8^2 + 9^2 - 2 \cdot 8 \cdot 9 \cos C$$
$$\Rightarrow 144 \cos C = 64 + 81 - 49$$
$$\Rightarrow \cos C = \frac{96}{144} = \frac{2}{3}$$
$$\Rightarrow C = 48°$$

Special right triangles

Special right triangles have set relationships between the hypotenuse and the legs.

The first of these is a 30°-60°-90° right triangle. In the diagram below the short leg (sl) is opposite the 30° angle, the long leg (ll) is opposite the 60° angle and h is the hypotenuse.

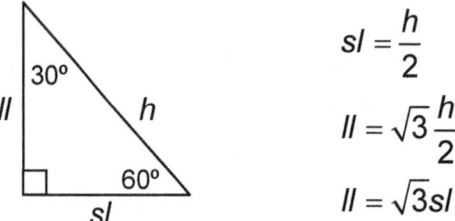

$$sl = \frac{h}{2}$$
$$ll = \sqrt{3}\frac{h}{2}$$
$$ll = \sqrt{3}sl$$

Example: A 20 ft ladder is propped up against a wall. If the distance from the bottom of the ladder to the wall is half the length of the ladder, how high up the wall is the top of the ladder?

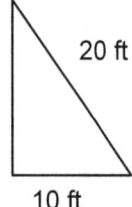

20 ft

10 ft

Since the length of the shorter leg of a 30°-60°-90° right triangle is half the length of the hypotenuse, the ladder forms a 30°-60°-90° right triangle with the wall and ground.

Thus, the longer leg of the right triangle = $10\sqrt{3} = 17.3$ ft and the top of the ladder is placed 17.3 ft up the wall.

The second special right triangle is a 45°-45°-90° right triangle. In the diagram below, the legs (*l*) are opposite the 45° angle and *h* is the hypotenuse.

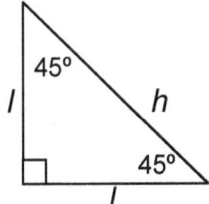

$$l = \frac{h}{\sqrt{2}}$$

Example: A woman is making a scarf in the shape of a right triangle. She wants the two shorter sides to be equal in length and the long side to be 15 inches long. What should the length of each of the shorter sides be?

Since the two shorter sides are equal in length, the scarf is an isosceles right triangle, i.e. a 45°-45°-90° right triangle.

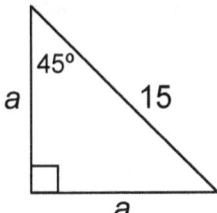

Thus the length of each short side = $\frac{15}{\sqrt{2}} = 10.6$ in.

Geometric mean

When an altitude is drawn to the hypotenuse of a right triangle, then the two triangles formed are similar to the original triangle and to each other.

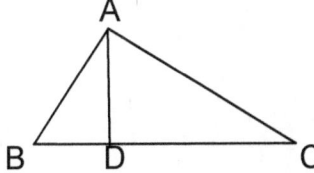

Given right triangle ABC with right angle at A, altitude AD drawn to hypotenuse BD at D, △ABC ~ △ABD ~ △ACD.

If a, b and c are positive numbers such that $\dfrac{a}{b} = \dfrac{b}{c}$, then b is called the **geometric mean** between a and c.

The geometric mean is significant when the altitude is drawn to the hypotenuse of a right triangle.

The length of the altitude is the geometric mean between each segment of the hypotenuse. Also, each leg is the geometric mean between the hypotenuse and the segment of the hypotenuse that is adjacent to the leg.

Example:

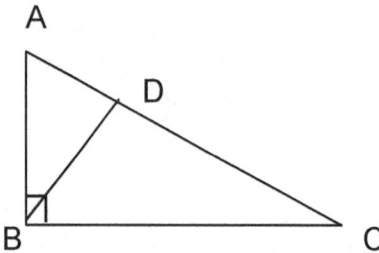

△ABC is a right triangle and ∠ABC is a right angle. AB = 6 and AC = 12. Find AD, CD, BD, and BC.

$\dfrac{12}{6} = \dfrac{6}{AD}$ $\dfrac{3}{BD} = \dfrac{BD}{9}$ $\dfrac{12}{BC} = \dfrac{BC}{9}$

12(AD) = 36   (BD)² = 27   (BC)² = 108

AD = 3
BD = $\sqrt{27}$ = $\sqrt{9 \cdot 3}$ = $3\sqrt{3}$
BC = $6\sqrt{3}$
CD = 12 - 3 = 9

2.2c. Understand, apply, and justify properties of polygons and circles from an advanced standpoint (e.g., derive the area formulas for regular polygons and circles from the area of a triangle)

Polygons

A polygon is a simple closed figure composed of line segments. Here we will consider only **convex polygons**, i.e. polygons for which the measure of each internal angle is less than 180°. Of the two polygons shown below, the one on the left is a convex polygon.

A **regular polygon** is one for which all sides are the same length and all interior angles are the same measure.

The sum of the measures of the **interior angles** of a polygon can be determined using the following formula, where n represents the number of angles in the polygon.

Sum of $\angle s = 180(n - 2)$

The measure of each angle of a regular polygon can be found by dividing the sum of the measures by the number of angles.

Measure of $\angle = \dfrac{180(n-2)}{n}$

Example: Find the measure of each angle of a regular octagon. Since an octagon has eight sides, each angle equals:

$$\frac{180(8-2)}{8} = \frac{180(6)}{8} = 135°$$

The sum of the measures of the **exterior angles** of a polygon, taken one angle at each vertex, equals 360°.

The measure of each exterior angle of a regular polygon can be determined using the following formula, where n represents the number of angles in the polygon.
Measure of exterior $\angle$ of regular polygon

$$= 180 - \frac{180(n-2)}{n} = \frac{360}{n}$$

Example: Find the measure of the interior and exterior angles of a regular pentagon.

Since a pentagon has five sides, each exterior angle measures:

$$\frac{360}{5} = 72°$$

Since each exterior angle is supplementary to its interior angle, the interior angle measures 180 – 72 or 108°.

A **quadrilateral** is a polygon with four sides. The sum of the measures of the angles of a convex quadrilateral is 360°.

A **trapezoid** is a quadrilateral with exactly one pair of parallel sides. The two parallel sides of a trapezoid are called the bases, and the two non-parallel sides are called the legs. If the two legs are the same length, then the trapezoid is called isosceles.

The segment connecting the two midpoints of the legs is called the median. The median has the following two properties:
1. The median is parallel to the two bases.
2. The length of the median is equal to one-half the sum of the length of the two bases.

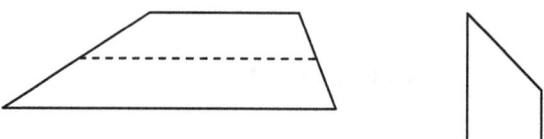

In an **isosceles trapezoid**, the non-parallel sides are congruent.

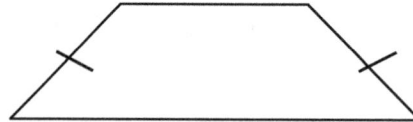

An isosceles trapezoid has the following properties:
1. The diagonals of an isosceles trapezoid are congruent.
2. The base angles of an isosceles trapezoid are congruent.

Example: An isosceles trapezoid has a diagonal of 10 and a base angle measure of 30°. Find the measure of the other 3 angles.

Based on the properties of trapezoids, the measure of the other base angle is 30° and the measure of the other diagonal is 10. The other two angles have a measure of

$$360 = 30(2) + 2x$$
$$x = 150°$$

The other two angles measure 150° each.

A **parallelogram** is a quadrilateral with two pairs of parallel sides and has the following properties:

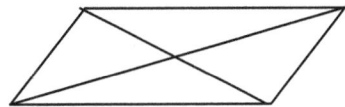

1. The diagonals bisect each other.
2. Each diagonal divides the parallelogram into two congruent triangles.
3. Both pairs of opposite sides are congruent.
4. Both pairs of opposite angles are congruent.
5. Two adjacent angles are supplementary.

Example: Find the measures of the other three angles of a parallelogram if one angle measures 38°.

Since opposite angles are equal, there are two angles measuring 38°. Since adjacent angles are supplementary, 180 – 38 = 142. Hence the other two angles measure 142° each.

Example: The measures of two adjacent angles of a parallelogram are 3x + 40 and x + 70. Find the measures of each angle.

$$2(3x + 40) + 2(x + 70) = 360$$
$$6x + 80 + 2x + 140 = 360$$
$$8x + 220 = 360$$
$$8x = 140$$
$$x = 17.5$$
$$3x + 40 = 92.5$$
$$x + 70 = 87.5$$

Thus the angles measure 92.5°, 92.5°, 87.5°, and 87.5°.

A **rectangle** is a parallelogram with a right angle. Since a rectangle is a special type of parallelogram, it exhibits all the properties of a parallelogram. All the angles of a rectangle are right angles because of congruent opposite angles. Additionally, the diagonals of a rectangle are congruent.

A **rhombus** is a parallelogram with all sides equal in length. A rhombus also has all the properties of a parallelogram. Additionally, its diagonals are perpendicular to each other and they bisect its angles.

A **square** is a rectangle with all sides equal in length. A **square** has all the properties of a rectangle <u>and</u> a rhombus.

Example: True or false?

All squares are rhombuses.	True
All parallelograms are rectangles.	False - <u>some</u> parallelograms are rectangles
All rectangles are parallelograms.	True
Some rhombuses are squares.	True
Some rectangles are trapezoids.	False - only <u>one</u> pair of parallel sides
All quadrilaterals are parallelograms.	False - some quadrilaterals are parallelograms
Some squares are rectangles.	False - all squares are rectangles
Some parallelograms are rhombuses.	True

Example: In rhombus ABCD side AB = 3x - 7 and side CD = x + 15. Find the length of each side.

Since all the sides are the same length, $3x - 7 = x + 15$
$$2x = 22$$
$$x = 11$$

Since $3(11) - 7 = 25$ and $11 + 15 = 25$, each side measures 25 units.

Perimeter and area of polygons

The **perimeter** of any polygon is the sum of the lengths of the sides. The **area** of a polygon is the number of square units covered by the figure or the space that a figure occupies. In the area formulae below, b refers to the base and h to the height or altitude of a figure. For a trapezoid, a and b are the two parallel bases.

FIGURE	AREA FORMULA	PERIMETER FORMULA
Rectangle	LW	$2(L+W)$
Triangle	$\frac{1}{2}bh$	$a+b+c$
Parallelogram	bh	sum of lengths of sides
Trapezoid	$\frac{1}{2}h(a+b)$	sum of lengths of sides

Even though different figures have different area formulae, the formulae are connected and one can go easily from one to another. For instance, it is easy to see from the diagram below that the area of the triangle ABD is half that of rectangle EABD and the area of triangle ADC is half that of rectangle AFDC. Thus, the area of triangle ABC is half that of rectangle EFBC and is equal to

$$\frac{1}{2}BC \cdot EB = \frac{1}{2}BC \cdot AD$$

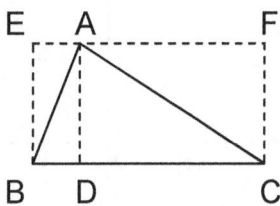

The area of a parallelogram may similarly be shown to be equal to that of an equivalent rectangle. Since triangles ACE and BDF are congruent in the diagram below (AE and BF are altitudes), parallelogram ABCD is equal in area to rectangle AEFB that has the same base (CD=EF) and height.

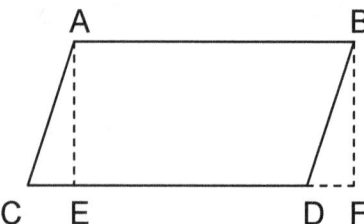

The area of a trapezoid is the sum of the areas of two triangles each of which has one of the parallel sides as a base. In the diagram below,
area of trapezoid ABCD = area of ABC + area of ACD
$$= \frac{1}{2}BC \cdot AE + \frac{1}{2}AD \cdot CF$$
$$= \frac{1}{2}AE(BC + AD) \quad \text{(Since AE = CF)}$$

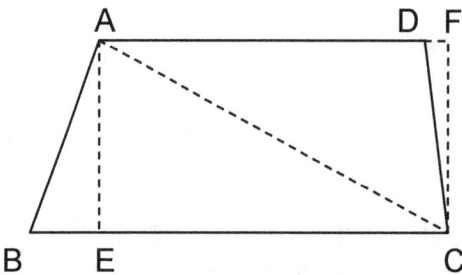

Example: A farmer has a piece of land shaped as shown below. He wishes to fence this land at an estimated cost of $25 per linear foot. What is the total cost of fencing this property to the nearest foot?

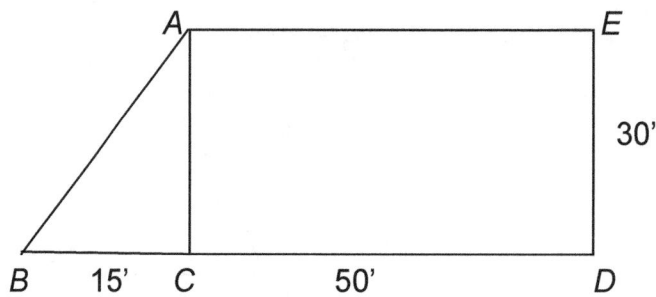

MATHEMATICS 96

From the right triangle ABC, AC = 30 and BC = 15.

Since $(AB) = (AC)^2 + (BC)^2$, $(AB) = (30)^2 + (15)^2$. So, $\sqrt{(AB)^2} = AB = \sqrt{1125} = 33.5410$ feet. To the nearest foot, AB = 34 feet. The perimeter of the piece of land is

$$AB + BC + CD + DE + EA = 34 + 15 + 50 + 30 + 50 = 179 \text{ feet}$$

The cost of fencing is $25 x 179 = $4, 475.00

The area of any regular polygon having *n* sides may be expressed as a sum of the areas of *n* congruent triangles. If each side of the polygon is of length *a*, and the apothem (distance from center of polygon to one side) is *h*,

area of the polygon = $n \times \frac{1}{2} \times a \times h$ (*n* times the area of one triangle)

Since *n* x *a* is the perimeter of the polygon, we can also write

area of the polygon = $\frac{1}{2} \times$ perimeter $\times$ apothem

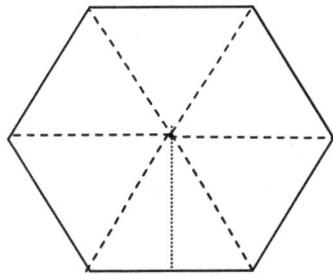

Circles

The distance around a circle is the **circumference**. The ratio of the circumference to the diameter is represented by the Greek letter pi, where $\pi \approx 3.14$. The circumference of a circle is given by the formula $C = 2\pi r$ or $C = \pi d$ where *r* is the radius of the circle and *d* is the diameter. The **area** of a circle is given by the formula $A = \pi r^2$.

We can extend the area formula of a regular polygon to get the area of a circle by considering the fact that a circle is essentially a regular polygon with an infinite number of sides. The radius of a circle is equivalent to the apothem of a regular polygon. Thus, applying the area formula for a regular polygon to a circle we get

$$\frac{1}{2} \times perimeter \times apothem = \frac{1}{2} \times 2\pi r \times r = \pi r^2$$

If **two circles** have radii that are in a ratio of $a:b$, then the following ratios also apply to the circles:

1. The diameters are in the ratio $a:b$.
2. The circumferences are in the ratio $a:b$.
3. The areas are in the ratio $a^2:b^2$, or the ratio of the areas is the square of the ratio of the radii.

If you draw two radii in a circle, the angle they form with the center as the vertex is a **central angle**. The piece of the circle "inside" the angle is an arc. Just like a central angle, an arc can have any degree measure from 0 to 360. The measure of an arc is equal to the measure of the central angle that forms the arc. Since a diameter forms a semicircle and the measure of a straight angle like a diameter is 180°, the measure of a semicircle is also 180°.

Given two points on a circle, the two points form two different arcs. Except in the case of semicircles, one of the two arcs will always be greater than 180° and the other will be less than 180°. The arc less than 180° is a **minor arc** and the arc greater than 180° is a **major arc**.

Examples:
1.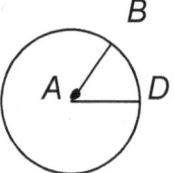

$m\angle BAD = 45°$
What is the measure of the major arc *BD*?

minor arc $BD = m\angle BAD = 45°$
$360 - 45 =$ major arc BD A major and minor arc always add up to $360°$.

Thus, major arc $BD = 315°$

2.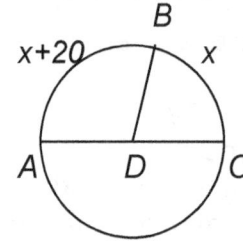

$\overline{AC}$ is a diameter of circle *D*.
What is the measure of $\angle BDC$?

$m\angle ADB + m\angle BDC = 180°$

$x + 20 + x = 180$

A diameter forms a semicircle that has a measure of $180°$.

$2x + 20 = 180$

$2x = 160$

$x = 80$

minor arc $BC = 80°$

$m\angle BDC = 80°$

A central angle has the same measure as the arc it forms.

Although an arc has a measure associated to the degree measure of a central angle, it also has a length that is a fraction of the circumference of the circle. For each central angle and its associated arc, there is a sector of the circle that resembles a pie piece. The area of such a sector is a fraction of the area of the circle. The fractions used for the area of a sector and length of its associated arc are both equal to the ratio of the central angle to 360°.

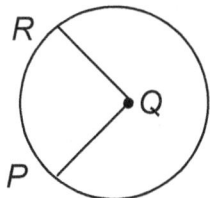

$$\frac{\angle PQR}{360°} = \frac{\text{length of arc RP}}{\text{circumference of circle}} = \frac{\text{area of sector PQR}}{\text{area of circle}}$$

Examples:

1.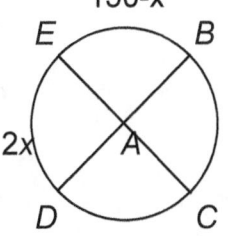

Circle A as a radius of 4 cm. What is the length of arc ED?

$2x + 150 - x = 180$

$x + 150 = 180$

$x = 30$

Arc BE and arc ED make a semicircle.

MATHEMATICS

Arc $ED = 2(30) = 60°$

$$\frac{60}{360} = \frac{\text{arc length } ED}{2\pi 4}$$

$$\frac{1}{6} = \frac{\text{arc length}}{8\pi}$$

$$\text{arc length} = \frac{8\pi}{6} = \frac{4\pi}{3}$$

The ratio 60° to 360° is equal to the ratio of arch length ED to the circumference of circle A.

Cross multiply and solve for the arc length.

2. The radius of circle M is 3 cm. The length of arc PF is 2π cm. What is the area of sector MPF?

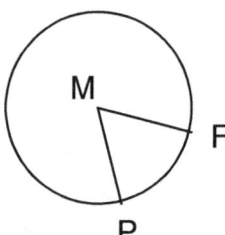

Circumference of circle M $= 2\pi(3) = 6\pi$

Area of circle M $= \pi \cdot 3^2 = 9\pi$

$$\frac{\text{area of } MPF}{9\pi} = \frac{2\pi}{6\pi}$$

$$\frac{\text{area of } MPF}{9\pi} = \frac{1}{3}$$

$$\text{area of } MPF = \frac{9\pi}{3}$$

$$\text{area of } MPF = 3\pi$$

Find the circumference and area of the circle.

The ratio of the sector area to the circle area is the same as the arc length to the circumference.

Solve for the area of the sector.

A **tangent line** intersects or touches a circle in exactly one point. If a radius is drawn to that point, the radius will be perpendicular to the tangent.

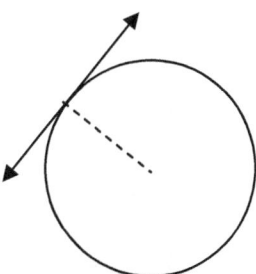

A **secant line** intersects a circle in two points and includes a **chord** which is a segment with endpoints on the circle. If a radius or diameter is perpendicular to a chord, the radius will cut the chord into two equal parts and vice-versa.

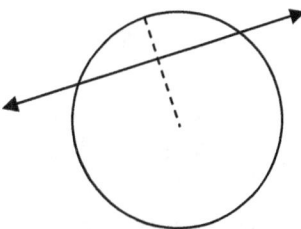

If **two chords** in the same circle have the same length, the two chords will have arcs that are the same length, and the two chords will be equidistant from the center of the circle. Distance from the center to a chord is measured by finding the length of a segment from the center perpendicular to the chord.

Examples:

1.
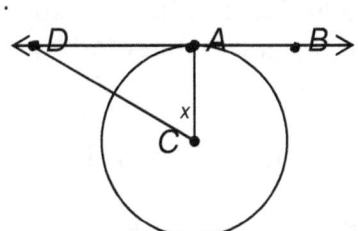

$\overrightarrow{DB}$ is tangent to circle C at A.
$m\angle ADC = 40°$ Find x.

$\overline{AC} \perp \overrightarrow{DB}$ A radius is $\perp$ to a tangent at the point of tangency.

$m\angle DAC = 90°$ Two segments that are $\perp$ form a $90°$ angle.

$40 + 90 + x = 180$ The sum of the angles of a triangle is 180°.

$x = 50°$ Solve for x.

2.

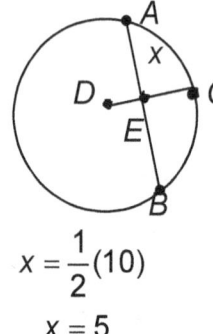

$\overline{CD}$ is a radius and $\overline{CD} \perp$ chord $\overline{AB}$. $\overline{AB} = 10$. Find x.

$x = \dfrac{1}{2}(10)$

$x = 5$

If a radius is $\perp$ to a chord, the radius bisects the chord.

Angles with their vertices on the circle

An **inscribed angle** is an angle whose vertex is on the circumference circle. Such an angle could be formed by two chords, two diameters, two secants, or a secant and a tangent. An inscribed angle has one arc of the circle in its interior. The measure of the inscribed angle is one-half the measure of its intercepted arc. If two inscribed angles intercept the same arc, the two angles are congruent (i.e. their measures are equal). If an inscribed angle intercepts an entire semicircle, the angle is a right angle.

Angles with their vertices in a circle's interior

When two chords intersect inside a circle, two sets of vertical angles are formed. Each set of vertical angles intercepts two arcs that are across from each other. The measure of an angle formed by two chords in a circle is equal to one-half the sum of the arc intercepted by the angle and the arc intercepted by its vertical angle.

Angles with their vertices in a circle's exterior

If an angle has its vertex outside of the circle and each side of the angle intersects the circle, then the angle contains two different arcs. The measure of the angle is equal to one-half the difference of the two arcs.

Examples:

1.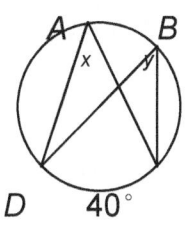

Find x and y.

$m\angle DAC = \frac{1}{2}(40) = 20°$

∠DAC and ∠DBC are both inscribed angles, so each one has a measure equal to one-half the measure of arc DC.

$m\angle DBC = \frac{1}{2}(40) = 20°$

$x = 20°$ and $y = 20°$

2. Find the measure of arc BC if the measure of arc DE is 30° and angle BAC = 20°.

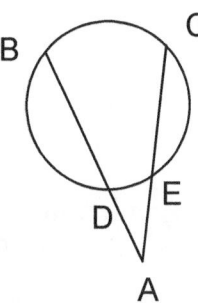

$m\angle BAC = \frac{1}{2}(mBC - mDE)$

$\Rightarrow 2 \times m\angle BAC = mBC - mDE$

$\Rightarrow mBC = 2 \times m\angle BAC + mDE = 2 \times 20° + 30° = 70°$

Intersecting chords:
If two chords intersect inside a circle, each chord is divided into two smaller segments. The product of the lengths of the two segments formed from one chord equals the product of the lengths of the two segments formed from the other chord.

Intersecting tangent segments:
If two tangent segments intersect outside of a circle, the two segments have the same length.

Intersecting secant segments:
If two secant segments intersect outside a circle, a portion of each segment will lie inside the circle and a portion (called the exterior segment) will lie outside the circle. The product of the length of one secant segment and the length of its exterior segment equals the product of the length of the other secant segment and the length of its exterior segment.

Tangent segments intersecting secant segments:
If a tangent segment and a secant segment intersect outside a circle, the square of the length of the tangent segment equals the product of the length of the secant segment and its exterior segment.

Examples:

1.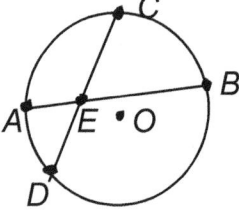

    $\overline{AB}$ and $\overline{CD}$ are chords.
    CE=10, ED=x, AE=5, EB=4

    $(AE)(EB) = (CE)(ED)$ Since the chords intersect in the circle, the products of the segment pieces are equal.

    $5(4) = 10x$
    $20 = 10x$
    $x = 2$ Solve for x.

2.

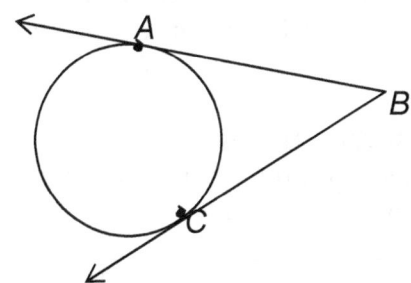

$\overline{AB}$ and $\overline{CD}$ are chords.
$\overline{AB} = x^2 + x - 2$
$\overline{CB} = 5 - 3x - x^2$
find the length of
$\overline{AB}$ and $\overline{BC}$

$\overline{AB} = x^2 + x - 2$ $\overline{BC} = x^2 - 3x + 5$	Given
$\overline{AB} = \overline{BC}$	Intersecting tangents are equal.
$x^2 + x - 2 = x^2 - 3x + 5$	Set the expression equal and solve.
$4x = 7$ $x = 1.75$	Substitute and solve.
$(1.75)^2 + 1.75 - 2 = \overline{AB}$ $\overline{AB} = \overline{BC} = 2.81$	

2.2d. Justify and perform the classical constructions (e.g., angle bisector, perpendicular bisector, replicating shapes, regular n-gons for n equal to 3, 4, 5, 6, and 8)

Classical construction refers to the use of a straightedge and compass for creating geometrical figures that match certain criteria. A construction consists of only segments, arcs, and points. Typical constructions includes the replication of line segments, angles or shapes, bisection of angles and lines, drawing lines that are parallel or perpendicular to a given line, as well as drawing different kinds of polygons and circles.

Duplication of line segments and angles

The easiest construction to make is to **duplicate a given line segment**. Given segment AB, construct a segment equal in length to segment AB by following these steps.

1. Place a point anywhere in the plane to anchor the duplicate segment. Call this point S.

2. Open the compass to match the length of segment AB. Keeping the compass rigid, swing an arc from S.

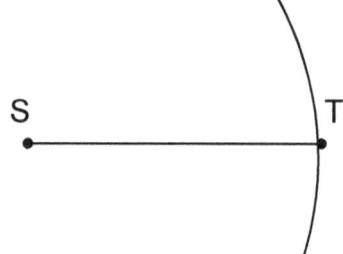

3. Draw a segment from S to any point on the arc. This segment will be the same length as AB.

To construct **an angle congruent to a given angle**:

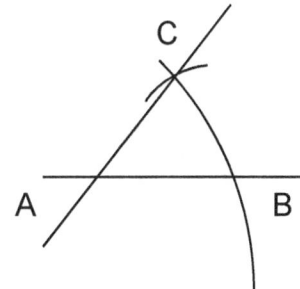

1. Given the angle A, draw an arc with any radius such that it intersects the sides of the angle at B and C.

2. On a working line w, select a point A' as the vertex of the angle to be drawn. With A' as the center and the same radius as the previous arc, draw an arc that intersects the line w in B'.

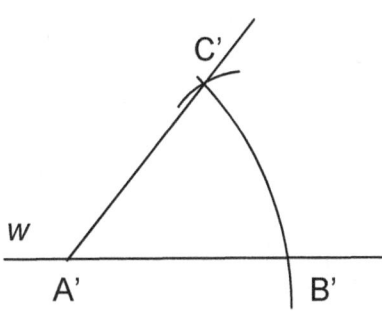

3. With B' as the center and radius equal to BC (measured off by placing ends of compass on B and C), draw a second arc that intersects the first arc at C'.

4. Join points A' and C'. The angle A' is congruent to the given angle A.

Construction of parallel lines

Angle duplication may be used to construct a line parallel to a given line AB through point W as shown below:

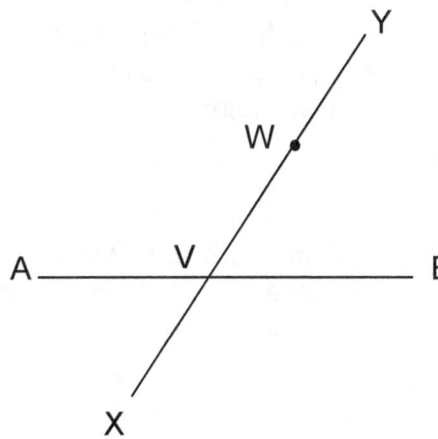

1. Draw a line XY through W intersecting AB in V.

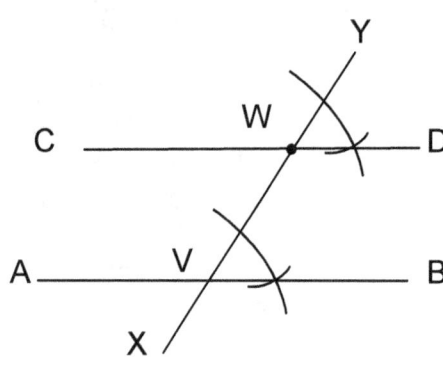

2. Construct angle YWD congruent to angle WVB. Then CD is the line parallel to AB.

Construction of perpendicular lines and bisectors

Given a line such as line l and a point P not on l, follow these steps to construct a **perpendicular line to l that passes through P**.

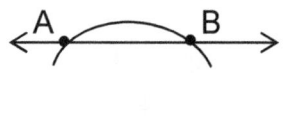

1. Swing an arc of any radius from P so that the arc intersects line l in two points A and B.

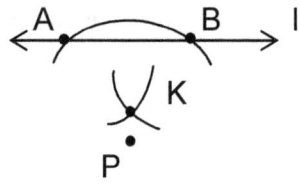

2. Open the compass to any length and swing two arcs of the same radius, one from A and the other from B. These two arcs will intersect at a new point K.

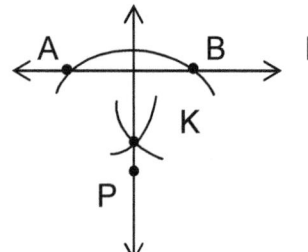

3. Connect K and P to form a line perpendicular to line l that passes through P.

Given a line segment with two endpoints such as A and B, follow these steps to **construct the line that both bisects and is perpendicular** to the line given segment.

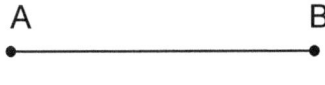

1. Swing an arc of any radius from point A. Swing another arc of the same radius from B. The arcs will intersect at two points. Label these points C and D.

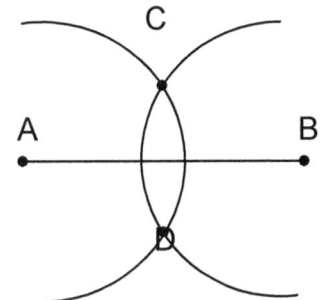

2. Connect C and D to form the perpendicular bisector of segment

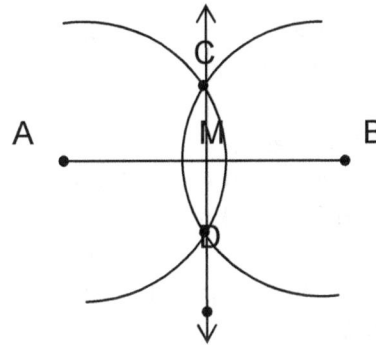

3. The point M where line CD and segment AB intersect is the midpoint of segment AB.

Construction of angle bisectors

To **bisect a given angle** such as angle *FUZ*, follow these steps.

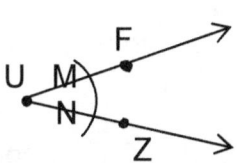

1. Swing an arc of any length with its center at point U. This arc will intersect rays *UF* and *UZ* at M and N.

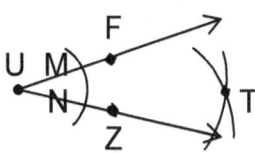
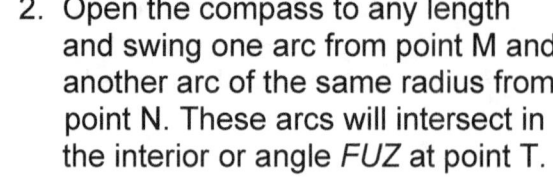

2. Open the compass to any length and swing one arc from point M and another arc of the same radius from point N. These arcs will intersect in the interior or angle *FUZ* at point T.

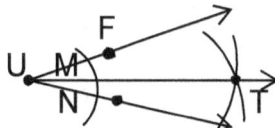

3. Connect U and T for the ray which bisects angle *FUZ*. Ray *UT* is the angle bisector of angle *FUZ*

Replicating shapes

The constructions we have done so far provide the building blocks of different shapes we may want to replicate. A shape consisting of a square topped by an equilateral triangle (shown below) may be replicated by following these steps:

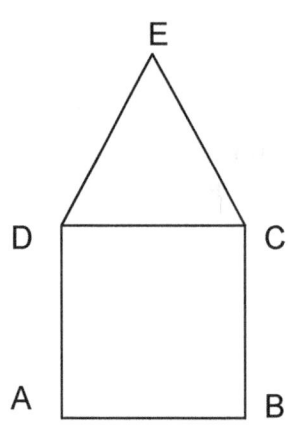

1. Draw a horizontal working line *w*.

2. Draw a line *l* perpendicular to the line *w* such that it intersects *w* in A'.

3. With A as center draw an arc with radius AB such that it intersects line *w* in B' and line *l* in D'.

4. Draw line *m* parallel to line A'B' through D'.

5. With D as center draw an arc that cuts line *m* in C'.

6. Join B'C' to complete the square.

7. With D' and C' as centers and radius equal to DE draw two arcs that intersect in E'.

8. Join D'E' and C'E' to complete the triangle.

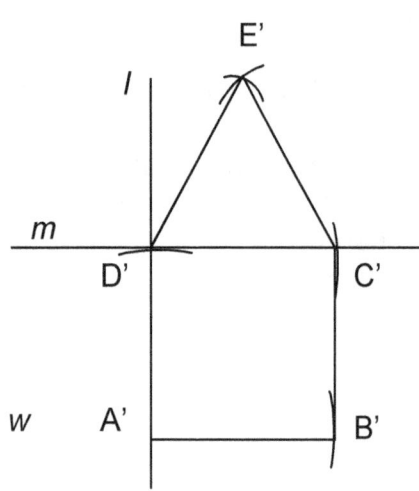

Construction of regular polygons

Not all regular polygons can be constructed with a compass and straightedge. The mathematician Gauss showed that a regular polygon with n sides can be constructed using a compass and ruler only if n is a product of a power of 2 and any number of distinct Fermat primes. Since the only known small Fermat primes are 3, 5, and 27, **a regular polygon can be constructed only if it has one of the following number of sides: 3, 4, 5, 6, 8, 10, 12, 15, 16, 17, 20, 24,**.. and so on.

We have already constructed an **equilateral triangle** and **square** in replicating a shape. Constructing a regular hexagon and **regular** octagon within a circle is also relatively simple. For construction of a **regular hexagon**, draw a diameter (AB in the figure below) in a circle. Then using the end points of the diameter A and B as centers, draw arcs with radius equal to the radius of the circle to intersect the circle in four points (C&D from A, E&F from B) that are the other vertices of the hexagon.

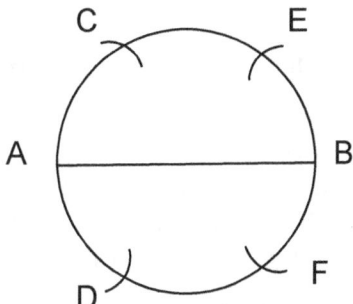

A **regular octagon** may be constructed by drawing two perpendicular diameters within a circle followed by lines that bisect the angles formed by the diameters. The points where all these lines intersect the circle are the vertices of a regular octagon.

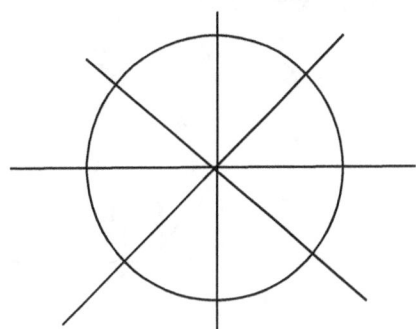

Construction of a **regular pentagon** is a little more involved. One method of construction is described below:

Make a circle with your compass, use the ruler to draw a line through the center of the circle (diameter). Then using compass and ruler, draw a vertical perpendicular line to the diameter (a radii). Next, using the same two tools, find the midpoint between point B and the center, point C, of the circle and draw another line from the midpoint of $\overline{BC}$ to point D. Next bisect ∠a in half to a point on $\overline{DC}$.

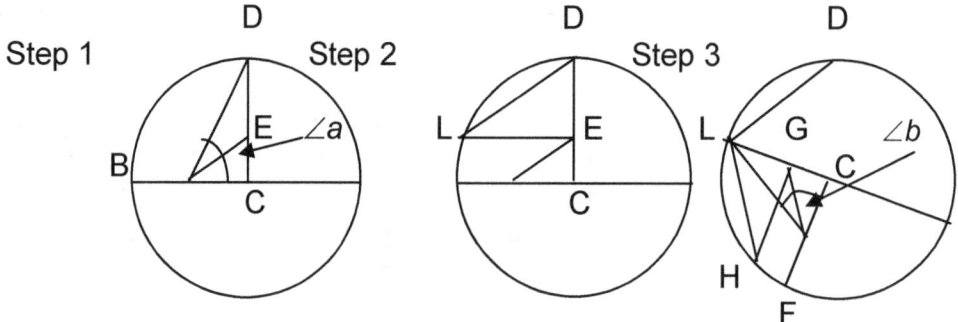

In Step 2, draw a line from point E to the edge of the circle that is parallel to $\overline{BC}$ and then connect points L and D with a line- this is the first side of your regular pentagon: $\overline{LD}$. To construct the second side, simply draw a line from point L through the center, point C to the other side of the circle that we'll call point F. Repeat the entire process of Steps 1 and 2 to find the second side of our regular pentagon: from the midpoint of $\overline{FC}$, draw a line to point L, then bisect ∠b to a point on $\overline{LC}$ which we'll call point G. Once again, draw a line that is parallel to $\overline{FC}$ from point G to the circle's edge, which can be called point H. Connect point L and point H and you have created the second side of the regular pentagon. Repeat these steps until all five sides have been drawn and to created a regular pentagon (all sides equal and all angles = 108°) just by using a compass and ruler.

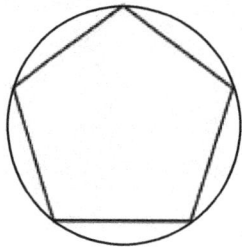

2.2e. **Use techniques in coordinate geometry to prove geometric theorems**

Coordinate geometry involves the application of algebraic methods to geometry. The locations of points in space are expressed in terms of coordinates on a Cartesian plane. The relationships between the coordinates of different points are expressed as equations.

Proofs using coordinate geometry techniques employ the following commonly used formulae and relationships:

1. **Midpoint formula**: The midpoint (x, y) of the line joining points (x_1, y_1) and (x_2, y_2) is given by

$$(x, y) = \left(\frac{x_1 + x_2}{2}, \frac{y_1 + y_2}{2} \right)$$

2. **Distance formula:** The distance between points (x_1, y_1) and (x_2, y_2) is given by

$$D = \sqrt{(x_2 - x_1)^2 + (y_2 - y_1)^2}$$

3. **Slope formula:** The slope m of a line passing through the points (x_1, y_1) and (x_2, y_2) is given by

$$m = \frac{y_2 - y_1}{x_2 - x_1}$$

3. **Equation of a line**: The equation of a line is given by $y = mx + b$, where m is the slope of the line and b is the y-intercept, i.e. the y-coordinate at which the line intersects the y-axis.

4. **Parallel and perpendicular lines**: Parallel lines have the same slope. The slope of a line perpendicular to a line with slope m is $-1/m$.

Example: Prove that quadrilateral ABCD with vertices A(-3,0), B(–1,0), C(0,3) and D(2,3) is in fact a parallelogram using coordinate geometry:

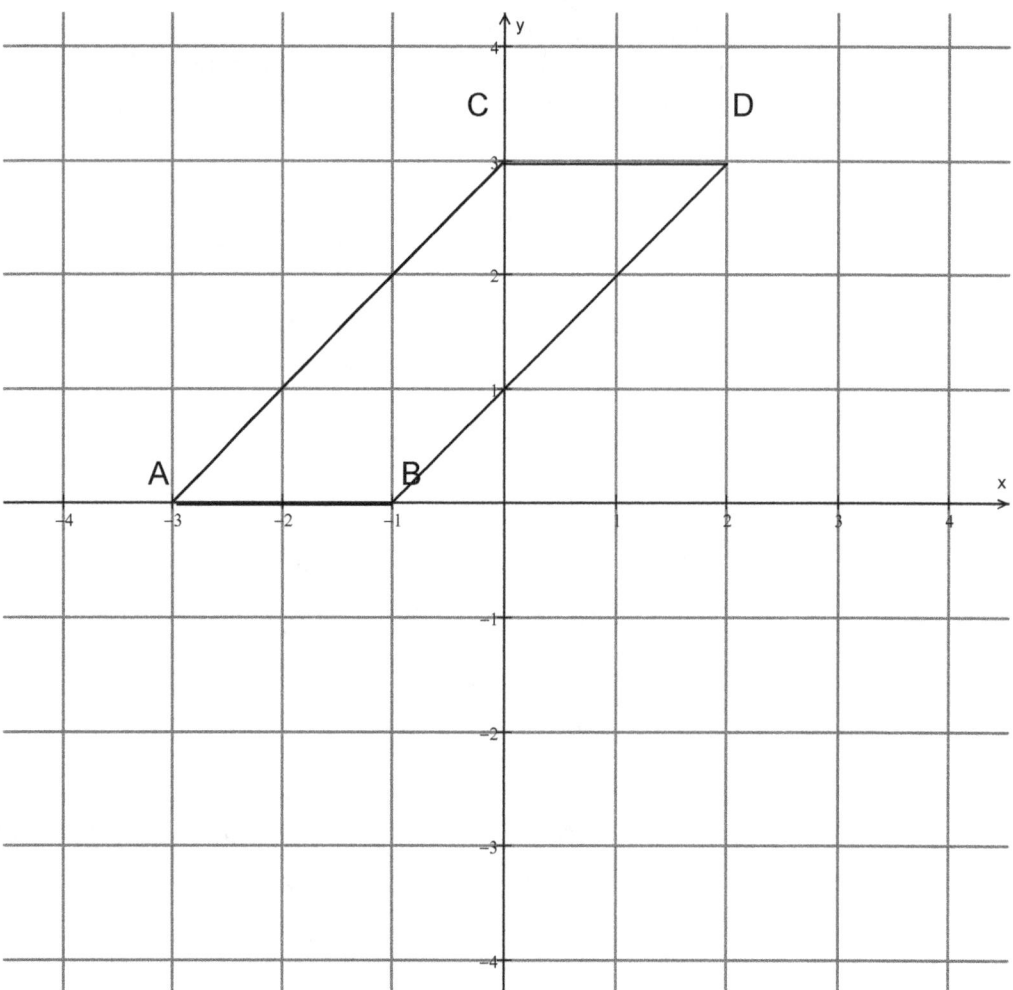

By definition, a parallelogram has diagonals that bisect each other. Using the midpoint formula, $(x,y) = \left(\dfrac{x_1+x_2}{2}, \dfrac{y_1+y_2}{2}\right)$, find the midpoints of $\overline{AD}$ and $\overline{BC}$.

The midpoint of $\overline{BC} = \left(\dfrac{-1+0}{2}, \dfrac{0+3}{2}\right) = \left(\dfrac{-1}{2}, \dfrac{3}{2}\right)$

The midpoint of $\overline{AD} = \left(\dfrac{-3+2}{2}, \dfrac{0+3}{2}\right) = \left(\dfrac{-1}{2}, \dfrac{3}{2}\right)$

Since the midpoints of the diagonals are the same, the diagonals bisect each other. Hence the polygon is a parallelogram.

In the above example the proof involved a specific geometrical figure with given coordinates. Coordinate geometry can also be used to prove more general results. This will be demonstrated in the examples that follow.

<u>Example:</u> Prove that the diagonals of a rhombus are perpendicular to each other.

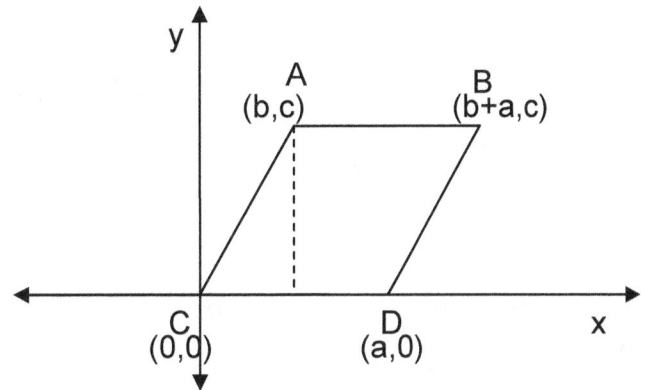

Draw a rhombus ABCD with side of length *a* such that the vertex C is at the origin and the side CD lies along the x-axis. The coordinates of the corners of the rhombus can then be written as shown above.

The slope m1 of the diagonal AD is given by $m1 = \dfrac{c}{b-a}$.

The slope m2 of the diagonal BC is given by $m2 = \dfrac{c}{b+a}$.

The product of the slopes is $m1 \cdot m2 = \dfrac{c}{b-a} \cdot \dfrac{c}{b+a} = \dfrac{c^2}{b^2 - a^2}$.

The length of side AC = $\sqrt{b^2 + c^2}$ = a (since each side of the rhombus is equal to a). Therefore,

$$b^2 + c^2 = a^2$$
$$\Rightarrow b^2 - a^2 = -c^2$$
$$\Rightarrow \dfrac{c^2}{b^2 - a^2} = -1$$

Thus the product of the slopes of the diagonals $m1 \cdot m2 = -1$. Hence the two diagonals are perpendicular to each other.

Example: Prove that the line joining the midpoints of two sides of a triangle is parallel to and half of the third side.

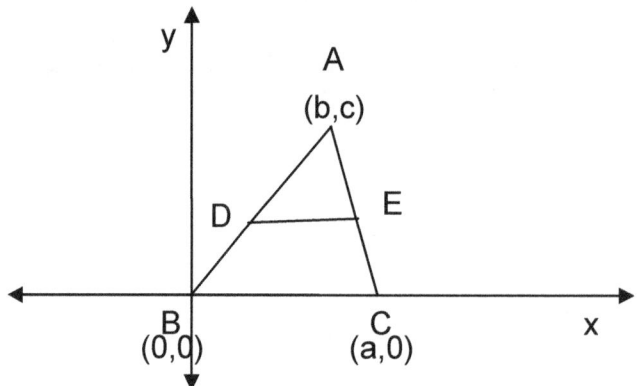

Draw triangle ABC on the coordinate plane in such a way that the vertex B coincides with the origin and the side BC lies along the x-axis. Let point C have coordinates (a,0) and A have coordinates (b,c). D is the midpoint of AB and E is the midpoint of AC.
We need to prove that DE is parallel to BC and is half the length of BC.

Using the midpoint formula,

coordinates of D = $\left(\dfrac{b}{2}, \dfrac{c}{2}\right)$; coordinates of E = $\left(\dfrac{b+a}{2}, \dfrac{c}{2}\right)$.

The slope of the line DE is then given by $\dfrac{\dfrac{c}{2} - \dfrac{c}{2}}{\dfrac{b+a}{2} - \dfrac{b}{2}} = 0$, which is equal to the slope of the x-axis. Thus DE is parallel to BC.

The length of the line segment DE =

$$\sqrt{\left(\dfrac{b+a}{2} - \dfrac{b}{2}\right)^2 + \left(\dfrac{c}{2} - \dfrac{c}{2}\right)^2} = \sqrt{\left(\dfrac{a}{2}\right)^2} = \dfrac{a}{2}$$

Thus the length of DE is half that of BC.

SKILL 2.3 THREE-DIMENSIONAL GEOMETRY

2.3a. Demonstrate an understanding of parallelism and perpendicularity of lines and planes in three dimensions

Parallelism of Lines and Planes

In two dimensions, parallelism and perpendicularity of lines can be defined in terms of a relatively small number of conditions. In three dimensions, however, the number of conditions must be increased. For instance, parallel lines in two dimensions can be sufficiently defined as lines that do not intersect. In three dimensions, however, this definition is insufficient. For example, the diagram below shows two parallel lines in three dimensions (planes that contain the lines are defined for clarity).

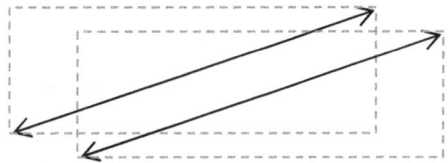

In the following case, however, two non-intersecting lines are shown that are clearly not parallel. (The intersection of the planes is shown with a dashed line.)

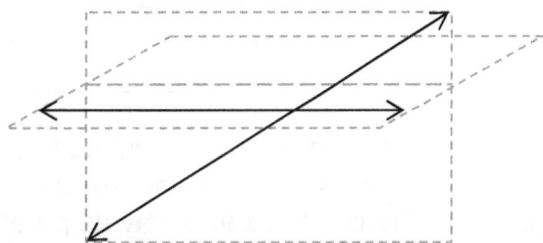

Parallel lines in three dimensions are defined as lines for which every pair of nearest points on the lines have a fixed distance. This definition is sufficient both for two- and three-dimensional parallelism, but it is necessary for the case of three dimensions. Notice, in the case above, the distance between nearest points for the parallel lines is constant, but it varies, depending on the pair of points chosen, for the non-parallel case. Lines in three dimensions that do not intersect and are not parallel are called **skew lines**.

Given two points (x_1, y_1, z_1) and (x_2, y_2, z_2), the distance d between them can be calculated as follows.

$$d = \sqrt{(x_2 - x_1)^2 + (y_2 - y_1)^2 + (z_2 - z_1)^2}$$

Alternative and equivalent definitions for parallel and skew lines can be formulated. For instance, skew lines are lines that do not intersect and do not lie on the same plane; parallel lines are lines that do not intersect and that *do* lie on the same plane. Since parallel lines are coplanar, then all the standard theorems apply in three dimensions if they are cut by a transversal. (For instance, alternate interior angles are still equal.)

For planes, parallelism is defined sufficiently as a lack of intersection. Thus, if two planes do not intersect, then they are parallel. Parallel and non-parallel planes are shown in the diagram below.

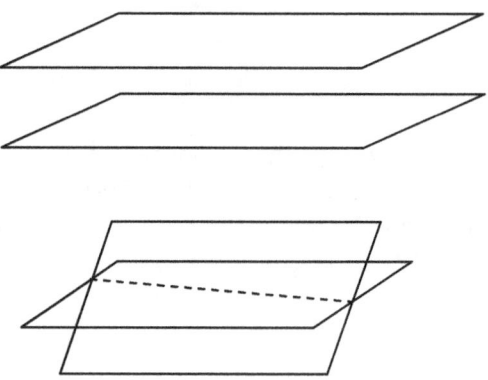

Two planes that intersect, assuming that they are not the same plane, intersect on a single line. Parallelism between two planes may also be defined in the same way as parallel lines: the distance between any pair of nearest points (one point on each plane) is constant.

Perpendicularity of Lines and Planes

Perpendicularity of lines and planes in three dimensions is largely similar to that of two dimensions. Two lines are **perpendicular**, in two or three dimensions, if they intersect at a point and form 90° angles between them. Consequently, perpendicular lines are always coplanar.

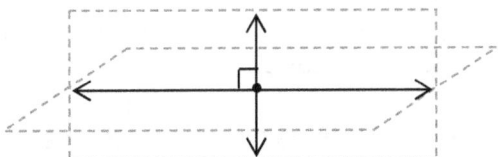

Notice that, for any line and coincident point on that line, there are an infinite number of perpendicular lines to the line through that point. In two dimensions, there is only one.

Two planes are perpendicular if they intersect and the angles formed between them are 90°. For any given plane and line on that plane, there is only one perpendicular plane.

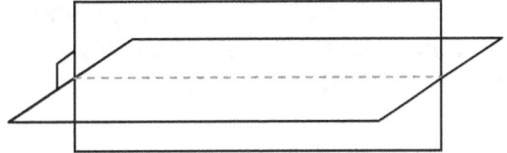

2.3b. Understand, apply, and justify properties of three-dimensional objects from an advanced standpoint (e.g., derive the volume and surface area formulas for prisms, pyramids, cones, cylinders, and spheres)

Three-dimensional figures require slightly more complicated mathematical manipulations to derive or apply such properties as surface area and volume. In some instances, two-dimensional concepts can be applied directly. In other instances, a more rigorous approach is needed.

To represent three-dimensional objects in a coordinate system, three coordinates are required. Thus, a point in three dimensions must be represented as (x, y, z), instead of simply (x, y) as is used in the two-dimensional representation.

Volume and Surface Area of Three-Dimensional Figures

The volume and surface area of three-dimensional figures can be derived most clearly (in some cases) using integral calculus. (See Skill 5.4d for more information on integrals relating to the area and volume of geometric figures.) For instance, the volume of a **sphere** of radius r can be derived by revolving a semicircular area around the axis defined by its diameter.

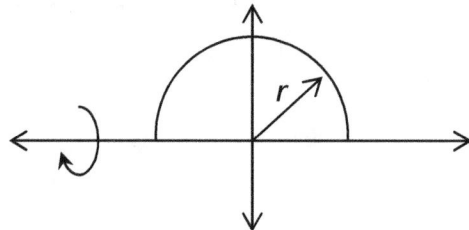

The result of this revolution is a solid sphere of radius r. To perform the integral, use the function $f(x)$ for the semicircle of radius r.

$$f(x) = \sqrt{r^2 - x^2}$$

$$V = \pi \int_{-r}^{r} \left[\sqrt{r^2 - x^2} \right]^2 dx$$

$$V = \pi \int_{-r}^{r} \left(r^2 - x^2 \right) dx$$

$$V = \pi \left[r^2 x - \frac{x^3}{3} \right]_{-r}^{r} = \pi \left[\left(r^3 + r^3 \right) - \left(\frac{r^3}{3} + \frac{r^3}{3} \right) \right]$$

$$V = \pi \left[2r^3 - \frac{2r^3}{3} \right] = \frac{4}{3}\pi r^3$$

The surface area can also be found by a similar integral that calculates the surface of revolution around the diameter, but there is a simpler method. Note that the differential change in volume of a sphere (dV) for a differential change in the radius (dr) is an infinitesimally thick spherical shell.

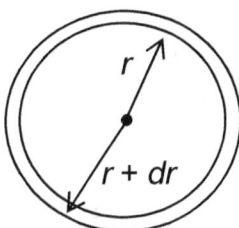

This infinitesimally thick shell is simply a surface with an area, but no volume. Find the derivative of the volume to get the surface area.

$$S = \frac{dV}{dr} = \frac{d}{dr}\frac{4}{3}\pi r^3$$
$$S = 4\pi r^2$$

The volume and surface area of a **right cone**, use an approach similar to that of the sphere. In this case, however, a line segment, rather than a semicircle, is revolved around the horizontal axis. The cone has a height h and a base radius r.

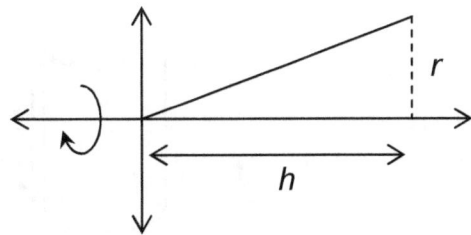

The function $f(x)$ that defines the line segment in this case is

$$f(x) = \frac{r}{h}x$$

from $x = 0$ to $x = h$.

$$V = \pi \int_0^h \left(\frac{r}{h}x \right)^2 dx$$

$$V = \pi\left(\frac{r}{h}\right)^2 \int_0^h x^2 dx = \pi\left(\frac{r}{h}\right)^2 \left[\frac{x^3}{3}\right]_0^h$$

$$V = \pi\left(\frac{r}{h}\right)^2 \frac{h^3}{3} = \frac{\pi r^2 h}{3}$$

To find the lateral surface area, an integral must be used to find the surface of revolution. This integral uses $f(x)$ as follows.

$$S = 2\pi \int_0^h f(x)\sqrt{1+\left[f'(x)\right]^2}\,dx$$

$$f'(x) = \frac{r}{h}$$

$$S = 2\pi\sqrt{1+\left(\frac{r}{h}\right)^2}\,\frac{r}{h}\int_0^h x\,dx = \frac{2\pi r}{h}\sqrt{1+\left(\frac{r}{h}\right)^2}\left[\frac{x^2}{2}\right]_0^h$$

$$S = \frac{2\pi r}{h}\sqrt{1+\left(\frac{r}{h}\right)^2}\left[\frac{h^2}{2}\right] = \pi r h\left(\frac{1}{h}\right)\sqrt{r^2 + h^2}$$

$$S = \pi r\sqrt{r^2 + h^2}$$

For right circular cylinders, the volume is simply the area of a cross section (a circle of radius r) multiplied by the height h of the cylinder. The **lateral surface area** (the surface area excluding the area on the ends of the figure) is simply the circumference of the circular cross section multiplied by the height h.

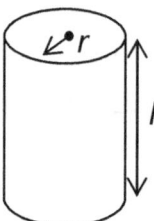

$V = \pi r^2 h$
$S = 2\pi r h$

The volumes and surface areas of these figures are summarized below.

Figure	Volume	Lateral Surface Area
Right Cylinder	$\pi r^2 h$	$2\pi r h + 2\pi r^2$

Right Cone	$\dfrac{\pi r^2 h}{3}$	$\pi r \sqrt{r^2 + h^2} + \pi r^2$
Sphere	$\dfrac{4}{3}\pi r^3$	$4\pi r^2$

For figures such as pyramids and prisms, the volume and surface areas must be derived by breaking the figure into portions for which these values can be calculated easily. For instance, consider the following figure.

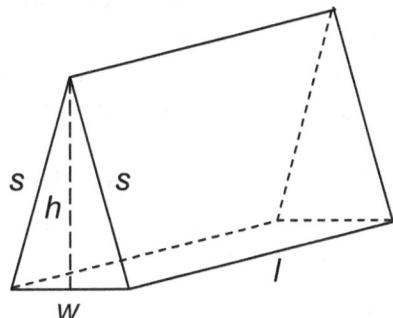

The volume of this figure can be found by calculating the area of the triangular cross section and then multiplying by *l*.

$$V = \frac{1}{2}hwl$$

The lateral surface area can be found by adding the areas of each side.

$$S = 2sl + lw$$

Similar reasoning applies to other figures composed of sides that are defined by triangles, quadrilaterals and other planar or linear elements.

SKILL 2.4 TRANSFORMATIONAL GEOMETRY

2.4a. **Demonstrate an understanding of the basic properties of isometries in two- and three-dimensional space (e.g., rotation, translation, reflection)**

An **isometry** is a linear transformation that maintains the dimensions of a geometric figure. A **transformation** is a change in the position, shape or size of a figure. **Transformational geometry** is the study of manipulating objects through movement, rotation and scaling. **Symmetry** is exact similarity between two parts or halves, as if one were a mirror image of the other. The transformation of an object is called its *image*. If the original object was labeled with letters, such as *ABCD*, the image can be labeled with the same letters followed by a prime symbol: *A'B'C'D'*.

A **translation** is a transformation that "slides" an object a fixed distance in a given direction. The original object and its translation have the same shape and size, and they face in the same direction.

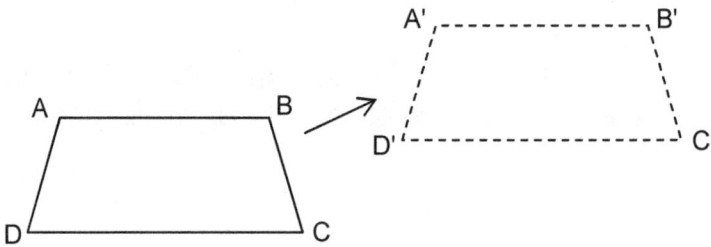

A **rotation** is a transformation that turns a figure about a fixed point, which is called the center of rotation. An object and its rotation are the same shape and size, but the figures may be oriented in different directions. Rotations can occur in either a clockwise or a counterclockwise direction.

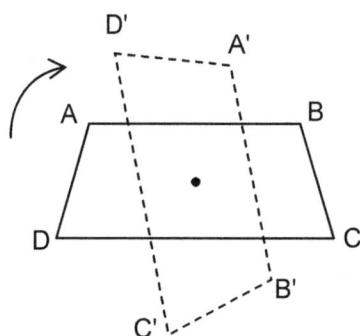

An object and its **reflection** have the same shape and size, but the figures face in opposite directions. The line (where a hypothetical mirror may be placed) is called the **line of reflection**. The distance from a point to the line of reflection is the same as the distance from the point's image to the line of reflection.

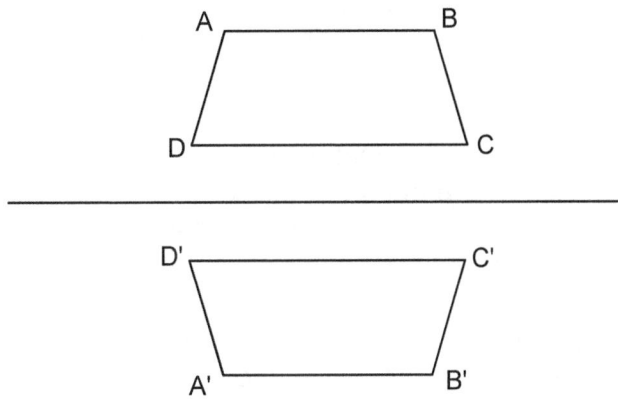

The line (where a mirror may be placed) is called the **line of reflection**. The distance from a point to the line of reflection is the same as the distance from the point's image to the line of reflection.

The examples of a translation, rotation and reflection given above are for polygons, but the same principles apply to the simpler geometrical elements of points and lines. In fact, a transformation performed on a polygon can be viewed equivalently as the same transformation performed on the set of points (vertices) and lines (sides) that compose the polygon. Thus, to perform complicated transformations on a figure, it is helpful to perform the transformations on all the points (or vertices) of the figure, then reconnect the points with lines as appropriate.

Multiple transformations can be performed on a geometrical figure. The order of these transformations may or may not be important. For instance, multiple translations can be performed in any order, as can multiple rotations (around a single fixed point) or reflections (across a single fixed line). The order of the transformations becomes important when several types of transformations are performed or when the point of rotation or the line of reflection change among transformations. For example, consider a translation of a given distance upward and a clockwise rotation by 90° around a fixed point. Changing the order of these transformations changes the result.

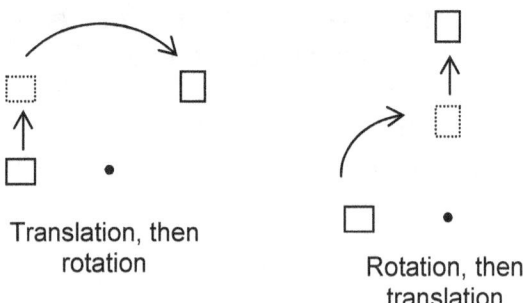

Translation, then rotation   Rotation, then translation

As shown, the final position of the box is different, depending on the order of the transformations. Thus, it is crucial that the proper order of transformations (whether determined by the details of the problem or some other consideration) be followed.

Example: Find the final location of a point at (1, 1) that undergoes the following transformations: rotate 90° counter-clockwise about the origin; translate distance 2 in the negative *y* direction; reflect about the *x*-axis.

First, draw a graph of the *x*- and *y*-axes and plot the point at (1, 1).

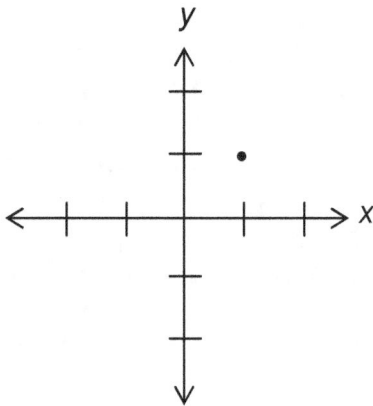

Next, perform the rotation. The center of rotation is the origin and is in the counter-clockwise direction. In this case, the even value of 90° makes the rotation simple to do by inspection. Next, perform a translation of distance 2 in the negative *y* direction (down). The results of these transformations are shown below.

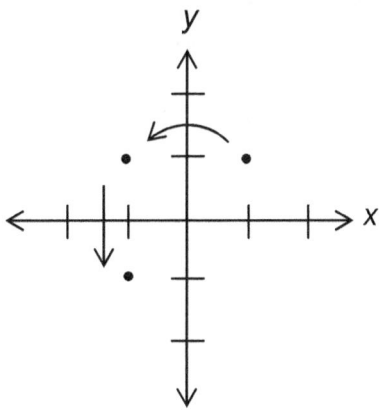

Finally, perform the reflection about the x-axis. The final result, shown below, is a point at (1, −1).

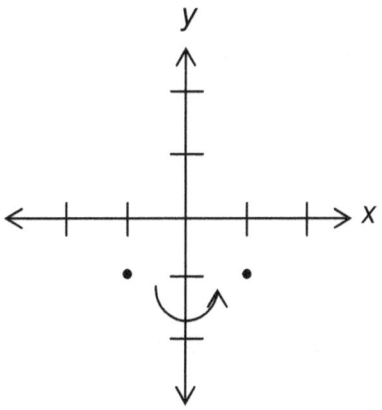

Using this approach, polygons can be transformed on a point-by-point basis.

For some problems, there is no need to work with coordinate axes. For instance, the problem may simply require transformations without respect to any absolute positioning.

Example: Rotate the following regular pentagon by 36° about its center and then reflect it about the horizontal line.

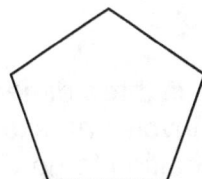

First, perform the rotation. In this case, the direction is not important because the pentagon is symmetric. As it turns out in this case, a rotation of 36° yields the same result as flipping the pentagon vertically (assuming the vertices of the pentagon are indistinguishable).

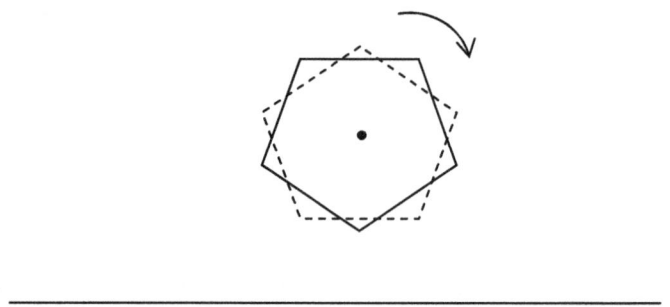

Finally, perform the reflection. Note that the result here is the same as a downward translation (assuming the vertices of the pentagon are indistinguishable).

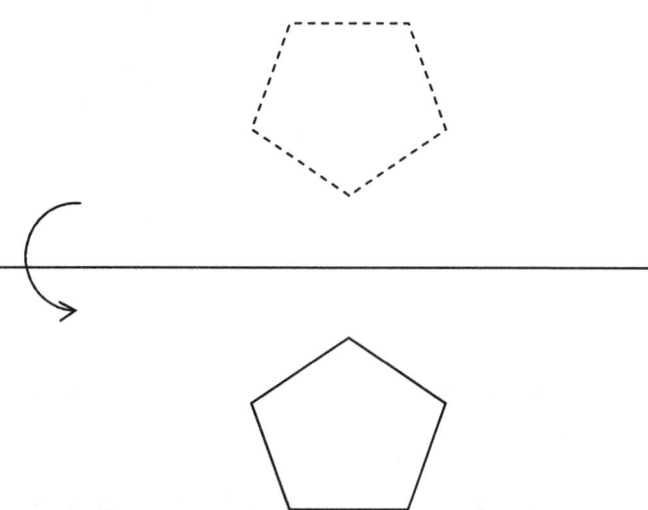

The above examples and illustrations primarily demonstrate isometries in **two dimensions**. These principles, however, apply also to **three dimensions**. The primary difference between two- and three-dimensional isometries is the additional degree of freedom in three dimensions, which allows for more complicated transformations.

Translations in three dimensions are the most easily understood, as they simply involve an extra direction along which a figure can be moved (in addition to up-down and left-right on the plane of this paper, three-dimensional transformations also permit movement into and out of the plane of the paper).

Rotations in three dimensions must be specified by a line of rotation, rather than a point. (In two dimensions, the point that serves as center of rotation is simply the intersection of the plane with a line that is perpendicular to it.) An example of a three-dimensional rotation is shown below. A view from the side of the figure is also shown to help elucidate the transformation.

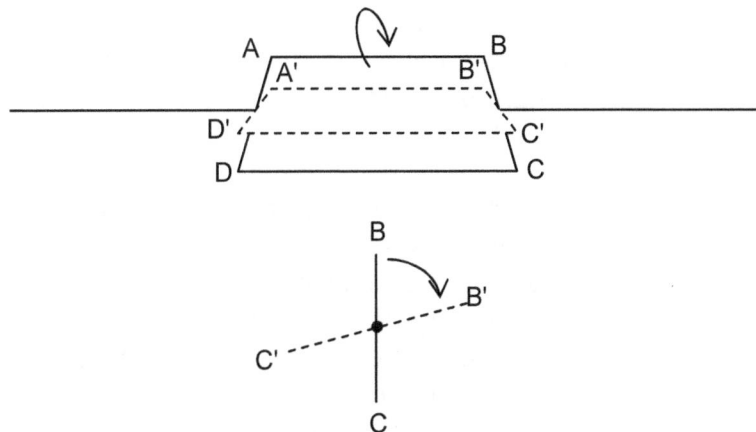

Thus, rotations, like transformations, can be more complicated in three dimensions. Likewise, reflections have an additional degree of freedom, and a plane of reflection is required in place of a line of reflection. (In two dimensions, the line of reflection is simply the intersection of the plane in which the figure is represented with the perpendicular plane of reflection.) The same "mirror image" principle applies to three-dimensional reflections, however.

It is also important to note that the order of transformations in three dimensions, as with that in two dimensions, is crucial. It is not generally the case that two different orderings of a set of transformations yield the same result. Thus, it is important to maintain the order of transformations as specified by the problem.

2.4b. Understand and prove the basic properties of dilations (e.g., similarity transformations or change of scale)

Dilations involve an expansion of a figure and a translation of that figure (the translation may be for a distance zero). These two transformations are obtained by first defining a **center of dilation**, C, which is some point that acts like an origin for the dilation. The distance from C to each point in a figure is then altered by a **scale factor** s. If the magnitude of s is greater than zero, the size of the figure is increased; if the magnitude of s is less than zero, the size is decreased.

The expansion of a geometric figure is a result of the scale factor, s. For instance, if $s = 2$, the expanded figure will be twice the size of the original figure. (A dilation maintains the angles and relative proportions of a figure.) The translation of a geometric figure is a result of the location of the center of dilation, C. If C is located at the center of the figure, for instance, the figure is dilated without and translation of its center.

Example: Dilate the figure shown by a scale factor of 2 using the origin of the coordinate system as the center of dilation.

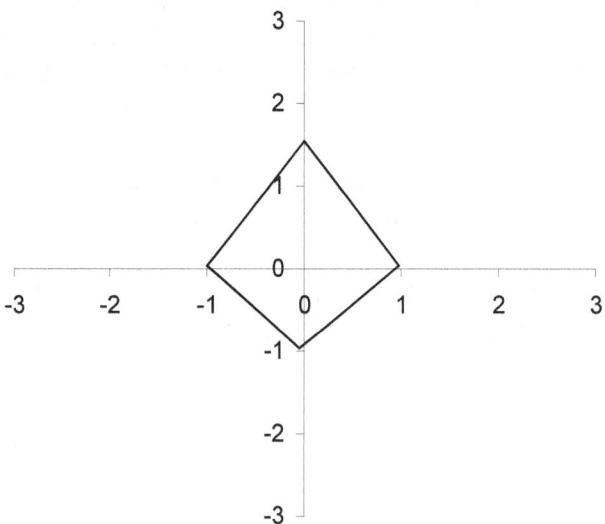

To perform this dilation, the distance between the origin and each point on the figure must be increased by a factor of 2. It is sufficient, however, to simply increase the distance of the vertices of the figure by a factor of 2 and then connect them to form the dilated figure.

MATHEMATICS

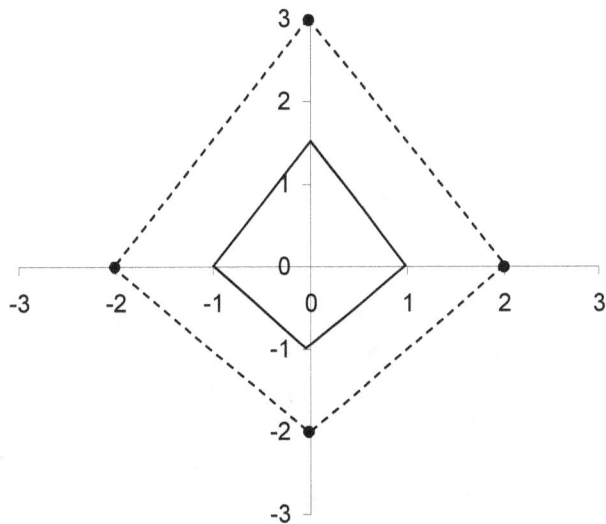

The resulting figure above (dashed line) is the dilation of the original figure.

Congruence of Angles Through Dilations

The points on a figure are dilated by increasing or decreasing their respective distances from a center of dilation C. As a result, each point P on a figure is essentially translated along the line through P and C. To show that a dilation of this type preserves angles, consider some angle formed by two line segments, with a center of dilation at some arbitrary location. The dilation is for some scale factor s.

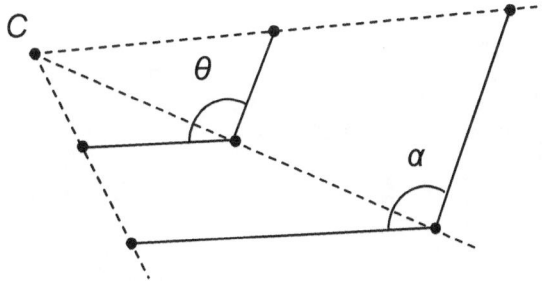

To show that the angles θ and α are equal, it is sufficient to show that the two pairs of overlapping triangles are similar. If they are similar, all the corresponding angles in the figure must be congruent.

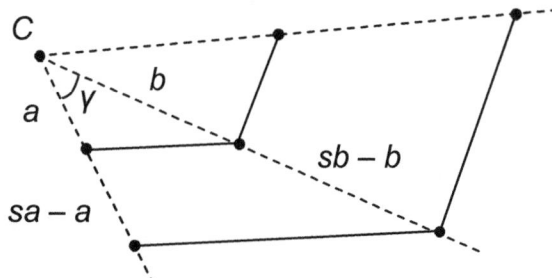

The smaller triangle in this case has sides of lengths a and b and an angle y between them. The larger triangle has sides of lengths sa (or $sa - a + a = sa$) and sb and an angle y between them. Thus, by SAS similarity, these two triangles are similar. Once this reasoning is applied to the other pair of overlapping triangles, it can be shown that angles θ and α are equal. Furthermore, due to the fact that these triangles have been shown to be similar, it is also true that line segments must scale by a factor s (this is necessary to maintain the similarity of the triangles above).

As a result of this reasoning, it can be shown that figures that are dilated using an arbitrary scale factor s and center of dilation C must maintain all angles through the dilation, and all line segments (or sides) of the figure must also scale by s. As a result, figures that are dilated are **similar** to the original figures.

Since dilations are transformations that maintain similarity of the figures being dilated, they can also be viewed as **changes of scale** about C. For instance, a dilation of a portion of a map would simply result in a change of the scale of the map.

TEACHER CERTIFICATION STUDY GUIDE

COMPETENCY 3.0 NUMBER THEORY

SKILL 3.1 NATURAL NUMBERS

3.1a. **Prove and use basic properties of natural numbers (e.g., properties of divisibility)**

The set of **natural numbers**, $\mathbb{N}$, includes 1, 2, 3, 4,.... (For some definitions, $\mathbb{N}$ includes zero.) The natural numbers are sometimes called the **counting numbers** (especially if the definition of $\mathbb{N}$ excludes zero). The set $\mathbb{N}$ constitutes neither a ring nor a field, because there is no additive inverse (since there are no negative numbers).

The set $\mathbb{N}$ obeys the properties of associativity, commutativity, distributivity and identity for multiplication and addition (assuming, for the case of addition, that zero is included in some sense in the natural numbers). The set of natural numbers does *not* obey additive or multiplicative inverses, however, as there are no non-integer fractions or negative numbers.

Divisibility Tests

a. A number is **divisible by 2** if that number is an even number (which means the last digit is 0, 2, 4, 6 or 8).

A number *abcd* defined by the digits *a*, *b*, *c* and *d* (for instance, 1,234). Rewrite the number as follows.

$$10abc + d = abcd$$

Note that 10*abc* is divisible by 2. Thus, the number *abcd* is only divisible by 2 if *d* is divisible by two; in other words, *abcd* is divisible by two only if it is an even number. For example, the last digit of 1,354 is 4, so it is divisible by 2. On the other hand, the last digit of 240,685 is 5, so it is not divisible by 2.

b. A number is **divisible by 3** if the sum of its digits is evenly divisible by 3.

Consider a number *abcd* defined by the digits *a*, *b*, *c* and *d*. The number can be written as

$$abcd = 1000a + 100b + 10c + d$$

MATHEMATICS

The number can also be rewritten as

$$abcd = (999+1)a + (99+1)b + (9+1)c + d$$
$$abcd = 999a + 99b + 9c + (a+b+c+d)$$

Note that the first three terms in the above expression are all divisible by 3. Thus, the number is evenly divisible by 3 only if $a + b + c + d$ is divisible by 3. The same logic applies regardless of the size of the number. This proves the rules for divisibility by 3.

The sum of the digits of 964 is 9+6+4 = 19. Since 19 is not divisible by 3, neither is 964. The digits of 86,514 is 8+6+5+1+4 = 24. Since 24 is divisible by 3, 86,514 is also divisible by 3.

c. A number is **divisible by 4** if the number in its last 2 digits is evenly divisible by 4.

Let a number *abcd* be defined by the digits *a*, *b*, *c* and *d*.

$$ab(100) + cd = abcd$$

Since 100 is divisible by 4, 100*ab* is also divisible by 4. Thus, *abcd* is divisible by 4 only if *cd* is divisible by 4.

$$25ab + \frac{cd}{4} = \frac{abcd}{4}$$

The number 113,336 ends with the number 36 for the last 2 digits. Since 36 is divisible by 4, 113,336 is also divisible by 4. The number 135,627 ends with the number 27 for the last 2 digits. Since 27 is not evenly divisible by 4, 135,627 is also not divisible by 4.

d. A number is **divisible by 5** if the number ends in either a 5 or a 0.

Use the same number *abcd*.

$$100ab + cd = abcd$$

The first term is evenly divisible by 5, but the second term is only evenly divisible by 5 if it is 0, 5, 10, 15,...,95. In other words, *abcd* is divisibly by 5 only if it ends in a 0 or 5. For instance, 225 ends with a 5, so it is divisible by 5. The number 470 is also divisible by 5 because its last digit is a 0. The number 2,358 is not divisible by 5 because its last digit is an 8.

e. A number is **divisible by 6** if the number is even and the sum of its digits is evenly divisible by 3 or 6.

Let a number *efgh* be defined by the digits *e*, *f*, *g* and *h*. If *efgh* is even, then it is divisible by 2. Write *abcd* as follows.

$$\frac{efgh}{2} = abcd = 999a + 99b + 9c + (a+b+c+d)$$
$$efgh = 2abcd = 2(999)a + 2(99)b + 2(9)c + 2(a+b+c+d)$$

Then divide *efgh* by 6.

$$\frac{efgh}{6} = \frac{2(999)}{6}a + \frac{2(99)}{6}b + \frac{2(9)}{6}c + \frac{2}{6}(a+b+c+d)$$
$$\frac{efgh}{6} = 333a + 33b + 3c + \frac{2}{6}(a+b+c+d)$$

Notice that *efgh* is divisible by 6 only if the sum of the digits is divisible by 3 or by 6. The number *efgh* must also be eve, since 2 is a factor of 6. For instance, 4,950 is an even number and its digits add to 18 (4 + 9 + 5 + 0 = 18). Since the number is even and the sum of its digits is 18 (which is divisible by 3 and 6), then 4,950 is divisible by 6. On the other hand, 326 is an even number, but its digits add up to 11. Since 11 is not divisible by 3 or 6, then 326 is not divisible by 6.

f. A number is **divisible by 8** if the number in its last 3 digits is evenly divisible by 8.

The logic for the proof of this case follows that of numbers divisible by 2 and 4. The number 113,336 ends with the 3-digit number 336 in the last 3 columns. Since 336 is divisible by 8, then 113,336 is also divisible by 8. The number 465,627 ends with the number 627 in the last 3 columns. Since 627 is not evenly divisible by 8, then 465,627 is also not divisible by 8.

g. A number is **divisible by 9** if the sum of its digits is evenly divisible by 9.

The logic for the proof of this case follows that for the case of numbers that are divisible by 3 and 6. The sum of the digits of 874, for example, is 8 + 7 + 4 = 19. Since 19 is not divisible by 9, neither is 874. The sum of the digits of 116,514 is 1 + 1 + 6 + 5 + 1 + 4 = 18. Since 18 is divisible by 9, 116,514 is also divisible by 9.

3.1b. Use the Principle of Mathematical Induction to prove results in number theory

The Principle of Mathematical Induction

Mathematical induction is a method for proving certain results (such as formulas or relations) in number theory. This method essentially involves showing first that a formula or relation works for an initial case ($i = 1$) and then showing that it works for the ($i + 1$)st case, assuming it works for the ith case.

Let $p(n)$ denote the relation involving the integer variable n. If $p(1)$ is true and $p(k + 1)$ is true for each integer $k \geq 1$ whenever $p(k)$ is true, then $p(n)$ is true for all $n \geq 1$. In other words, the relation is true for all numbers if the following two statements are true:

1. The statement is true for $n = 1$.
2. If the statement is true for $n = k$, then it is also true for $n = k + 1$.

The four basic components of mathematical induction proofs are:

1. Identify the statement to be proved
2. Prove the initial case ("let $n = 1$")
3. Make the assumption ("let $n = k$ and assume the statement is true for k")
4. Prove the induction step ("let $n = k+1$")

<u>Example:</u> Prove that the sum of all numbers from 1 to n is equal to $\dfrac{n(n+1)}{2}$.

First, identify the relation to be proved.

$$\sum_{i=1}^{n} i = \frac{n(n+1)}{2}$$

Next, show that this relation is valid for $n = 1$.

$$\sum_{i=1}^{1} i = 1$$

$$\frac{n(n+1)}{2} = \frac{1(1+1)}{2} = \frac{2}{2} = 1$$

Assume that this relation works for $n = k$. For the induction step, prove that the relation works for $n = k + 1$. Since the relation is assumed to work for $n = k$,

$$\sum_{i=1}^{k+1} i = \sum_{i=1}^{k} i + (k+1) = \frac{k(k+1)}{2} + (k+1)$$

Manipulate this expression to find the equivalent form of $\frac{n(n+1)}{2}$ for $k + 1$.

$$\sum_{i=1}^{k+1} i = \frac{k(k+1)}{2} + \frac{2(k+1)}{2} = \frac{k^2 + k + 2k + 2}{2}$$

$$\sum_{i=1}^{k+1} i = \frac{k^2 + 3k + 2}{2} = \frac{(k+1)(k+2)}{2}$$

$$\sum_{i=1}^{k+1} i = \frac{(k+1)([k+1]+1)}{2}$$

Thus, it has been proven that the formula works for $n = k + 1$. The induction is complete, and $\frac{n(n+1)}{2}$ is the correct formula for the sum $1 + 2 + 3 + \ldots + n$.

3.1c. Know and apply the Euclidean Algorithm

The **Euclidean Algorithm** is a method for determining the **greatest common devisor** (GCD) of two positive integers. (The GCD is also known as the **greatest common factor**, or GCF.) The algorithm can be formulated in a recursive manner that simply involves repetition of a few steps until a terminating point is reached. The algorithm can be summarized as follows, where a and b are the two integers for which determination of the GCD is to be undertaken. (Assign a and b such that $a > b$.)

1. If $b = 0$, a is the GCD.
2. Calculate $c = a \bmod b$.
3. If $c = 0$, b is the GCD.
4. Go back to step 2, replacing a with b and b with c.

Note that the "**mod**" operator in this case is simply a remainder operator. Thus, $a \bmod b$ is the remainder of division of a by b.

Example: Find the GCD of 299 and 351.

To find the GCD, first let $a = 351$ and $b = 299$. Begin the algorithm as follows.

1. $b \neq 0$.
2. $c = 351 \bmod 299 = 52$
3. $c \neq 0$

Perform the next iteration, starting with step 2.

2. $c = 299 \bmod 52 = 39$
3. $c \neq 0$

Continue to iterate recursively until a solution is found.

2. $c = 52 \bmod 39 = 13$
3. $c \neq 0$

2. $c = 39 \bmod 13 = 0$
3. $c = 0$: GCD = 13

Thus, the GCD of 299 and 351 is thus 13.

3.1d. **Apply the Fundamental Theorem of Arithmetic (e.g., find the greatest common factor and the least common multiple, show that every fraction is equivalent to a unique fraction where the numerator and denominator are relatively prime, prove that the square root of any number, not a perfect square number, is irrational)**

The Fundamental Theorem of Arithmetic

Every integer greater than 1 can be written uniquely in the form

$$p_1^{e_1} \, p_2^{e_2} \cdots p_k^{e_k}.$$

The p_i are distinct primes and the e_i are positive integers.

GCF is the abbreviation for the **greatest common factor**. The GCF is the largest number that is a factor of all the numbers given in a problem. The GCF can be no larger than the smallest number given in the problem. If no other number is a common factor, then the GCF will be the number 1. To find the GCF, list all possible factors of the smallest number given (include the number itself). Starting with the largest factor (which is the number itself), determine if it is also a factor of all the other given numbers. If so, that is the GCF. If that factor does not work, try the same method on the next smaller factor. Continue until a common factor is found. This is the GCF. Note: There can be other common factors besides the GCF.

Example: Find the GCF of 12, 20, and 36.

The smallest number in the problem is 12. The factors of 12 are 1,2,3,4,6 and 12. 12 is the largest factor, but it does not divide evenly into 20. Neither does 6, but 4 will divide into both 20 and 36 evenly. Therefore, 4 is the GCF.

Example: Find the GCF of 14 and 15.

Factors of 14 are 1,2,7 and 14. 14 is the largest factor, but it does not divide evenly into 15. Neither does 7 or 2. Therefore, the only factor common to both 14 and 15 is the number 1, which is the GCF.

LCM is the abbreviation for **least common multiple**. The least common multiple of a group of numbers is the smallest number that all of the given numbers will divide into. The least common multiple will always be the largest of the given numbers or a multiple of the largest number.

Example: Find the LCM of 20, 30 and 40.

The largest number given is 40, but 30 will not divide evenly into 40. The next multiple of 40 is 80 (2 x 40), but 30 will not divide evenly into 80 either. The next multiple of 40 is 120. 120 is divisible by both 20 and 30, so 120 is the LCM (least common multiple).

Example: Find the LCM of 96, 16 and 24.

The largest number is 96. 96 is divisible by both 16 and 24, so 96 is the LCM.

The Fundamental Theorem of Arithmetic can be used to show that **every fraction is equivalent to a unique fraction where the numerator and denominator are relatively prime.**

Given a fraction $\frac{a}{b}$, the integers a and b can both be written uniquely as a product of prime factors.

$$\frac{a}{b} = \frac{p_1^{x_1} p_2^{x_2} p_3^{x_3} \ldots p_n^{x_n}}{q_1^{y_1} q_2^{y_2} q_3^{y_3} \ldots q_m^{y_m}}$$

When all the common factors are cancelled, the resulting numerator a_1 (the product of remaining factors $p_n^{x_n}$) and the resulting denominator b_1 (the product of remaining factors $q_m^{y_m}$) have no common divisor other than 1; i.e., they are **relatively prime**.

Since, according to the Fundamental Theorem of Arithmetic, the initial prime decomposition of the integers a and b is unique, the new reduced fraction $\frac{a_1}{b_1}$ is also **unique**. Hence, any fraction is equivalent to a unique fraction where the numerator and denominator are relatively prime.

The proof that **the square root of any integer, not a perfect square number, is irrational** may also be demonstrated using prime decomposition.

Let n be an integer. Assuming that the square root of n is rational, we can write

$$\sqrt{n} = \frac{a}{b}$$

Since every fraction is equivalent to a unique fraction where the numerator and denominator are relatively prime (shown earlier), we can reduce the fraction $\frac{a}{b}$ to the fraction $\frac{a_1}{b_1}$ and write

$$\sqrt{n} = \frac{a_1}{b_1}; \; n = \frac{a_1^2}{b_1^2}$$

where a_1 and b_1 are relatively prime.

Since a_1 and b_1 are relatively prime, a_1^2 and b_1^2 must also be relatively prime. Also, since n is an integer, $\frac{a_1^2}{b_1^2}$ must be an integer.

The only way the above two conditions can be satisfied is if the denominator $b_1^2 = 1$. Thus, $n = a_1^2$

As a result, the square root of an integer can be rational only if the integer is a perfect square. Stated in an alternative manner, the square root of an integer, not a perfect square, is irrational.

COMPETENCY 4.0 PROBABILITY AND STATISTICS

SKILL 4.1 PROBABILITY

4.1a. Prove and apply basic principles of permutations and combinations

A **permutation** is the number of possible arrangements of items, without repetition, where order of selection is important.

A **combination** is the number of possible arrangements, without repetition, where order of selection is not important.

Example: If any two numbers are selected from the set {1, 2, 3, 4}, list the possible permutations and combinations.

Combinations	Permutations
12, 13, 14, 23, 24, 34	12, 21, 13, 31, 14, 41,
	23, 32, 24, 42, 34, 43,
six ways	twelve ways

Note that the list of permutations includes 12 and 21 as separate possibilities since the order of selection is important. In the case of combinations, however, the order of selection is not important and, therefore, 12 is the same combination as 21. Hence, 21 is not listed separately as a possibility.

The number of permutations and combinations may also be found by using the formulae given below.

The number of possible permutations in selecting r objects from a set of n is given by

$$_nP_r = \frac{n!}{(n-r)!}$$

The notation $_nP_r$ is read "the number of permutations of n objects taken r at a time."

In our example, two objects are being selected from a set of four.

$$_4P_2 = \frac{4!}{(4-2)!}$$ Substitute known values.

$$_4P_2 = 12$$

The number of possible combinations in selecting r objects from a set of n is given by

$$_nC_r = \frac{n!}{(n-r)!r!}$$ The number of combinations when r objects are selected from n objects.

In our example,

$$_4C_2 = \frac{4!}{(4-2)!2!}$$ Substitute known values.
$$_4C_2 = 6$$

It can be shown that $_nP_n$, **the number of ways n objects can be arranged in a row, is equal to $n!$.** We can think of the problem as n positions being filled one at a time. The first position can be filled in n ways using any one of the n objects. Since one of the objects has already been used, the second position can be filled only in $n - 1$ ways. Similarly, the third position can be filled in $n - 2$ ways and so on. Hence, the total number of possible arrangements of n objects in a row is given by

$$_nP_n = n(n-1)(n-2)........1 = n!$$

Example: Five books are placed in a row on a bookshelf. In how many different ways can they be arranged?

The number of possible ways in which 5 books can be arranged in a row is 5! = 1x2x3x4x5 = 120.

The formula given above for $_nP_r$, **the number of possible permutations of r objects selected from n objects** can also be proven in a similar manner. If r positions are filled by selecting from n objects, the first position can be filled in n ways, the second position can be filled in $n - 1$ ways and so on (as shown before). The rth position can be filled in $n-(r-1) = n-r+1$ ways. Hence,

$$_nP_r = n(n-1)(n-2).....(n-r+1) = \frac{n!}{(n-r)!}$$

The formula for the **number of possible combinations of r objects selected from n**, $_nC_r$, may be derived by using the above two formulae. For the same set of *r* objects, the number of permutations is *r*!. All of these permutations, however, correspond to the same combination. Hence,

$$_nC_r = \frac{_nP_r}{r!} = \frac{n!}{(n-r)!r!}$$

The number of permutations of n objects in a ring is given by (n – 1)!. This can be demonstrated by considering the fact that the number of permutations of *n* objects in a row is *n*!. When the objects are placed in a ring, moving every object one place to its left will result in the same arrangement. Moving each object two places to its left will also result in the same arrangement. We can continue this kind of movement up to *n* places to get the same arrangement. Thus the count *n*! is *n* times too many when the objects are arranged in a ring. Hence, the number of permutations of *n* objects in a ring is given by $\frac{n!}{n} = (n-1)!$.

Example: There are 20 people at a meeting. Five of them are selected to lead a discussion. How many different combinations of five people can be selected from the group? If the five people are seated in a row, how many different seating permutations are possible? If the five people are seated around a circular table, how many possible permutations are there?

The number of possible combinations of 5 people selected from the group of 20 is

$$_{20}C_5 = \frac{20!}{15!5!} = \frac{16 \times 17 \times 18 \times 19 \times 20}{1 \times 2 \times 3 \times 4 \times 5} = \frac{1860480}{120} = 15504$$

The number of possible permutations of the five seated in a row is

$$_{20}P_5 = \frac{20!}{15!} = 16 \times 17 \times 18 \times 19 \times 20 = 1860480$$

The number of possible permutations of the five seated in a circle is

$$\frac{_{20}P_5}{5} = \frac{20!}{5 \times 15!} = \frac{16 \times 17 \times 18 \times 19 \times 20}{5} = 372096$$

If the set of *n* objects contains some objects that are exactly alike, the number of permutations will again be different than *n*!. For instance, if n_1 of the *n* objects are exactly alike, then switching those objects among themselves will result in the same arrangement. Since we already know that n_1 objects can be arranged in n_1! ways, *n*! must be reduced by a factor of n_1! to get the correct number of permutations. Thus, the number of permutations of *n* objects of which n_1 are exactly alike is given by $\frac{n!}{n_1!}$. Generalizing this, we can say that **the number of different permutations of *n* objects of which n_1 are alike, n_2 are alike,... n_j are alike, is**

$$\frac{n!}{n_1! n_2! ... n_j!} \text{ where } n_1 + n_2 ..... + n_j = n$$

Example: A box contains 3 red, 2 blue and 5 green marbles. If all the marbles are taken out of the box and arranged in a row, how many different permutations are possible?

The number of possible permutations is

$$\frac{10!}{3!2!5!} = \frac{6 \times 7 \times 8 \times 9 \times 10}{6 \times 2} = 2520$$

4.1b. **Illustrate finite probability using a variety of examples and models (e.g., the fundamental counting principles)**

The following discussion of finite probability uses the symbols $\cap$ to mean "and," $\cup$ to mean "or" and $P(x)$ to mean "the probability of x." Also, $N(x)$ means "the number of ways that x can occur."

Fundamental Counting Principles

The Addition Principle of Counting states that if A and B are arbitrary events, then

$$N(A \cup B) = N(A) + N(B) - N(A \cap B)$$

Furthermore, if A and B are **mutually exclusive** events, then

$$N(A \cup B) = N(A) + N(B)$$

Correspondingly, the probabilities associated with arbitrary events are

$$P(A \cup B) = P(A) + P(B) - P(A \cap B)$$

For mutually exclusive events,

$$P(A \cup B) = P(A) + P(B)$$

Example: In how many ways can you select a black card or a Jack from an ordinary deck of playing cards?

Let B denote selection of a black card and let J denote selection of a jack. Then, since half the cards (26) are black and four are jacks,

$$N(B) = 26$$
$$N(J) = 26$$

Also, since a card can be both black and a jack (the jack of spades and the jack of clubs),

$$N(B \cap J) = 2$$

Thus, the solution is

$$N(B \cup J) = N(B) + N(J) - N(B \cap J) = 26 + 4 - 2 = 28$$

Example: A travel agency offers 40 possible trips: 14 to Asia, 16 to Europe and 10 to South America. In how many ways can you select a trip to Asia or Europe through this agency?

Let A denote selection of a trip to Asia and let E denote selection of a trip to Europe. Since these are mutually exclusive events, then

$$N(A \cup E) = N(A) + N(E) = 14 + 16 = 30$$

Therefore, there are 30 ways you can select a trip to Asia or Europe.

The Multiplication Principle of Counting for Dependent Events states that if A and B are arbitrary events, then the number of ways that A and B can occur in a two-stage experiment is given by

$$N(A \cap B) = N(A)N(B|A)$$

where $N(B|A)$ is the number of ways B can occur given that A has already occurred. If A and B are mutually exclusive events, then

$$N(A \cap B) = N(A)N(B)$$

Also, the probabilities associated with arbitrary events are

$$P(A \cap B) = P(A)P(B|A)$$

For mutually exclusive events,

$$P(A \cap B) = P(A)P(B)$$

Example: How many ways from an ordinary deck of 52 cards can two jacks be drawn in succession if the first card is not replaced into the deck before the second card is drawn (that is, without replacement)?

This is a two-stage experiment. Let A be selection of a jack in the first draw and let B be selection of a jack in the second draw. It is clear that

$$N(A) = 4$$

If the first card drawn is a jack, however, then there are only three remaining jacks remaining for the second draw. Thus, drawing two cards without replacement means the events A and B are dependent, and

$$N(B|A) = 3$$

The solution is then

$$N(A \cap B) = N(A)N(B|A) = (4)(3) = 12$$

Example: How many six-letter code "words" can be formed if repetition of letters is not allowed?

Since these are code words, a word does not have to be in the dictionary; for example, *abcdef* could be a code word. Since the experiment requires choosing each letter without replacing the letters from previous selections, the experiment has six stages.

Repetition is not allowed; thus, there are 26 choices for the first letter, 25 for the second, 24 for the third, 23 for the fourth, 22 for the fifth and 21 for the sixth. Therefore, if A is the selection of a six-letter code word without repetition, then

$$N(A) = (26)(25)(24)(23)(22)(21) = 165,765,600$$

There are over 165 million ways to choose a six-letter code word with six unique letters.

Finite Probability

Using the fundamental counting principles described above, finite probability problems can be solved. Generally, finding the probability of a particular event or set of events involves dividing the number of ways the particular event can take place by the total number of possible outcomes for the experiment. Thus, by appropriately counting these possible outcomes using the above rules, probabilities can be determined.

Example: Determine the probability of rolling three even numbers on three successive rolls of a six-sided die.

This is a three-stage experiment. First, determine the total number of possible outcomes for three rolls of a die. For each roll,

$$N(\text{roll}) = 6$$

There are three possible even rolls for a die: 2, 4 and 6.

$$N(\text{even}) = 3$$

The probability of rolling an even number on any particular roll is then

$$P(\text{even}) = \frac{N(\text{even})}{N(\text{roll})} = \frac{3}{6} = \frac{1}{2}$$

For three successive rolls, use the multiplication rule for mutually exclusive events.

$$P(3 \text{ even rolls}) = P(\text{even})^3 = \left(\frac{1}{2}\right)^3 = \frac{1}{8} = 0.125$$

Thus, the probability of rolling three successive even numbers using a six-sided die is 0.125.

4.1c.   Use and explain the concept of conditional probability

Dependent events occur when the probability of the second event depends on the outcome of the first event. For example, consider the two events: the home team wins the semifinal round (event A) and the home team wins the final round (event B). The probability of event B is contingent on the probability of event A. If the home team fails to win the semifinal round, it has a zero probability of winning in the final round. On the other hand, if the home team wins the semifinal round, then it may have a finite probability of winning in the final round. Symbolically, the probability of event B given event A is written $P(B|A)$. The conditional probability can be calculated according to the following definition.

$$P(B|A) = \frac{P(A \cap B)}{P(A)}$$

Consider a pair of dice: one red and one green. First the red die is rolled, followed by the green die. It is apparent that these events do not depend on each other, since the outcome of the roll of the green die is not affected by the outcome of the roll of the red die. The total probability of the two independent events can be found by multiplying the separate probabilities.

$$P(A \cap B) = P(A)P(B)$$
$$P(A \cap B) = \left(\frac{1}{6}\right)\left(\frac{1}{6}\right) = \frac{1}{36}$$

In many instances, however, events are not independent. Suppose a jar contains 12 red marbles and 8 blue marbles. If a marble is selected at random and then replaced, the probability of picking a certain color is the same in the second trial as it is in the first trial. If the marble is *not* replaced, then the probability of picking a certain color is *not* the same in the second trial, because the total number of marbles is decreased by one. This is an illustration of conditional probability. If R_n signifies selection of a red marble on the *n*th trial and B_n signifies selection of a blue marble on the *n*th trial, then the probability of selecting a red marble in two trials *with replacement* is

$$P(R_1 \cap R_2) = P(R_1)P(R_2) = \left(\frac{12}{20}\right)\left(\frac{12}{20}\right) = \frac{144}{400} = 0.36$$

The probability of selecting a red marble in two trials *without replacement* is

$$P(R_1 \cap R_2) = P(R_1)P(R|R_1) = \left(\frac{12}{20}\right)\left(\frac{11}{19}\right) = \frac{132}{360} \approx 0.367$$

Example: A car has a 75% probability of traveling 20,000 miles without breaking down. It has a 50% probability of traveling 10,000 additional miles without breaking down if it first makes it to 20,000 miles without breaking down. What is the probability that the car reaches 30,000 miles without breaking down?

Let event A be that the car reaches 20,000 miles without breaking down.

$$P(A) = 0.75$$

Event B is that the car travels an additional 10,000 miles without breaking down (assuming it didn't break down for the first 20,000 miles). Since event B is contingent on event A, write the probability as follows:

$$P(B|A) = 0.50$$

Use the conditional probability formula to find the probability that the car travels 30,000 miles $(A \cap B)$ without breaking down.

$$P(B|A) = \frac{P(A \cap B)}{P(A)}$$
$$0.50 = \frac{P(A \cap B)}{0.75}$$
$$P(A \cap B) = (0.50)(0.75) = 0.375$$

Thus, the car has a 37.5% probability of traveling 30,000 consecutive miles without breaking down.

4.1d. Interpret the probability of an outcome

The **probability** of an outcome, given a random experiment (a structured, repeatable experiment where the outcome cannot be predicted—or, alternatively, where the outcome is dependent on "chance"), is the relative frequency of the outcome. The relative frequency of an outcome is the number of times an experiment yields that outcome for a very large (ideally, infinite) number of trials. For instance, if a "fair" coin is tossed a very large number of times, then the relative frequency of a "heads-up" outcome is 0.5, or 50% (that is, one out of every two trials, on average, should be heads up). The probability is this relative frequency.

A **Bernoulli trial** is an experiment whose outcome is random and can be either of two possible outcomes, which are called "success" or "failure." Tossing a coin would be an example of a Bernoulli trial. The probability of success is represented by p, with the probability of failure being $q = 1 - p$. Bernoulli trials can be applied to any real-life situation in which there are only two possible outcomes. For example, concerning the birth of a child, the only two possible outcomes for the sex of the child are male or female.

Probability can also be expressed in terms of **odds**. Odds are defined as the ratio of the number of favorable outcomes to the number of unfavorable outcomes. The sum of the favorable outcomes and the unfavorable outcomes should always equal the total possible outcomes.

For example, given a bag of 12 red marbles and 7 green marbles, compute the odds of randomly selecting a red marble.

$$\text{Odds of red} = \frac{12}{19}$$

$$\text{Odds of not getting red} = \frac{7}{19}$$

In the case of flipping a coin, it is equally likely that a head or a tail will be tossed. The odds of tossing a head are 1:1. This is called **even odds**.

4.1e. Use normal, binomial, and exponential distributions to solve and interpret probability problems

The Normal Distribution

A **normal distribution** is the distribution associated with most sets of real-world data. It is frequently called a **bell curve**. A normal distribution has a **continuous random variable** X with mean μ and variance σ^2. The normal distribution has the following form.

$$f(x) = \frac{1}{\sigma\sqrt{2\pi}} e^{-\frac{1}{2}\left(\frac{x-\mu}{\sigma}\right)^2}$$

The total area under the normal curve is one. Thus,

$$\int_{-\infty}^{\infty} f(x)\,dx = 1$$

Since the area under the curve of this function is one, the distribution can be used to determine probabilities through integration. If a continuous random variable x follows the normal distribution, then the probability that x has a value between a and b is

$$P(a < X \le b) = \int_a^b f(x)\,dx = F(b) - F(a)$$

Since this integral is difficult to evaluate analytically, tables of values are often used. Often, however, the tables use the integral

$$\frac{1}{\sqrt{2\pi}} \int_a^b e^{-\frac{t^2}{2}}\,dt = F(b) - F(a)$$

To use this form, simply convert x values to t values using

$$t = \frac{x_i - \mu}{\sigma}$$

where x_i is a particular value for the random variable X. This formula is often called the **z-score**.

Example: Albert's Bagel Shop's morning customer load follows a normal distribution, with **mean** (average) 50 and **standard deviation** 10. Determine the probability that the number of customers on a particular morning will be less than 42.

First, convert to a form that allows use of normal distribution tables:

$$t = \frac{x - \mu}{\sigma} = \frac{42 - 50}{10} = -0.8$$

Next, use a table to find the probability corresponding to the z-score. The actual integral in this case is

$$P(X < 42) = \frac{1}{\sqrt{2\pi}} \int_{-\infty}^{-0.8} e^{-\frac{t^2}{2}} dt$$

The table gives a value for $x = 0.8$ of 0.7881. To find the value for $x < -0.8$, subtract this result from one.

$$P(X < 42) = 1 - 0.7881 = 0.2119$$

This means that there is about a 21.2% chance that there will be fewer than 42 customers in a given morning.

Example: The scores on Mr. Rogers' statistics exam follow a normal distribution with mean 85 and standard deviation 5. A student is wondering what is the probability that she will score between a 90 and a 95 on her exam.

To compute $P(90 < x < 95)$, first compute the z-scores for each raw score.

$$z_{90} = \frac{90 - 85}{5} = 1$$

$$z_{95} = \frac{95 - 85}{5} = 2$$

Use the tables to find $P(1 < z < 2)$. To do this, subtract as follows.

$$P(1 < z < 2) = P(z < 2) - P(z < 1)$$

The table yields

$$P(1 < z < 2) = 0.9772 - 0.8413 = 0.1359$$

It can then be concluded that there is a 13.6% chance that the student will score between a 90 and a 95 on her exam.

The Binomial Distribution

The **binomial distribution** is a probability distribution for discrete random variables and is expressed as follows.

$$f(x) = \binom{n}{x} p^x q^{n-x}$$

where a sequence of n trials of an experiment are performed and where p is the probability of "success" and q is the probability of "failure." The value x is the number of times the experiment yields a successful outcome. Notice that this probability function is the product of p^x (the probability of successful outcomes in x trials) and q^{n-x} (the probability of unsuccessful outcomes in the remainder of the trials). The factor $\binom{n}{x}$ indicates that the x successful trials can be chosen $\binom{n}{x}$ ways (combinations) from the n total trials. (In other words, the successful trials may occur at different points in the sequence.)

Example: A loaded coin has a probability 0.6 of landing heads up. What is the probability of getting three heads in four successive tosses?

Use the binomial distribution. In this case, p is the probability of the coin landing heads up, and $q = 1 - p$ is the probability of the coin landing tails up. Also, the number of "successful" trials (heads up) is 3. Then,

$$f(3) = \binom{4}{3}(0.6)^3 (1-0.6)^{4-3}$$

$$f(3) = \frac{4!}{3!(4-3)!}(0.6)^3 (0.4)^1$$

$$f(3) = \frac{24}{6(1)}(0.216)(0.4) = 0.3456$$

Thus, there is a 34.56% chance that the loaded coin will land heads up three out of four times.

The Exponential Distribution

The exponential distribution is for continuous random variables and has the following form.

$$f(x) = \lambda e^{-\lambda x}$$

Here, $x \geq 0$. The parameter λ is called the **rate parameter**. For instance, the exponential distribution is often applied to failure rates. If a certain device has a failure rate λ failures per hour, then the probability that a device has failed at time T hours is

$$P(T) = \lambda \int_0^T e^{-\lambda t} dt = -\lambda \frac{1}{\lambda} e^{-\lambda t} \Big|_0^T = -\left[e^{-\lambda T} - e^0\right] = 1 - e^{-\lambda T}$$

Example: Testing has revealed that a newly designed widget has a failure rate of 1 per 5,000 hours of use. What is the probability that a particular part will be operational after a year of continual use?

Use the formula given above for the exponential distribution.

$$P(1\,\text{year}) = 1 - e^{-\lambda(1\,\text{year})}$$

Write λ in terms of failures per year.

$$\lambda = \frac{1\,\text{failure}}{5,000\,\text{hours}} \left(\frac{24\,\text{hours}}{1\,\text{day}}\right)\left(\frac{365\,\text{days}}{1\,\text{year}}\right) = 1.752 \frac{\text{failures}}{\text{year}}$$

Then

$$P(1\,\text{year}) = 1 - e^{-1.752(1)} = 1 - 0.173 = 0.827$$

Thus, there is an 82.7% probability that the device will be operational after one year of continual use.

SKILL 4.2 STATISTICS

4.2a. Compute and interpret the mean, median, and mode of both discrete and continuous distributions

The mean, median and mode are measures of central tendency (i.e., the average or typical value) in a data set. They can be defined both for discrete and continuous data sets. A **discrete variable** is one that can only take on certain specific values. For instance, the number of students in a class can only be a whole number (e.g., 15 or 16, but not 15.5). A **continuous variable**, such as the weight of an object, can take on a continuous range of values.

For discrete data, the **mean** is the average of the data items, or the value obtained by adding all the data values and dividing by the total number of data items. For a data set of n items with data values $x_1, x_2, x_3, \ldots, x_n$, the mean is given by

$$\bar{x} = \frac{x_1 + x_2 + x_3 + \ldots + x_n}{n}$$

The **median** is found by putting the data in order from smallest to largest and selecting the item in the middle (or the average of the two values in the middle if the number of data items is even). The **mode** is the most frequently occurring datum. There can be more than one mode in a data set.

Example: Find the mean, median, and mode of the test scores listed below:

85	77	65
92	90	54
88	85	70
75	80	69
85	88	60
72	74	95

Mean: sum of all scores ÷ number of scores = 78
Median: put numbers in order from smallest to largest. Pick the middle number.
54, 60, 65, 69, 70, 72, 74, 75, <u>77</u>, <u>80</u>, 85, 85, 85, 88, 88, 90, 92, 95

Both values are in the middle.

Therefore, median is average of two numbers in the middle, or 78.5
Mode: most frequent number = 85

MATHEMATICS

Discrete data is typically displayed in a table as shown in the example above. If the data set is large, it may be expressed in compact form as a **frequency distribution**. The number of occurrences of each data point is the **frequency** of that value. The **relative frequency** is defined as the frequency divided by the total number of data points. Since the sum of the frequencies equals the number of data points, the relative frequencies add up to 1. The relative frequency of a data point, therefore, represents the probability of occurrence of that value. Thus, a distribution consisting of relative frequencies is known as a **probability distribution**.

For data expressed as a frequency distribution, the mean is given by

$$\overline{x} = \frac{\sum x_i f_i}{\sum f_i} = \sum x_i f_i'$$

where x_i represents a data value, f_i the corresponding frequency and f_i' the corresponding relative frequency.

The **cumulative frequency** of a data point is the sum of the frequencies from the beginning up to that point. The median of a frequency distribution is the point at which the cumulative frequency reaches half the value of the total number of data points.

The mode is the point at which the frequency distribution reaches a maximum. There can be more than one mode in which case the distribution is **multimodal**.

Example: The frequency distribution below shows the summary of some test results where people scored points ranging from 0 to 45 in increments of 5. One person scored 5 points, 4 people scored 10 points and so on. Find the mean, median and mode of the data set.

Points	Frequency	Cumulative Frequency	Relative Frequency
5	1	1	0.009
10	4	5	0.035
15	12	17	0.105
20	22	39	0.193
25	30	69	0.263
30	25	94	0.219
35	13	107	0.114
40	6	113	0.053
45	1	114	0.009

The mean score is the following:
(5x1+10x4+15x12+20x22+25x30+30x25+35x13+40x6+45x1)/114
= (5+40+180+440+750+750+455+240+45)/114 = 25.5.

The median score (the point at which the cumulative frequency reaches or surpasses the value 57) is 25.

The mode (or value with the highest frequency) is 25.

The frequency distribution from the above example is displayed below as a histogram.

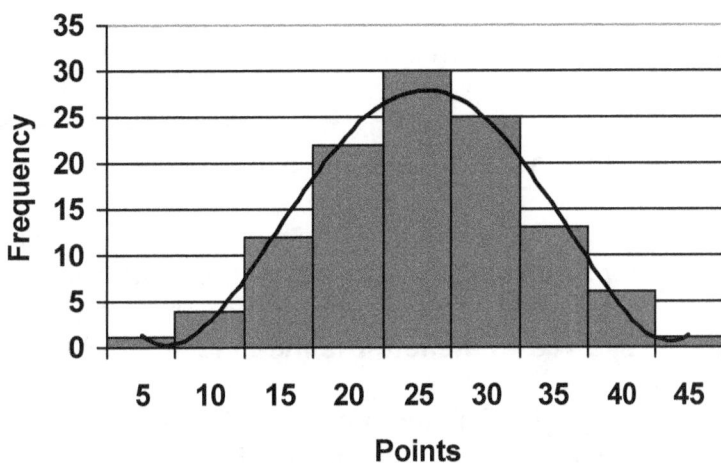

The histogram shows the reason why the mean, median and mode of this distribution are practically identical. This is due to the fact that the distribution is symmetric with one peak exactly in the middle. A trend line has been added to the histogram. Notice that this approximates the most common **continuous distribution**, a **normal or bell curve** for which the mean, median and mode are identical.

A frequency distribution may also be created by subdividing the range of the data into sub-ranges. In this case, the count in each subdivision or **bin** is the frequency. Discrete as well as continuous data may be represented in this way.

A large data set of continuous data is often represented using a **probability distribution** expressed as a **probability density function.** The integral of the probability density function over a certain range gives the probability of a data point being in that range of values. The integral of the probability density function over the whole range of values is equal to 1.

The **mean** value for a distribution of a variable x represented by a probability density function $f(x)$ is given by

$$\int_{-\infty}^{+\infty} xf(x)dx$$

(Compare this with its discrete counterpart $\bar{x} = \sum x_i f_i'$).

The **median** is the upper bound for which the integral of the probability density function is equal to 0.5; i.e., if $\int_{-\infty}^{a} f(x)dx = 0.5$, then a is the median of the distribution.

The mode is the maximum value or values of the probability density function within the range of the function.

As mentioned before, the mean and median are very close together for symmetric distributions. **If the distribution is skewed to the right, the mean is greater than the median. If the distribution is skewed to the left, the mean is smaller than the median.**

Example: Find the mean, median and mode for the distribution given by the probability density function

$$f(x) = \begin{cases} 4x(1-x^2) & 0 \leq x \leq 1 \\ 0 & \text{otherwise} \end{cases}$$

Mean = $\int_0^1 4x^2(1-x^2)dx = \frac{4x^3}{3}\Big|_0^1 - \frac{4x^5}{5}\Big|_0^1 = \frac{4}{3} - \frac{4}{5} = \frac{20-12}{15} = \frac{8}{15} = 0.53$

If $x = a$ is the median, then

$$\int_0^a 4x(1-x^2)dx = 0.5$$

$$\Rightarrow \frac{4x^2}{2}\Big|_0^a - \frac{4x^4}{4}\Big|_0^a = 0.5$$

$$\Rightarrow 2a^2 - a^4 = 0.5$$

$$\Rightarrow 2a^4 - 4a^2 + 1 = 0$$

Solving for a yields

$$a^2 = \frac{4 \pm \sqrt{16-8}}{4} = 1 \pm \frac{2\sqrt{2}}{4} = 1 - \frac{\sqrt{2}}{2}$$ (to keep x within the range 0 to 1)

$$a = \sqrt{1 - \frac{1}{\sqrt{2}}} = 0.54$$

The mode is obtained by taking the derivative of the probability density function and setting it to zero as shown below. (Notice that the second derivative is negative at $x = 0.58$, and, hence, this is clearly a maximum.)

$$\frac{d}{dx}(4x - 4x^3) = 4 - 12x^2 = 0$$
$$\Rightarrow 12x^2 = 4$$
$$\Rightarrow x^2 = \frac{1}{3}$$
$$\Rightarrow x = \frac{1}{\sqrt{3}} = 0.58$$

4.2b. Compute and interpret quartiles, range, variance, and standard deviation of both discrete and continuous distributions

Statistics for Discrete Distributions

Range is a measure of variability that is calculated by subtracting the smallest value from the largest value in a set of discrete data.

The **variance** and **standard deviation** are measures of the "spread" of data around the mean. It is noteworthy that descriptive statistics involving such parameters as variance and standard deviation can be applied to a set of data that spans the entire population (parameters, typically represented using Greek symbols) or to a set of data that only constitutes a portion of the population (sample statistics, typically represented by Latin letters).

The mean of a set of data, whether for a population (μ) or for a sample ($\bar{x}$), uses the formula discussed in Skill a, and can be represented as either a set of individual data or as a set of data with associated frequencies. The variance and standard deviation for the population differ slightly from those of a sample. The population variance (σ^2) and the population standard deviation (σ) are as follows.

$$\sigma^2 = \frac{1}{n}\sum(x_i - \mu)^2$$
$$\sigma = \sqrt{\sigma^2}$$

For a sample, the data does not include the entire population. As a result, it should be expected that the sample data might not be perfectly representative of the population. To account for this shortcoming in the sample variance (s^2) and standard deviation (s), the sum of the squared differences between the data and the mean is divided by ($n - 1$) instead of just n. This increases the variance and standard deviation slightly, which in turn increases slightly the data spread to account for the possibility that the sample may not accurately represent the population.

$$s^2 = \frac{1}{n-1}\sum(x_i - \bar{x})^2$$
$$s = \sqrt{s^2}$$

Example: Calculate the range, variance and standard deviation for the following data set: {3, 3, 5, 7, 8, 8, 8, 10, 12, 21}.

The range is simply the largest data value minus the smallest. In this case, the range is 21 – 3 = 18.

To calculate the variance and standard deviation, first calculate the mean. If it is not stated whether a data set constitutes a population or sample, assume it is a population. (In this case, if the data was labeled as "ages of the 10 people in a room," this would be a population. If the data was labeled "ages of males at a crowded circus event," the data would be a sample.)

$$\mu = \frac{3+3+5+7+8+8+8+10+12+21}{10} = 8.5$$

Use this mean to calculate the variance.

$$\sigma^2 = \frac{1}{10}\sum(x_i - 8.5)^2$$
$$\sigma^2 = \frac{1}{10}\{(3-8.5)^2 + (3-8.5)^2 + (5-8.5)^2 + ... + (21-8.5)^2\}$$
$$\sigma^2 = \frac{246.5}{10} = 24.65$$

The standard deviation is

$$\sigma = \sqrt{\sigma^2} = \sqrt{24.65} \approx 4.96$$

Statistics for Continuous Distributions

The range for a continuous data distribution is the same as that for a discrete distribution: the largest value minus the smallest value. Calculation of the mean, variance and standard deviation are similar, but slightly different. Since a continuous distribution does not permit a simple summation, integrals must be used. The mean μ of a distribution function $f(x)$ is expressed below (and is discussed further in Skill a).

$$\mu = \int_{-\infty}^{\infty} xf(x)dx$$

The variance σ^2 over also has an integral form, and has a form similar to that of a discrete distribution.

$$\sigma^2 = \int_{-\infty}^{\infty}(x-\mu)^2 f(x)dx$$

The standard deviation σ is simply

$$\sigma = \sqrt{\sigma^2}$$

Example: Calculate the standard deviation of a data distribution function $f(x)$ where

$$f(x) = \begin{cases} 0 & x < 1 \\ -2x^2 + 2 & -1 \leq x \leq 1 \\ 0 & x > 1 \end{cases}$$

First calculate the mean of the function. Since the function is zero except between 1 and −1, the integral can likewise be evaluated from −1 to 1. (For further discussion of integrals, see Domain 5.4.)

$$\mu = \int_{-1}^{1}\left(-2x^2+2\right)x\,dx$$

$$\mu = -2\int_{-1}^{1}\left(x^3-x\right)dx$$

$$\mu = -2\left[\frac{x^4}{4}-\frac{x^2}{2}\right]_{x=-1}^{x=1}$$

$$\mu = -2\left\{\left[\frac{(1)^4}{4}-\frac{(1)^2}{2}\right]-\left[\frac{(-1)^4}{4}-\frac{(-1)^2}{2}\right]\right\} = 0$$

The mean can also be seen clearly by the fact that the graph of the function $f(x)$ is symmetric about the y-axis, indicating that its center (or mean) is at $x = 0$. Next, calculate the variance of f.

$$\sigma^2 = \int_{-1}^{1}(x-0)^2\left(-2x^2+2\right)dx = -2\int_{-1}^{1}x^2\left(x^2-1\right)dx$$

$$\sigma^2 = -2\int_{-1}^{1}(x^4 - x^2)dx$$

$$\sigma^2 = -2\left[\frac{x^5}{5} - \frac{x^3}{3}\right]_{x=-1}^{x=1} = -2\left\{\left[\frac{(1)^5}{5} - \frac{(1)^3}{3}\right] - \left[\frac{(-1)^5}{5} - \frac{(-1)^3}{3}\right]\right\}$$

$$\sigma^2 = -2\left\{\frac{1}{5} - \frac{1}{3} - \left(-\frac{1}{5}\right) + \left(-\frac{1}{3}\right)\right\} = -2\left(\frac{2}{5} - \frac{2}{3}\right)$$

$$\sigma^2 = \frac{8}{15} \approx 0.533$$

The standard deviation is

$$\sigma = \sqrt{\sigma^2} = \sqrt{\frac{8}{15}} \approx 0.730$$

Percentiles and Quartiles

Percentiles divide data into 100 equal parts. A datum that falls in the nth percentile means that this datum exceeds (by whatever measure) n percent of the other data and that $(100 - n)$ percent of the data exceed this datum. For instance, a person whose score on a test falls in the 65th percentile has outperformed 65 percent of all those who took the test. This does not mean that the score was 65 percent out of 100, nor does it mean that 65 percent of the questions answered were correctly. Instead, this score means that the grade was higher than 65 percent of all those who took the test.

Quartiles divide the data into four segments. To find the quartile of a particular datum, first determine the median of the data set (which is labeled Q2), then find the median of the upper half (labeled Q3) and the median of the lower half (labeled Q1) of the data set. There is some confusion in determining the upper and lower quartile, and statisticians do not agree on the appropriate method to use. Tukey's method for finding the quartile values is to find the median of the data set, then find the median of the upper and lower halves of the data set. If there is an odd number of values in the data set, include the median value in both halves when finding the quartile values. For example, consider the following data set:

$$\{1, 4, 9, 16, 25, 36, 49, 64, 81\}$$

First, find the median value, which is 25. This is the value Q2. Since there is an odd number of values in the data set (nine), include the median in both halves. To find the quartile values, find the medians of the two sets

{1, 4, 9, 16, 25} and {25, 36, 49, 64, 81}

Since each of these subsets has an odd number of elements (five), use the middle value. Thus, the lower quartile value (Q1) is 9 and the upper quartile value (Q3) is 49.

Another method to find quartile values (if the total data set has an odd number of values) excludes the median from both halves when finding the quartile values. Using this approach on the data set above, exclude the median (25) from each half. To find the quartile values, find the medians of

{1, 4, 9, 16} and {36, 49, 64, 81}

Since each of these data sets has an even number of elements (four), average the middle two values. Thus the lower quartile value (Q1) is (4+9)/2 = 6.5 and the upper quartile value (Q3) is (49+64)/2 = 56.5. The middle quartile value (Q2) remains 25.

Other methods for calculating quartiles also exist, but these two methods are the most straightforward.

Percentiles and quartiles are typically applied to discrete data distributions, but application to continuous distributions is also possible. In such a case, percentiles and quartiles would be calculated by dividing the area under the curve of the distribution into either 100 (for percentile) or 4 (for quartile) even or approximately even segments. The boundaries of these segments are the percentile or quartile values.

Example: Find the percentile of a student who scored 80 on an exam, where the distribution of scores for the entire class is {68, 72, 73, 75, 78, 80, 81, 85, 92, 96}.

The total number of test scores is 10. Find the number of scores that were less than or equal to 80. In this case, the result is 6. The percentile is

$$\frac{6}{10} 100\% = 60\%$$

Thus, the student who scored 80 on the test is in the 60th percentile. Notice that the student's score is, in this case, much higher than the percentile. Thus, percentile is a relative scoring mechanism. (Conceivably, a student with an almost-perfect score could rank in a very low percentile, assuming all or most of the other students received a perfect score.)

4.2c. **Select and evaluate sampling methods appropriate to a task (e.g., random, systematic, cluster, convenience sampling) and display the results**

In cases where the number of events or individuals is too large to collect data on each one, scientists collect information from only a small percentage. This is known as **sampling** or **surveying**. If sampling is done correctly, it should give the investigator nearly the same information he would have obtained by testing the entire population. The survey must be carefully designed, considering both the sampling technique and the size of the sample.

There are a variety of sampling techniques, both **random** and **non-random**. Random sampling is also known as **probability sampling** since the methods of probability theory can be used to ascertain the odds that the sample is representative of the whole population. Statistical methods may be used to determine how large a sample is necessary to give an investigator a specified level of certainty (95% is a typical confidence interval). Conversely, if an investigator has a sample of certain size, those same statistical methods can be used to determine how confident one can be that the sample accurately reflects the whole population.

A truly **random** sample must choose events or individuals without regard to time, place or result. **Simple random sampling** is ideal for populations that are relatively homogeneous with respect to the data being collected.

In some cases an accurate representation of distinct sub-populations requires **stratified random sampling** or **quota sampling**. For instance, if men and women are likely to respond very differently to a particular survey, the total sample population can be separated into these two subgroups and then a random group of respondents selected from each subgroup. This kind of sampling not only provides balanced representation of different subgroups, it also allows comparison of data between subgroups. Stratified sampling is sometimes **proportional**; i.e., the number of samples selected from each subgroup reflects the fraction of the whole population represented by the subgroup.

Sometimes compromises must be made to save time, money or effort. For instance, when conducting a phone survey, calls are typically only made in a certain geographical area and at a certain time of day. This is an example of **cluster random sampling**. There are three stages to cluster or area sampling: the target population is divided into many regional clusters (groups), a few clusters are randomly selected for study and a few subjects are randomly chosen from within a cluster

Systematic random sampling involves the collection of a sample at defined intervals (for instance, every tenth part to come off a manufacturing line). Here, it is assumed that the population is ordered randomly and there is no hidden pattern that may compromise the randomness of the sampling.

Non-random sampling is also known as **non-probability sampling**. **Convenience sampling** is the method of choosing items arbitrarily and in an unstructured manner from the frame. **Purposive sampling** targets a particular section of the population. **Snowball sampling** (e.g., having survey participants recommend others) and **expert sampling** are other types of non-random sampling. Obviously, non-random samples are far less representative of the whole population than random ones. They may, however, be the only methods available or may meet the needs of a particular study.

The data obtained from sampling may be categorical (e.g., yes or no responses) or numerical. In both cases, results are displayed using a variety of graphical techniques. Geographical data is often displayed superposed on maps.

Bar graphs are used to compare various quantities using bars of different lengths.

Example: A class had the following grades:
4 A's, 9 B's, 8 C's, 1 D, 3 F's.
Graph these on a bar graph.

Bar graph

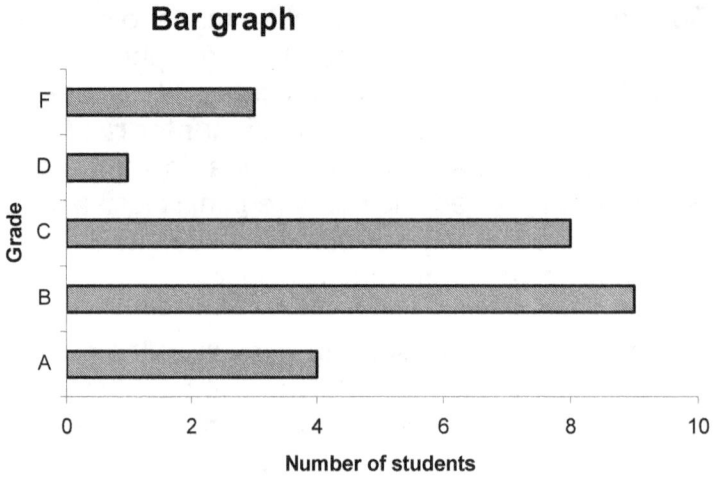

Line graphs are used to show trends, often over a period of time.

Example: Graph the following information using a line graph.

The number of National Merit finalists/school year

School	90-91	91-92	92-93	93-94	94-95	95-96
Central	3	5	1	4	6	8
Wilson	4	2	3	2	3	2

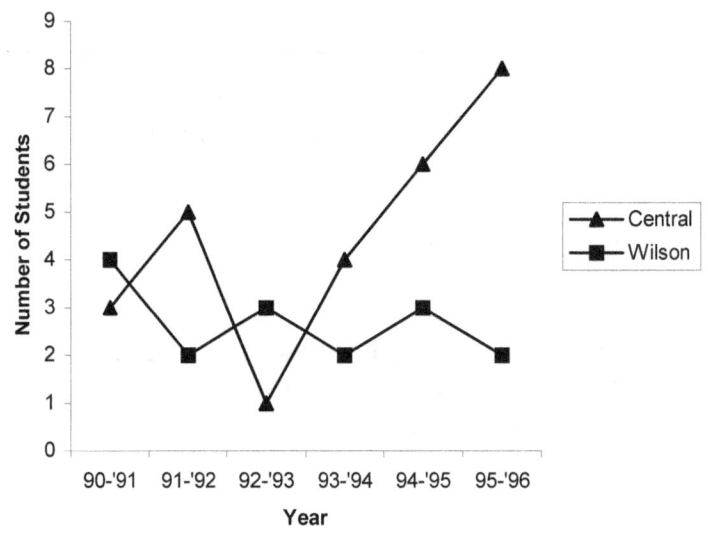

Circle graphs or **Pie charts** show the relationship of various parts of a data set to each other and the whole. Each part is shown as a percentage of the total and occupies a proportional sector of the circular area. To make a circle graph, total all the information that is to be included on the graph. Determine the central angle to be used for each sector of the graph using the following formula:

$$\frac{\text{information}}{\text{total information}} \times 360° = \text{degrees in central} \angle$$

Lay out the central angles according to these sizes, label each section and include its percentage.

Example: Graph this information on a circle graph:

Monthly expenses:
- Rent, $400
- Food, $150
- Utilities, $75
- Clothes, $75
- Church, $100
- Misc., $200

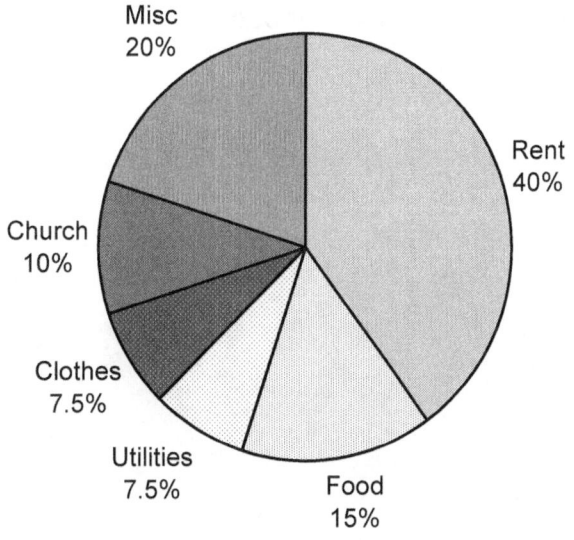

Scatter plots compare two characteristics of the same group of things or people and usually consist of a large body of data. They show how much one variable is affected by another. The relationship between the two variables is their **correlation**. The closer the data points come to making a straight line when plotted, the closer the correlation.

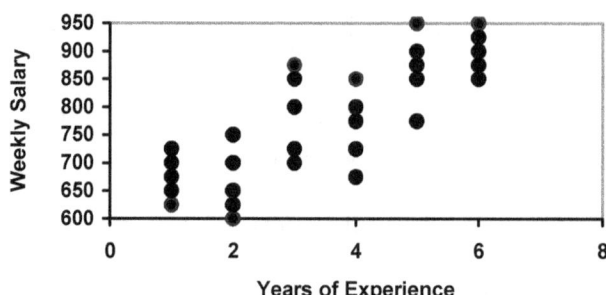

The most common form of graphical display used for numerical data obtained from random sampling is the **histogram**. A trend line can be superposed on a histogram to observe the general shape of the distribution. In some cases, the trend line may also be fitted to a probability density function. Typical statistical measures such as the mean, median, mode and standard deviation can be computed using the frequency distribution.

4.2d. Know the method of least squares and apply it to linear regression and correlation

Method of least squares

Given a set of data, a curve approximation can be fitted to the data by using the **method of least squares**. The best-fit curve, defined by the function $f(x)$, is assumed to approximate a set of data with coordinates (x_i, y_i) by minimizing the sum of squared differences between the curve and the data. Mathematically, the sum of these squared differences (errors) can be written as follows for a data set with n points.

$$S = \sum_{i=1}^{n}\left[f(x_i) - y_i\right]^2$$

Thus, the best-fit curve approximation to a set of data (x_i, y_i) is $f(x)$ such that S is minimized.

Shown below is a set of data and a linear function that approximates it. The vertical distances between the data points and the line are the errors that are squared and summed to find S.

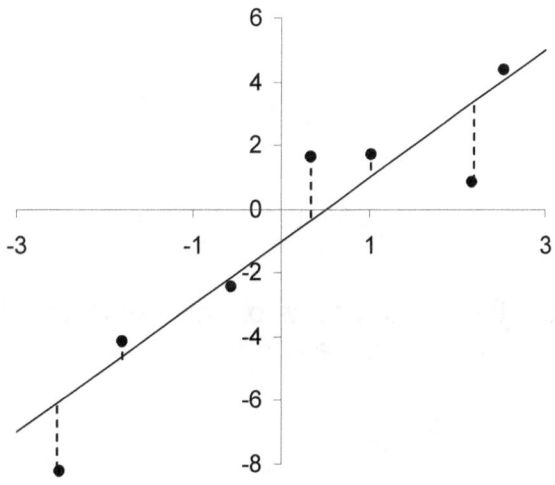

Linear least squares regression

If the curve $f(x)$ that is used to approximate a set of data by minimizing the sum of squared errors, S, then $f(x)$ is called a **least squares regression line**. The process of determining $f(x)$ is called **linear least squares regression**. In this case, $f(x)$ has the following form:

$$f(x) = ax + b$$

Given a set of data $\{(x_1, y_1), (x_2, y_2), (x_3, y_3), \ldots, (x_n, y_n)\}$, the sum S for linear regression is the following.

$$S = \sum_{i=1}^{n} [ax_i + b - y_i]^2$$

To find $f(x)$, it is necessary to find a and b. This can be done by minimizing S. Since S is a function of both a and b, S must be minimized through the use of partial derivatives. (A partial derivative is exactly the same as a full derivative, except that all variables other than the one being differentiated are treated as constants. Partial derivatives often use the symbol ∂ in place of d.) Therefore, find the partial derivative with respect to a and the partial derivative with respect to b.

$$\frac{\partial S}{\partial a} = \frac{\partial}{\partial a} \sum_{i=1}^{n} [ax_i + b - y_i]^2 \qquad \frac{\partial S}{\partial b} = \frac{\partial}{\partial b} \sum_{i=1}^{n} [ax_i + b - y_i]^2$$

$$\frac{\partial S}{\partial a} = \sum_{i=1}^{n} 2x_i [ax_i + b - y_i] \qquad \frac{\partial S}{\partial b} = \sum_{i=1}^{n} 2[ax_i + b - y_i]$$

Set these equal to zero. This yields a system of equations that can be solved to find a and b.

$$\frac{\partial S}{\partial a} = 0 \qquad \frac{\partial S}{\partial b} = 0$$

$$0 = 2a \sum_{i=1}^{n} x_i^2 + 2b \sum_{i=1}^{n} x_i - 2 \sum_{i=1}^{n} x_i y_i$$

$$0 = 2a \sum_{i=1}^{n} x_i + 2 \sum_{i=1}^{n} b - 2 \sum_{i=1}^{n} y_i = 2a \sum_{i=1}^{n} x_i + 2nb - 2 \sum_{i=1}^{n} y_i$$

Solve the second equation for b:

$$0 = 2a\sum_{i=1}^{n} x_i + 2nb - 2\sum_{i=1}^{n} y_i$$

$$2nb = 2\sum_{i=1}^{n} y_i - 2a\sum_{i=1}^{n} x_i$$

$$b = \frac{1}{n}\sum_{i=1}^{n} y_i - \frac{a}{n}\sum_{i=1}^{n} x_i$$

Substitute this result into the first equation and solve for a.

$$0 = 2a\sum_{i=1}^{n} x_i^2 + 2\left\{\frac{1}{n}\sum_{i=1}^{n} y_i - \frac{a}{n}\sum_{i=1}^{n} x_i\right\}\sum_{i=1}^{n} x_i - 2\sum_{i=1}^{n} x_i y_i$$

$$0 = 2a\sum_{i=1}^{n} x_i^2 + \frac{2}{n}\sum_{i=1}^{n} x_i \sum_{i=1}^{n} y_i - \frac{2a}{n}\left[\sum_{i=1}^{n} x_i\right]^2 - 2\sum_{i=1}^{n} x_i y_i$$

$$a\left\{\sum_{i=1}^{n} x_i^2 - \frac{1}{n}\left[\sum_{i=1}^{n} x_i\right]^2\right\} = \sum_{i=1}^{n} x_i y_i - \frac{1}{n}\sum_{i=1}^{n} x_i \sum_{i=1}^{n} y_i$$

$$a = \frac{\sum_{i=1}^{n} x_i y_i - \frac{1}{n}\sum_{i=1}^{n} x_i \sum_{i=1}^{n} y_i}{\sum_{i=1}^{n} x_i^2 - \frac{1}{n}\left[\sum_{i=1}^{n} x_i\right]^2} = \frac{n\sum_{i=1}^{n} x_i y_i - \sum_{i=1}^{n} x_i \sum_{i=1}^{n} y_i}{n\sum_{i=1}^{n} x_i^2 - \left[\sum_{i=1}^{n} x_i\right]^2}$$

Note that the average x value for the data (which is the sum of all x values divided by n) and the average y value for the data (which is the sum of all y values divided by n) can be used to simplify the expression. The average x value is defined as $\bar{x}$ and the average y value is defined as $\bar{y}$.

$$a = \frac{\sum_{i=1}^{n} x_i y_i - n\bar{x}\bar{y}}{\sum_{i=1}^{n} x_i^2 - n\bar{x}^2}$$

Since the expression for b is complicated, it suffices to the above expression for b in terms of a.

MATHEMATICS

$$b = \frac{1}{n}\left(\sum_{i=1}^{n} y_i - a\sum_{i=1}^{n} x_i\right)$$

$$b = \bar{y} - a\bar{x}$$

Thus, given a set of data, the linear least squares regression line can be found by calculating a and b as shown above.

The **correlation coefficient**, r, can be used as a measure of the quality of $f(x)$ as a fit to the data set. The value of r ranges from zero (for a poor fit) to one (for a good fit). The correlation coefficient formula is given below.

$$r^2 = \frac{\left[\sum_{i=1}^{n} x_i y_i - \frac{1}{n}\sum_{i=1}^{n} x_i \sum_{i=1}^{n} y_i\right]^2}{\left[\sum_{i=1}^{n} x_i^2 - \frac{1}{n}\left(\sum_{i=1}^{n} x_i\right)^2\right]\left[\sum_{i=1}^{n} y_i^2 - \frac{1}{n}\left(\sum_{i=1}^{n} y_i\right)^2\right]}$$

$$r^2 = \frac{\left(\sum_{i=1}^{n} x_i y_i - n\bar{x}\bar{y}\right)^2}{\left(\sum_{i=1}^{n} x_i^2 - n\bar{x}^2\right)\left(\sum_{i=1}^{n} y_i^2 - n\bar{y}^2\right)}$$

Example: A company has collected data comparing the age of its employees to their respective income (in thousands of dollars). Find the line that best fits the data (using a least squares approach). Also calculate the correlation coefficient for the fit. The data is given below in the form of (age, income).

$$\{(35,42),(27,23),(54,43),(58,64),(39,51),(31,40)\}$$

The data are plotted in the graph below.

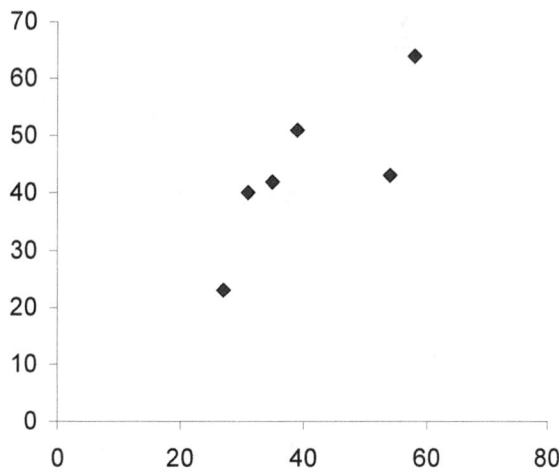

Note that there are six pieces of data. It is helpful to first calculate the following sums:

$$\sum_{i=1}^{6} x_i = 35 + 27 + 54 + 58 + 39 + 31 = 244$$

$$\sum_{i=1}^{6} y_i = 42 + 23 + 43 + 64 + 51 + 40 = 263$$

$$\sum_{i=1}^{6} x_i y_i = 35(42) + 27(23) + 54(43) + 58(64) + 39(51) + 31(40)$$
$$= 11354$$

$$\sum_{i=1}^{6} x_i^2 = 35^2 + 27^2 + 54^2 + 58^2 + 39^2 + 31^2 = 10716$$

$$\sum_{i=1}^{6} y_i^2 = 42^2 + 23^2 + 43^2 + 64^2 + 51^2 + 40^2 = 12439$$

Based on these values, the average x and y values are given below.

$$\bar{x} = \frac{244}{6} \approx 40.67$$

$$\bar{y} = \frac{263}{6} \approx 43.83$$

To find the equation of the least squares regression line, calculate the values of a and b.

$$a = \frac{\sum_{i=1}^{n} x_i y_i - n\bar{x}\bar{y}}{\sum_{i=1}^{n} x_i^2 - n\bar{x}^2} = \frac{11354 - 6(40.67)(43.83)}{10716 - 6(40.67)^2} \approx 0.832$$

$$b = \bar{y} - a\bar{x} = 43.83 - 0.832(40.67) = 9.993$$

Thus, the equation of the least squares regression line is

$$f(x) = 0.832x + 9.993$$

This result can be displayed on the data graph to ensure that there are no egregious errors in the result.

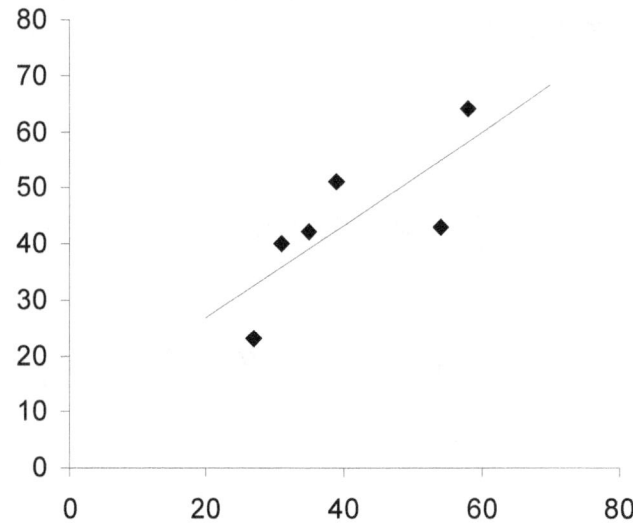

The regression line in the graph above appears to do a good job of approximating the trend of the data. To quantify how well the line fits the data, calculate the correlation coefficient using the formula given above.

$$r^2 = \frac{(11354 - 6(40.67)(43.83))^2}{(10716 - 6(40.67)^2)(12439 - 6(43.83)^2)}$$

$$r^2 = \frac{(658.603)^2}{(791.707)(912.587)} = 0.600$$

$$r = 0.775$$

Thus, the fit to the data is reasonably good.

4.2e. **Know and apply the chi-square test**

Chi-square tests are used to determine the acceptability of a null hypothesis. They are useful for testing the "goodness-of-fit" between an observed distribution and an expected distribution or for testing the independence of two variables. (A **null hypothesis** is assumed to be true and is then tested for potential rejection.)

The chi-square value is calculated using the observed and expected frequencies of a distribution. Given that O_i is the observed frequency for the *i*th value of a data set and E_i is the expected frequency, then the chi-square (χ^2) value is the following.

$$\chi^2 = \sum_{i=1}^{N} \frac{(O_i - E_i)^2}{E_i}$$

Here, N is the total number of values in the observed data set. Notice that NO_i and NE_i are the total number of observed and expected samples, respectively, of the *i*th value of the data set. Notice also that χ^2 is a measure of the deviation of the observed values from the expected values. If the observed values are precisely the same as the expected values, then χ^2 is zero. A high χ^2 means that there is large variation.

Another important parameter in the chi-square test is the **degrees of freedom**, n. The number of degrees of freedom is the total number of possible values or value classes, less one. Thus, if a problem involves rolling a six-sided die, the number of degrees of freedom is the six possible outcomes minus one, or five.

Problems may either involve finding or using the significance parameter α, which is the probability that χ^2 will exceed a certain amount c.

$$\alpha = P(\chi^2 > c) = 1 - P(\chi^2 \leq c)$$

Again, if the hypothesis is true, α is the probability that χ^2 will exceed c. A common value for α is 0.05, which is intended to ensure that a hypothesis is rejected only if it can reasonably be assumed that the lack of a fit or dependence results from intention rather than chance.

The critical values, c, corresponding to various significance levels, α, and degrees of freedom, n, can be found in χ^2 tables. A sample portion of the χ^2 table is shown below. Note that the probability values, P, correspond to $1 - \alpha$. (The values in the table have limited numerical accuracy, and cases where greater accuracy is needed may require direct calculation of the critical value.)

$$P(\chi^2 \le c)$$

	0.99	0.95	0.90	0.75	0.50	0.25	0.10	0.05
1	6.63	3.84	2.71	1.32	0.46	0.10	0.02	0.00
2	9.21	5.99	4.61	2.77	1.39	0.58	0.21	0.10
3	11.3	7.81	6.25	4.11	2.37	1.21	0.58	0.35
4	13.3	9.49	7.78	5.39	3.36	1.92	1.06	0.71
5	15.1	11.1	9.24	6.63	4.35	2.67	1.61	1.15

Example: A coin is flipped 200 times and lands heads up 92 times and tails up 108 times. Determine if the coin is a fair coin.

The "fairness" of the coin can be determined using a chi-square test. First, establish a null hypothesis. In this example, the null hypothesis is that the coin should be equally likely to land heads up or tails up for a given flip. This null hypothesis allows us to state expected frequencies. For 200 tosses we would expect 100 heads and 100 tails.

Next, prepare a table.

	Heads	Tails	Total
Observed	92	108	200
Expected	100	100	200
Total	192	208	400

The observed values are the data gathered. The expected values are the frequencies expected, based on the null hypothesis.

Calculate χ^2 as follows, noting that there are two sample values: heads up and tails up.

$$\chi^2 = \sum_{i=1}^{2}\frac{(O_i - E_i)^2}{E_i} = \frac{(92-100)^2}{100} + \frac{(108-100)^2}{100}$$

$$\chi^2 = \frac{64}{100} + \frac{64}{100} = \frac{128}{100} = 1.28$$

Next, determine the degrees of freedom (n) by subtracting one from the number of sample values. In this example, there are two possible sample values (heads and tails), so $n = 1$.

An appropriate significance level (α) must also be chosen. For instance, assume that there should only be a 5% chance that the χ^2 value is greater than the critical value c. Next, consult the table of critical values of the chi-squared distribution.

The chi-squared value corresponding to $n = 1$ is 1.28. In the table above, the corresponding critical value c is 3.84. Since 1.28 < 3.84, the hypothesis should not be rejected.

Notice, however, that if the number of heads was 114 and the number of tails 86, then the χ^2 value would be 3.92, which exceeds the critical value of $c = 3.84$. In this case, for the chosen significance level, there would be evidence that the coin was loaded, and the hypothesis (the coin is fair) would be rejected.

COMPETENCY 5.0 CALCULUS

SKILL 5.1 TRIGONOMETRY

5.1a. Prove that the Pythagorean Theorem is equivalent to the trigonometric identity $\sin^2 x + \cos^2 x = 1$ and that this identity leads to $1 + \tan^2 x = \sec^2 x$ and $1 + \cot^2 x = \csc^2 x$

The Pythagorean Theorem can be shown to be equivalent to the trigonometric identity $\sin^2 x + \cos^2 x = 1$ by examining a generic right triangle, as shown below (not necessarily drawn to scale).

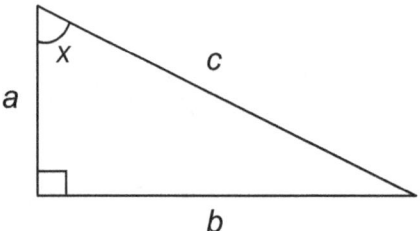

The Pythagorean Theorem in this case is expressed as follows.

$$a^2 + b^2 = c^2$$

This expression can be rewritten in the following form.

$$\left(\frac{a}{c}\right)^2 + \left(\frac{b}{c}\right)^2 = 1$$

Notice, however, that the sine and cosine functions for the angle x can be written in terms of a, b and c.

$$\sin x = \frac{b}{c}$$

$$\cos x = \frac{a}{c}$$

Substitute these functions into the revised form of the Pythagorean Theorem.

$$(\cos x)^2 + (\sin x)^2 = 1$$
$$\sin^2 x + \cos^2 x = 1$$

Likewise, this expression can be modified to prove other identities. There are two methods that can be used to prove trigonometric identities. One method is to choose one side of the equation and manipulate it until it equals the other side; the other method is to replace expressions on both sides of the equation with equivalent expressions until both sides are equal. In this case, to prove that $1 + \tan^2 x = \sec^2 x$, divide both sides of the above identity by $\cos^2 x$.

$$\frac{\sin^2 x}{\cos^2 x} + \frac{\cos^2 x}{\cos^2 x} = \frac{1}{\cos^2 x}$$

Use the relationships among the trigonometric functions to simplify this expression.

$$\tan^2 x + 1 = \sec^2 x$$
$$1 + \tan^2 x = \sec^2 x$$

Also, the identity $1 + \cot^2 x = \csc^2 x$ can also be derived from the original identity, in this case by dividing by $\sin^2 x$ and simplifying.

$$\frac{\sin^2 x}{\sin^2 x} + \frac{\cos^2 x}{\sin^2 x} = \frac{1}{\sin^2 x}$$
$$1 + \cot^2 x = \csc^2 x$$

A summary of the relationships among trigonometric functions is given below for reference. It is noteworthy that each identity can be proven by analyzing the right triangle diagram above.

$$\sin x = \frac{1}{\csc x} \qquad \cos x = \frac{1}{\sec x} \qquad \tan x = \frac{1}{\cot x}$$

$$\tan x = \frac{\sin x}{\cos x}$$

5.1b. Prove the sine, cosine, and tangent sum formulas for all real values, and derive special applications of the sum formulas (e.g., double angle, half angle)

Trigonometric functions involving the sum or difference of two angles can be expressed in terms of functions of each individual angle using the following formulae.

$$\cos(\alpha + \beta) = \cos\alpha\cos\beta - \sin\alpha\sin\beta$$
$$\cos(\alpha - \beta) = \cos\alpha\cos\beta + \sin\alpha\sin\beta$$
$$\sin(\alpha + \beta) = \sin\alpha\cos\beta + \cos\alpha\sin\beta$$
$$\sin(\alpha - \beta) = \sin\alpha\cos\beta - \cos\alpha\sin\beta$$
$$\tan(\alpha + \beta) = \frac{\tan\alpha + \tan\beta}{1 - \tan\alpha\tan\beta}$$
$$\tan(\alpha - \beta) = \frac{\tan\alpha - \tan\beta}{1 + \tan\alpha\tan\beta}$$

The **cosine sum formula** can be proven by considering the relationships between the angles and distances in the unit circle shown below.

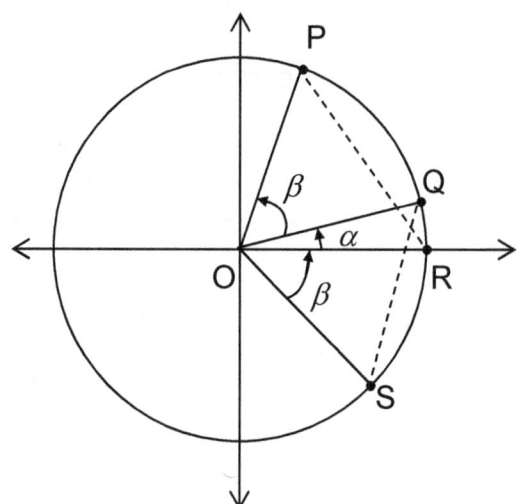

The coordinates of point P are $(\cos(\alpha + \beta), \sin(\alpha + \beta))$, the coordinates of point Q are $(\cos\alpha, \sin\alpha)$, the coordinates of point R are (1, 0) and the coordinates of point S are $(\cos\beta, -\sin\beta)$.

Since ∠POR = ∠QOS = $\alpha + \beta$, PR = QS.

Using the distance formula to express the lengths PR and QS in terms of their coordinates, the result is the following.

$$PQ = \sqrt{(\cos(\alpha+\beta)-1)^2 + (\sin(\alpha+\beta)-0)^2}$$
$$QS = \sqrt{(\cos\alpha-\cos\beta)^2 + (\sin\alpha-(-\sin\beta))^2}$$

Squaring both expressions and simplifying yields the following.

$$PQ = (\cos(\alpha+\beta)-1)^2 + \sin^2(\alpha+\beta)$$
$$PQ = \cos^2(\alpha+\beta) + 1 - 2\cos(\alpha+\beta) + \sin^2(\alpha+\beta)$$
$$QS = (\cos\alpha-\cos\beta)^2 + (\sin\alpha+\sin\beta)^2$$
$$QS = \cos^2\alpha + \cos^2\beta - 2\cos\alpha\cos\beta + \sin^2\alpha + \sin^2\beta + 2\sin\alpha\sin\beta$$

Apply the Pythagorean identities $\cos^2(\alpha+\beta) + \sin^2(\alpha+\beta) = 1$, $\sin^2\alpha + \cos^2\alpha = 1$ and $\sin^2\beta + \cos^2\beta = 1$ to the above expressions.

$$PQ = 1 + 1 - 2\cos(\alpha+\beta) = 2 - 2\cos(\alpha+\beta)$$
$$QS = 2 - 2\cos\alpha\cos\beta + 2\sin\alpha\sin\beta$$

Equate these two expressions and simplify.

$$PQ = QS$$
$$2 - 2\cos(\alpha+\beta) = 2 - 2\cos\alpha\cos\beta + 2\sin\alpha\sin\beta$$
$$-2\cos(\alpha+\beta) = -2\cos\alpha\cos\beta + 2\sin\alpha\sin\beta$$
$$\cos(\alpha+\beta) = \cos\alpha\cos\beta - \sin\alpha\sin\beta$$

This is the cosine sum formula.

The **sine sum formula** can be proven using the cosine sum formula and the Pythagorean identity.

$$\sin^2(\alpha+\beta) = 1 - \cos^2(\alpha+\beta)$$
$$\sin^2(\alpha+\beta) = 1 - (\cos\alpha\cos\beta - \sin\alpha\sin\beta)^2$$
$$\sin^2(\alpha+\beta) = 1 - \cos^2\alpha\cos^2\beta - \sin^2\alpha\sin^2\beta + 2\cos\alpha\cos\beta\sin\alpha\sin\beta$$

Replacing the 1 on the right hand side of the above equation using $\sin^2\alpha + \cos^2\alpha = 1$ yields the following.

$$\sin^2(\alpha+\beta) = \sin^2\alpha + \cos^2\alpha - \cos^2\alpha\cos^2\beta - \sin^2\alpha\sin^2\beta$$
$$+ 2\cos\alpha\cos\beta\sin\alpha\sin\beta$$

Combining terms 1 & 4 and terms 2 & 3 on the right hand side,

$$\sin^2(\alpha+\beta) = \sin^2\alpha - \sin^2\alpha\sin^2\beta + \cos^2\alpha - \cos^2\alpha\cos^2\beta$$
$$+ 2\cos\alpha\cos\beta\sin\alpha\sin\beta$$
$$= \sin^2\alpha(1-\sin^2\beta) + \cos^2\alpha(1-\cos^2\beta) + 2\cos\alpha\cos\beta$$

Since $1-\sin^2\beta = \cos^2\beta$ and $1-\cos^2\beta = \sin^2\beta$,

$$\sin^2(\alpha+\beta) = \sin^2\alpha\cos^2\beta + \cos^2\alpha\sin^2\beta + 2\cos\alpha\cos\beta$$
$$= (\sin\alpha\cos\beta + \cos\alpha\sin\beta)^2$$
$$\sin(\alpha+\beta) = \sin\alpha\cos\beta + \cos\alpha\sin\beta$$

This is the sine sum formula.

The **tangent sum formula** can be obtained by combining the sine and cosine sum formulae.

$$\tan(\alpha+\beta) = \frac{\sin(\alpha+\beta)}{\cos(\alpha+\beta)} = \frac{\sin\alpha\cos\beta + \cos\alpha\sin\beta}{\cos\alpha\cos\beta - \sin\alpha\sin\beta}$$

Dividing both numerator and denominator by $\cos\alpha\cos\beta$,

$$\tan(\alpha+\beta) = \frac{\dfrac{\sin\alpha\cos\beta}{\cos\alpha\cos\beta} + \dfrac{\cos\alpha\sin\beta}{\cos\alpha\cos\beta}}{1 - \dfrac{\sin\alpha\sin\beta}{\cos\alpha\cos\beta}}$$

$$= \frac{\dfrac{\sin\alpha}{\cos\alpha} + \dfrac{\sin\beta}{\cos\beta}}{1 - \dfrac{\sin\alpha\sin\beta}{\cos\alpha\cos\beta}}$$

$$\tan(\alpha+\beta) = \frac{\tan\alpha + \tan\beta}{1 - \tan\alpha\tan\beta}$$

This is the tangent sum formula.

The difference formulae can be easily derived from the sum formulae. For instance,

$$\cos(\alpha - \beta) = \cos(\alpha + (-\beta))$$
$$= \cos\alpha \cos(-\beta) - \sin\alpha \sin(-\beta)$$
$$= \cos\alpha \cos\beta + \sin\alpha \sin\beta$$

Example: Evaluate the following using the appropriate identity:

$$\sin(35°)\cos(55°) + \cos(35°)\sin(55°)$$

Using the sine sum formula,

$$\sin 35° \cos 55° + \cos 35° \sin 55°$$
$$= \sin(35° + 55°) = \sin(90°) = 1$$

Example: Show that $\dfrac{\cos(x+y)}{\cos x \cos y} = 1 - \tan x \tan y$

Applying the cosine sum formula

$$\frac{\cos(x+y)}{\cos x \cos y} = \frac{\cos x \cos y - \sin x \sin y}{\cos x \cos y}$$
$$= 1 - \frac{\sin x \sin y}{\cos x \cos y}$$
$$= 1 - \tan x \tan y$$

The **double angle identities** can be obtained using the sum formulae:

$$\cos 2\alpha = \cos(\alpha + \alpha)$$
$$= \cos\alpha \cos\alpha - \sin\alpha \sin\alpha$$
$$\cos 2\alpha = \cos^2\alpha - \sin^2\alpha$$

Also,

$$\cos 2\alpha = 1 - 2\sin^2\alpha \quad (\text{Since } \cos^2\alpha = 1 - \sin^2\alpha)$$

or

$$\cos 2\alpha = 2\cos^2\alpha - 1 \quad (\text{Since } \sin^2\alpha = 1 - \cos^2\alpha)$$

$$\sin 2\alpha = \sin(\alpha + \alpha)$$
$$= \sin\alpha\cos\alpha + \cos\alpha\sin\alpha$$
$$= 2\sin\alpha\cos\alpha$$

$$\tan 2\alpha = \tan(\alpha + \alpha)$$
$$= \frac{\tan\alpha + \tan\alpha}{1 - \tan\alpha\tan\alpha}$$
$$= \frac{2\tan\alpha}{1 - \tan^2\alpha}$$

Example: Show that $\sin(3x) = \sin x(3\cos^2 x - \sin^2 x)$

$$\sin(3x) = \sin(2x + x)$$
$$= \sin 2x \cos x + \cos 2x \sin x \quad \text{Sine Sum Formula}$$
$$= 2\sin x \cos x \cos x$$
$$\quad + (\cos^2 x - \sin^2 x)\sin x \quad \text{Double Angle Identities}$$
$$= 2\sin x \cos^2 x + \sin x \cos^2 x - \sin^3 x$$
$$= 3\sin x \cos^2 x - \sin^3 x$$
$$= \sin x(3\cos^2 x - \sin^2 x)$$

The **half angle identities** can be derived by solving the double angle identities for the sine, cosine or tangent of a single angle.

$$\cos 2\alpha = 2\cos^2\alpha - 1$$
$$2\cos^2\alpha = 1 + \cos 2\alpha$$
$$\cos^2\alpha = \frac{1 + \cos 2\alpha}{2}$$
$$\cos\alpha = \pm\sqrt{\frac{1 + \cos 2\alpha}{2}}$$

Since this identity is valid for all values of α, it will continue to be valid if we replace α with $\frac{\alpha}{2}$. Therefore,

$$\cos\frac{\alpha}{2} = \pm\sqrt{\frac{1 + \cos\alpha}{2}}$$

Similarly,

$$\cos 2\alpha = 1 - 2\sin^2 \alpha$$
$$2\sin^2 \alpha = 1 - \cos 2\alpha$$
$$\sin^2 \alpha = \frac{1 - \cos 2\alpha}{2}$$
$$\sin \alpha = \pm\sqrt{\frac{1 - \cos 2\alpha}{2}}$$
$$\sin \frac{\alpha}{2} = \pm\sqrt{\frac{1 - \cos \alpha}{2}}$$
$$\tan \frac{\alpha}{2} = \frac{\sin \frac{\alpha}{2}}{\cos \frac{\alpha}{2}} = \frac{\pm\sqrt{\frac{1 - \cos \alpha}{2}}}{\pm\sqrt{\frac{1 + \cos \alpha}{2}}} = \pm\sqrt{\frac{1 - \cos \alpha}{1 + \cos \alpha}}$$

Alternatively, multiplying the numerator and denominator of the above identity by $\sqrt{1 - \cos \alpha}$,

$$\tan \frac{\alpha}{2} = \pm\sqrt{\frac{(1 - \cos \alpha)(1 - \cos \alpha)}{(1 + \cos \alpha)(1 - \cos \alpha)}}$$
$$= \pm\sqrt{\frac{(1 - \cos \alpha)^2}{(1 - \cos^2 \alpha)}}$$
$$= \pm\sqrt{\frac{(1 - \cos \alpha)^2}{\sin^2 \alpha}} = \frac{1 - \cos \alpha}{\sin \alpha}$$

Similarly, multiplying the numerator and denominator of the first identity by $\sqrt{1 + \cos \alpha}$,

$$\tan \frac{\alpha}{2} = \pm\sqrt{\frac{(1 - \cos \alpha)(1 + \cos \alpha)}{(1 + \cos \alpha)(1 + \cos \alpha)}}$$
$$= \pm\sqrt{\frac{(1 - \cos^2 \alpha)}{(1 + \cos \alpha)^2}}$$
$$= \pm\sqrt{\frac{\sin^2 \alpha}{(1 + \cos \alpha)^2}} = \frac{\sin \alpha}{1 + \cos \alpha}$$

Example: Given that $\sin 30° = \dfrac{1}{2}$, find the value of $\tan 15°$.

$$\cos 30° = \sqrt{1 - \sin^2 30°} = \sqrt{1 - \dfrac{1}{4}}$$

$$= \sqrt{\dfrac{3}{4}} = \dfrac{\sqrt{3}}{2}$$

$\tan 15° = \dfrac{1 - \cos 30°}{\sin 30°}$ \hspace{1em} Half angle identity

$$= \dfrac{1 - \dfrac{\sqrt{3}}{2}}{\dfrac{1}{2}} = 2 - \sqrt{3} = 0.27$$

5.1c. **Analyze properties of trigonometric functions in a variety of ways (e.g., graphing and solving problems)**

Trigonometric functions can be analyzed with respect to their individual behavior or with respect to solving problems that include them.

One crucial issue is the type of argument used. The argument of a trigonometric function is an angle that is typically expressed in either degrees or radians. A **degree** constitutes an angle corresponding to a sector that is 1/360th of a circle. Therefore, a circle has 360 degrees. A **radian**, on the other hand, is the angle corresponding to a sector of a circle where the arc length of the sector is equal to the radius of the circle. In the case of the unit circle (a circle of radius 1), the circumference is 2π. Thus, there are 2π radians in a circle. Conversion between degrees and radians is a simple matter of using the ratio between the total degrees in a circle and the total radians in a circle.

$$(\text{degrees}) = \frac{180}{2\pi} \times (\text{radians})$$

$$(\text{radians}) = \frac{2\pi}{180} \times (\text{degrees})$$

Graphs of trigonometric functions

The trigonometric functions sine, cosine and tangent are **periodic functions**. The values of periodic functions repeat on regular intervals. The period, amplitude and phase shift are critical properties of periodic functions that can be determined by observation of the graph or by detailed study of the functions themselves.

The **period** is the smallest domain containing the complete cycle of the function. For example, the period of a sine or cosine function is the distance between the adjacent peaks or troughs of the graph. The **amplitude** of a function is half the distance between the maximum and minimum values of the function. The **phase shift** is the amount of horizontal displacement of a function from a given reference position.

Below is a generic sinusoidal graph with the period and amplitude labeled.

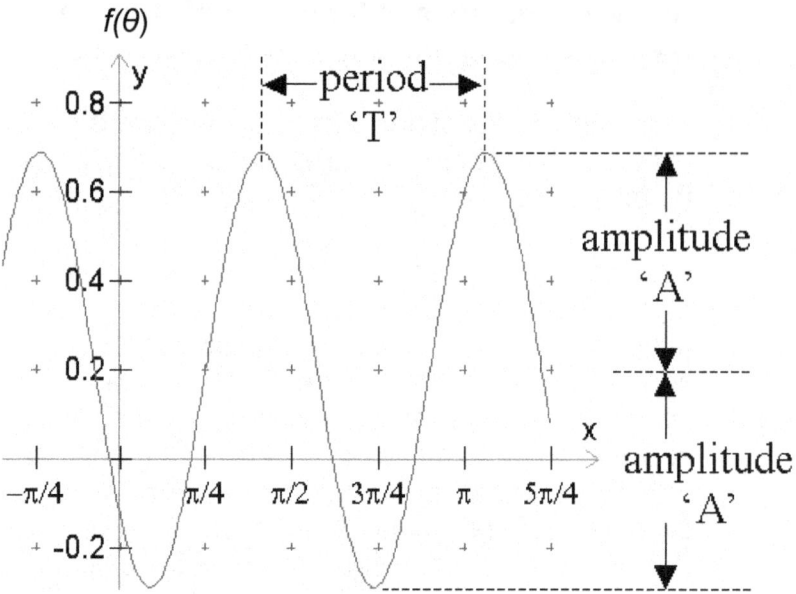

The phase and amplitude for the three basic trigonometric functions are provided in the table below.

Function	Period (radians)	Amplitude
$\sin \theta$	2π	1
$\cos \theta$	2π	1
$\tan \theta$	π	Undefined

Below are the graphs of the basic trigonometric functions, (a) y = sin x; (b) y = cos x; and (c) y = tan x.

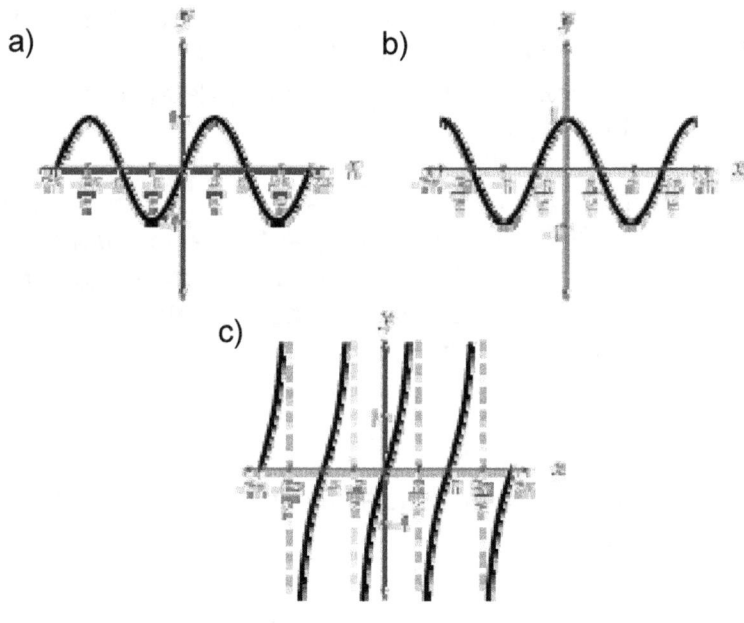

Graphing a trigonometric function by hand typically requires a calculator for determining the value of the function for various angles. Nevertheless, simple functions can often be graphed by simply determining the amplitude, period and phase shift. Once these parameters are known, the graph can be sketched approximately. The amplitude of a simple sine or cosine function is simply the multiplicative constant (or function) associated with the trigonometric function. Thus, 2cos x, for instance, has an amplitude of 2. The phase shift is typically just a constant added to the argument of the function. For instance, sin(x + 1) includes a phase shift of 1. A positive phase shift constant indicates that the graph of the function is shifted to the left; a negative phase shift indicates that the graph is shifted to the right.

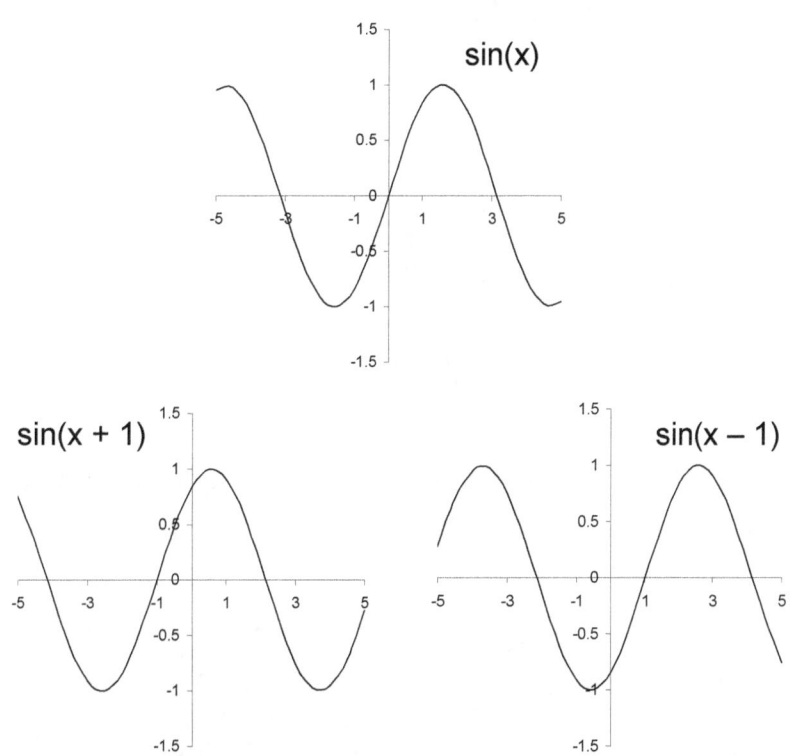

Example: Sketch the graph of the function $f(x) = 4\sin\left(2x + \dfrac{\pi}{2}\right)$.

Notice, first, that the amplitude of the function is 4. Since there is no constant term added to the sine function, the function is centered on the x-axis. Find crucial points on the graph by setting f equal to zero and solving for x to find the roots.

$$f(x) = 0 = 4\sin\left(2x + \dfrac{\pi}{2}\right)$$

$$\sin\left(2x + \frac{\pi}{2}\right) = 0$$

$$2x + \frac{\pi}{2} = n\pi$$

In the above expression, n is an integer.

$$2x = \left(n - \frac{1}{2}\right)\pi$$

$$x = \left(n - \frac{1}{2}\right)\frac{\pi}{2}$$

So, the roots of the function are at

$$x = \pm\frac{\pi}{4}, \pm\frac{3\pi}{4}, \pm\frac{5\pi}{4}, \ldots$$

The maxima and minima of the function are halfway between successive roots. Determine the location of a maximum by testing the function. Try $x = 0$.

$$f(0) = 4\sin\left(2[0] + \frac{\pi}{2}\right) = 4\sin\left(\frac{\pi}{2}\right) = 4$$

Thus, f is maximized at $x = 4$. The function can then be sketched.

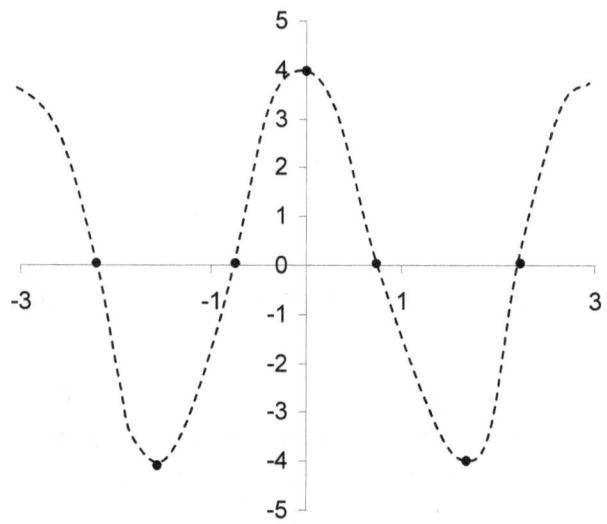

Solving trigonometry problems

Unlike trigonometric identities that are true for all values of the defined variable, trigonometric equations are true for some, but not all, of the values of the variable. Most often, trigonometric equations are solved for values between 0 and 360 degrees or 0 and 2π radians. Solving trigonometric problems is largely the same as solving algebraic equations. Care must be taken, however, due to the periodic nature of trigonometric functions. This often yields multiple (or an infinite number of) solutions.

Trigonometric identities, including sum and difference formulas, are often indispensable in the problem-solving process. These identities allow many complicated functions to be simplified to forms that are more easily managed, algebraically.

Some algebraic operation, such as squaring both sides of an equation, will yield extraneous answers. Avoid incorrect solutions by remembering to check all solutions to be sure they satisfy the original equation.

<u>Example:</u> Solve the following equation for x: $\cos x = 1 - \sin x$, where $0° \leq x \leq 360°$.

Start by squaring both sides of the equation.

$$\cos^2 x = (1 - \sin x)^2 = 1 - 2\sin x + \sin^2 x$$

Substitute using the Pythagorean identity to replace the cosine term.

$$1 - \sin^2 x = 1 - 2\sin x + \sin^2 x$$

Simplify the results.

$$2\sin^2 x - 2\sin x = 0$$
$$\sin x (\sin x - 1) = 0$$

There are two possible solutions to the equation:

$\sin x = 0$ and $\sin x = 1$
$x = 0°, 180°$ $\quad\quad\quad x = 90°$

Thus, the apparent solutions to the problem are $x = 0°$, $90°$ and $180°$. By checking each solution, however, it is found that $x = 180°$ is not a legitimate solution and must be discarded. The actual solutions to the equation are thus $x = 0°$ and $90°$.

Example: Solve the following equation: $\cos^2 x = \sin^2 x$ for $0 \leq x \leq 2\pi$.

First, use the Pythagorean identity to convert either the cosine or sine term.

$$\cos^2 x = 1 - \cos^2 x$$

Simplify the results.

$$2\cos^2 x = 1$$
$$\cos^2 x = \frac{1}{2}$$
$$\cos x = \pm \frac{1}{\sqrt{2}}$$

Familiarity with the properties of trigonometric functions should lead to the realization that this corresponds to odd integer multiples of $\frac{\pi}{4}$. Alternatively, a calculator can be used to calculate the inverse function. (A more detailed review of inverse trigonometric functions is provided in the Skill 5.1d.)

$$x = \arccos\left(\pm \frac{1}{\sqrt{2}}\right)$$

In either case, the solution is the following:

$$x = \frac{\pi}{4}, \frac{3\pi}{4}, \frac{5\pi}{4}, \frac{7\pi}{4}$$

5.1d. Know and apply the definitions and properties of inverse trigonometric functions (i.e., arcsin, arccos, and arctan)

The inverse sine function of x is written as arcsin x or $\sin^{-1} x$ and is the angle for which the sine is x; i.e., $\sin(\arcsin x) = x$. Since the sine function is periodic, many values of arcsin x correspond to a particular x. In order to define arcsin as a function, therefore, its range needs to be restricted.

The function **y = arcsin x** has a domain [-1,1] and range $\left[-\dfrac{\pi}{2}, \dfrac{\pi}{2}\right]$.

In some books, a restricted inverse function is denoted by a capitalized beginning letter such as in Sin^{-1} or Arctan. The arcsin function is shown below.

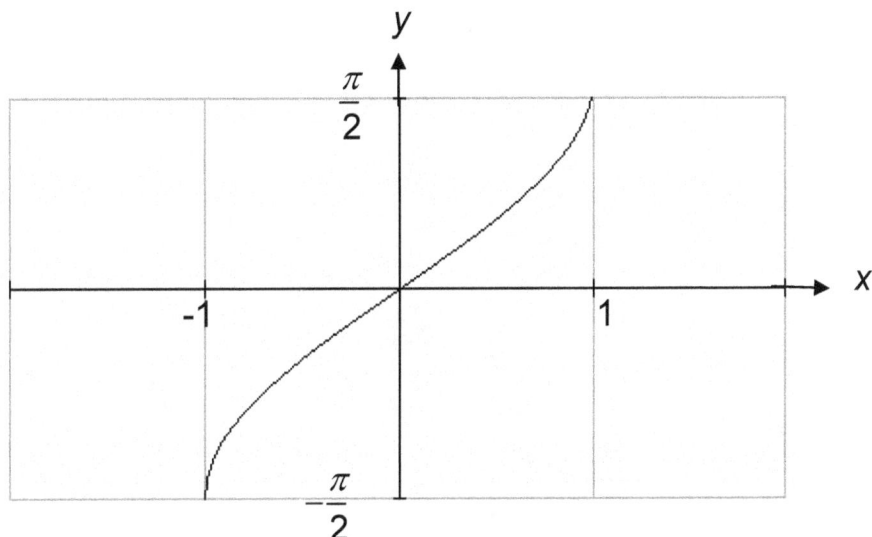

The inverse cosine and tangent functions are defined in the same way: $\cos(\arccos x) = x$; $\tan(\arctan x) = x$.

The function **y = arccos x** has a domain [-1,1] and range $[0, \pi]$. The graph of this function is shown below.

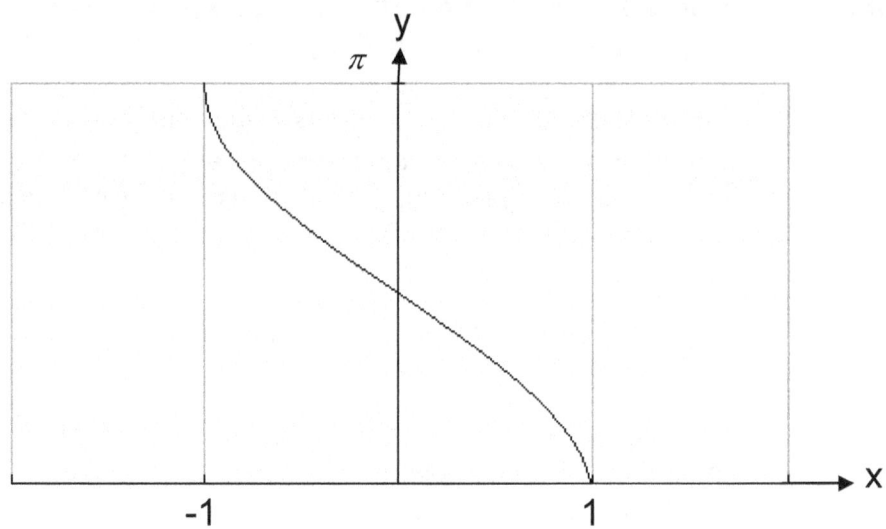

The function **y = arctan x** has a domain $[-\infty, +\infty]$ and range $\left[-\dfrac{\pi}{2}, \dfrac{\pi}{2}\right]$. The plot of the function is shown below.

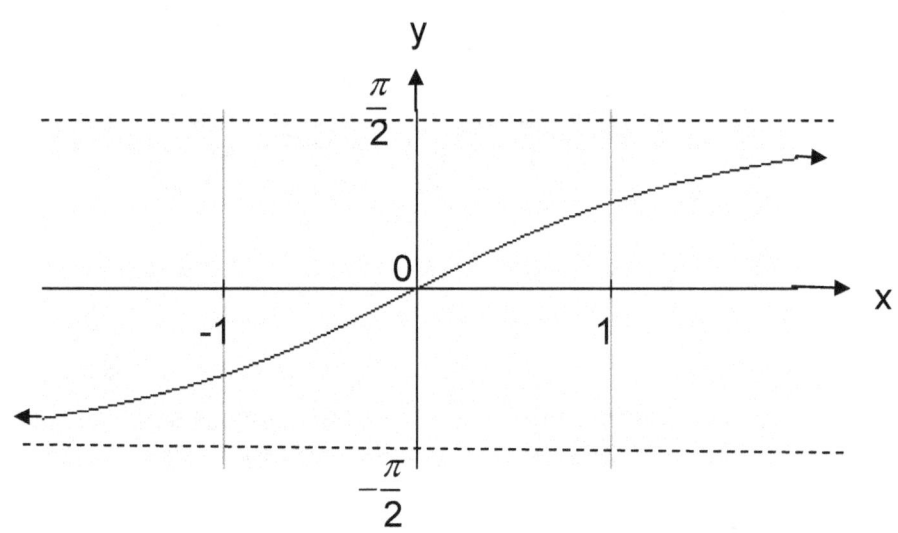

Example: Evaluate the following: (i) $\sin^{-1}(0)$ and (ii) $\arccos(-1)$

(i) $\sin(\sin^{-1}(0)) = 0$.
The value of the inverse sine function must lie in the range $\left[-\dfrac{\pi}{2}, \dfrac{\pi}{2}\right]$. Since 0 is the only argument in the range $\left[-\dfrac{\pi}{2}, \dfrac{\pi}{2}\right]$ for which the sine function is zero, $\sin^{-1}(0) = 0$.

(ii) $\cos(\arccos(-1)) = -1$

The value of the inverse cosine function must lie in the range $[0, \pi]$. π is the only argument for which the cosine function is equal to -1 in the range $[0, \pi]$.

Hence, $\arccos(-1) = \pi$.

The following are some **identities for the inverse trigonometric functions**:

$$\csc^{-1}(x) = \sin^{-1}(1/x) \text{ for } |x| \geq 1$$

$$\sec^{-1}(x) = \cos^{-1}(1/x) \text{ for } |x| \geq 1$$

$$\cot^{-1}(x) = \begin{cases} \tan^{-1}(1/x) & \text{for } x > 0 \\ \tan^{-1}(1/x) + \pi & \text{for } x < 0 \\ \pi/2 & \text{for } x = 0 \end{cases}$$

$$\sin^{-1} x = \cos^{-1}(\sqrt{1-x^2}) \qquad \cos^{-1} x = \sin^{-1}(\sqrt{1-x^2})$$

$$\tan^{-1} x = \cos^{-1}\left(\frac{1}{\sqrt{1+x^2}}\right) \qquad \cos^{-1} x = \tan^{-1}\left(\frac{\sqrt{1-x^2}}{x}\right)$$

$$\tan^{-1} x = \sin^{-1}\left(\frac{x}{\sqrt{1+x^2}}\right) \qquad \sin^{-1} x = \tan^{-1}\left(\frac{x}{\sqrt{1-x^2}}\right)$$

<u>Example</u>: Simplify the expression $\cos(\arcsin x) + \sin(\arccos x)$

$\arcsin x = \arccos(\sqrt{1-x^2})$ identity

$\Rightarrow \cos(\arcsin x) = \sqrt{1-x^2}$

$\arccos x = \arcsin(\sqrt{1-x^2})$ identity

$\Rightarrow \sin(\arccos x) = \sqrt{1-x^2}$

Hence, $\cos(\arcsin x) + \sin(\arccos x) = \sqrt{1-x^2} + \sqrt{1-x^2} = 2\sqrt{1-x^2}$

Example: Using the identities given above, prove the identity

$$\sin^{-1} x + \cos^{-1} x = \frac{\pi}{2}$$

Since $\sin\left(\dfrac{\pi}{2}\right) = 1$, the identity may be proven by showing that

$$\sin\left(\sin^{-1} x + \cos^{-1} x\right) = 1$$
$$\sin\left(\sin^{-1} x + \cos^{-1} x\right) = \sin(\sin^{-1} x)\cos(\cos^{-1} x)$$
$$\hspace{3cm} + \cos(\sin^{-1} x)\sin(\cos^{-1} x) \quad \text{sine sum formula}$$
$$= x \cdot x + \sqrt{1-x^2}\sqrt{1-x^2} \quad \text{inverse identities}$$
$$= x^2 + 1 - x^2 = 1$$

Other similar identities include the following:

$$\tan^{-1} x + \cot^{-1} x = \pi/2$$
$$\sec^{-1} x + \csc^{-1} x = \pi/2$$

5.1e. Understand and apply polar representations of complex numbers (e.g., DeMoivre's Theorem)

Complex numbers can be plotted graphically in a Cartesian complex plane, where the x-axis represents real numbers and the y-axis represents imaginary numbers. An equivalent representation, following a graphical approach, is to use polar coordinates (a magnitude and angle). These two representations are shown below for the example of 2+3i.

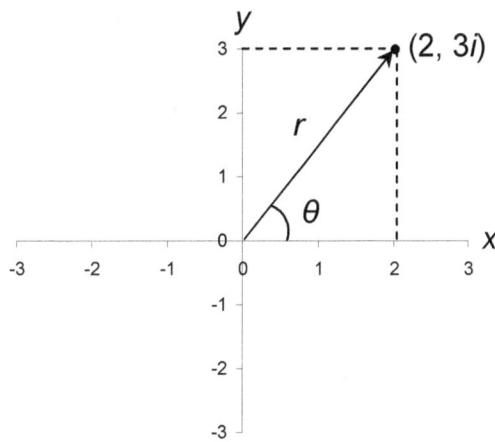

Thus, a complex number $a + bi$ can be represented using a vector length r and an angle θ, measured in the counter-clockwise direction from the x-axis. Using trigonometry, the complex number $a + bi$ can be written as follows.

$$a + bi = r(\cos\theta + i\sin\theta)$$

Note that

$$r = \sqrt{a^2 + b^2}$$
$$\theta = \arctan\frac{b}{a}$$

In addition to the use of trigonometric functions for a polar representation, complex numbers can also be represented in polar form using exponentials. To derive Euler's formula, define z as follows.

$$z = \cos\theta + i\sin\theta$$

Differentiate z with respect to θ and form a differential equation.

$$\frac{dz}{d\theta} = \frac{d}{d\theta}(\cos\theta + i\sin\theta)$$

$$\frac{dz}{d\theta} = -\sin\theta + i\cos\theta$$

$$dz = (-\sin\theta + i\cos\theta)d\theta$$

Note that dz can be rewritten as follows using the definition of i.

$$dz = (i^2 \sin\theta + i\cos\theta)d\theta$$

$$dz = i(\cos\theta + i\sin\theta)d\theta = iz\,d\theta$$

$$\frac{dz}{z} = i\,d\theta$$

Integrate the result.

$$\int \frac{dz}{z} = \int i\,d\theta$$

$$\ln z = i\theta$$

Use the rules of exponentials to find z.

$$e^{\ln z} = e^{i\theta}$$

$$z = \cos\theta + i\sin\theta = e^{i\theta}$$

This is **Euler's formula**. Thus, complex numbers can be written in either trigonometric or exponential polar form.

$$a + bi = r(\cos\theta + i\sin\theta) = re^{i\theta}$$

The exponential polar form is particularly beneficial for fast multiplication and division of complex numbers, because these operations simply involve multiplying or dividing the multiplicative factors (r) and adding or subtracting the exponents ($i\theta$).

Using Euler's formula, **de Moivre's Theorem** can be derived. Consider z defined as follows.

$$z = (\cos\theta + i\sin\theta)^n$$

Apply Euler's formula.

$$z = (\cos\theta + i\sin\theta)^n = (e^{i\theta})^n$$
$$z = e^{in\theta}$$

Rewrite using Euler's formula once more.

$$z = e^{in\theta} = \cos(n\theta) + i\sin(n\theta)$$

The result is de Moivre's Theorem (or de Moivre's identity):

$$(\cos\theta + i\sin\theta)^n = \cos(n\theta) + i\sin(n\theta)$$

<u>Example</u>: Write $2 - 5i$ in polar form.

This complex number can either be written in terms of sine and cosine or in terms of an exponential. In either case, first calculate r and θ.

$$r = \sqrt{2^2 + (-5)^2} = \sqrt{4+25} = \sqrt{29} \approx 5.385$$
$$\theta = \arctan\left(-\frac{5}{2}\right) \approx -1.190$$

Thus,

$$2 - 5i \approx 5.385\left[\cos(-1.190) + i\sin(-1.190)\right]$$
$$= 5.385[\cos 1.190 - i\sin 1.190]$$

or

$$2 - 5i \approx 5.385e^{-1.190i}$$

In the first case, the result can be checked by evaluating the trigonometric functions and multiplying.

$$5.385[\cos 1.190 - i\sin 1.190] \approx 5.385[0.372 - i0.928]$$
$$5.385[\cos 1.190 - i\sin 1.190] \approx 2.003 - i4.998$$

Although a lack of numerical accuracy yields a result that is not exact, it is close enough to assume that it is correct. To be more certain, simply use greater numerical accuracy throughout the problem.

Example: Express $x + ix \tan x$ in polar form.

Calculate r and θ, noting that the real and imaginary parts of this complex number are functions instead of numbers.

$$r = \sqrt{x^2 + (x\tan x)^2} = \sqrt{x^2 + x^2 \tan^2 x} = \sqrt{x^2(1+\tan^2 x)}$$
$$r = \sqrt{x^2 \sec^2 x} = x\sec x$$
$$\theta = \arctan\left(\frac{x\tan x}{x}\right) = \arctan(\tan x) = x$$

Write the polar form.

$$x + i\tan x = x\sec x(\cos x + i\sin x)$$
$$x + i\tan x = (x\sec x)e^{ix}$$

Expand the trigonometric polar form to test the result.

$$x\sec x(\cos x + i\sin x) = x\sec x\cos x + ix\sec x\sin x$$
$$x\sec x(\cos x + i\sin x) = x\frac{\cos x}{\cos x} + ix\frac{\sin x}{\cos x} = x + ix\tan x$$

The result is confirmed.

SKILL 5.2 LIMITS AND CONTINUITY

5.2a. **Derive basic properties of limits and continuity, including the Sum, Difference, Product, Constant Multiple, and Quotient Rules, using the formal definition of a limit**

Limits

The limit of a function is the *y* value that the graph approaches as the value of *x* approaches a certain number. The **formal definition of a limit** is as follows:

A function *f(x)* has a limit *L* as *x* approaches the value *a*, expressed as

$$\lim_{x \to a} f(x) = L$$

if and only if for a given $\varepsilon > 0$ there exists a $\delta > 0$ such that $|f(x) - L| < \varepsilon$ when $0 < |x - a| < \delta$.

This definition essentially means that for a value of *x* arbitrarily close to *a*, *f(x)* must have a value arbitrarily close to *L*.

A function f(x) is **continuous** at *x* = *a* if $\lim_{x \to a} f(x)$ exists and is equal to *f(a)*. This essentially means that the graph of the function *f(x)* does not have a break (or discontinuity) at *x* = *a*.

According to the **sum rule for limits**, if $\lim_{x \to a} f(x) = L$ and $\lim_{x \to a} g(x) = M$, then $\lim_{x \to a} (f(x) + g(x)) = L + M$.

Proof: By the definition of the limits of *f(x)* and *g(x)* at *x* = *a*, we know that we can select an $\varepsilon > 0$ with a corresponding $\delta > 0$ for which $0 < |x - a| < \delta$ such that

$$|f(x) - L| < \varepsilon/2 \text{ and } |g(x) - M| < \varepsilon/2$$

Combining the two inequalities yields

$$|f(x) + g(x) - L - M| < \varepsilon$$

Since this satisfies the criterion for the existence of a limit,

$$\lim_{x \to a}(f(x)+g(x))=L+M$$

Using the sum rule for limits and the definition of continuity, we can conclude that if functions f(x) and g(x) are continuous at x = a—i.e. L = f(a) and M = g(a)—then the function f(x) + g(x) is also continuous at x = a.

The **difference rule for limits** states that if $\lim_{x \to a} f(x) = L$ and $\lim_{x \to a} g(x) = M$, then $\lim_{x \to a}(f(x)-g(x))=L-M$.

Proof: By the definition of the limits of f(x) and g(x) at x = a, we know that we can select an $\varepsilon > 0$ with a corresponding $\delta > 0$ for which $0 < |x - a| < \delta$ such that

$$|f(x)-L| < \varepsilon/2 \text{ and } |g(x)-M| < \varepsilon/2$$

This can be rewritten as

$$-\varepsilon/2 < f(x)-L < \varepsilon/2 \text{ and } -\varepsilon/2 < g(x)-M < \varepsilon/2$$

Multiplying the second inequality by –1 yields

$$\varepsilon/2 > -g(x)+M > -\varepsilon/2 \text{ or } -\varepsilon/2 < -g(x)+M < \varepsilon/2$$

Combining the inequalities for f(x) and g(x) yields

$$-\varepsilon < f(x)-g(x)-(L-M) < \varepsilon \text{ or } |f(x)-g(x)-(L-M)| < \varepsilon$$

Since this satisfies the criterion for the existence of a limit,

$$\lim_{x \to a}(f(x)-g(x))=L-M$$

As before, using the difference rule for limits and the definition of continuity, we can conclude that if functions f(x) and g(x) are continuous at x = a then the function f(x) – g(x) is also continuous at x = a.

According to the **constant multiple rule for limits** if $\lim_{x \to a} f(x) = L$, then, for any constant c, $\lim_{x \to a}(cf(x)) = cL$.

Proof: By the definition of the limit of $f(x)$ at $x = a$, we know that we can select an $\varepsilon > 0$ with a corresponding $\delta > 0$ for which $0 < |x - a| < \delta$ such that

$$|f(x) - L| < \frac{\varepsilon}{|c|}$$

where c is a non-zero constant. Multiplying both sides of the inequality by $|c|$ yields

$$|cf(x) - cL| < \varepsilon$$

Since this satisfies the criterion for the existence of a limit,

$$\lim_{x \to a}(cf(x)) = cL$$

As before, we can conclude that if the function $f(x)$ is continuous at $x = a$ then the function $cf(x)$ is also continuous at $x = a$.

According to the **product rule for limits**, if $\lim_{x \to a} f(x) = L$ and $\lim_{x \to a} g(x) = M$ then $\lim_{x \to a}(f(x)g(x)) = LM$.

Proof: First prove that the limit of the square of a function is the square of its limit; i.e., $\lim_{x \to a} f^2(x) = L^2$

We consider the cases $L = 0$ and $L \neq 0$ separately.

For $L = 0$, we can select an $0 < \varepsilon < 1$ such that $-\varepsilon < f(x) < \varepsilon$. Then $0 < f^2(x) < \varepsilon^2 < \varepsilon$ or $|f^2(x) - 0| < \varepsilon$ satisfies the criterion for a limit to exist at 0.

For $L \neq 0$, we consider $g(x) = \frac{f(x)}{L}$ for which $\lim_{x \to a} g(x) = \lim_{x \to a} \frac{f(x)}{L} = 1$. To prove $\lim_{x \to a} f^2(x) = L^2$, we need to prove that $\lim_{x \to a} g^2(x) = 1$. Since $\lim_{x \to a} g(x) = 1$, we can find an $0 < \varepsilon < 1$ such that

$$\frac{2}{3} < 1 - \frac{\varepsilon}{3} < g(x) < 1 + \frac{\varepsilon}{3} < \frac{4}{3}$$

Then:

$$|g(x)+1||g(x)-1| < \frac{\varepsilon}{3}\left(\frac{4}{3}+1\right)$$

$$|g^2(x)-1| < \frac{7}{9}\varepsilon < \varepsilon$$

Thus we have proved that $\lim_{x \to a} g^2(x) = 1$ and, therefore, $\lim_{x \to a} f^2(x) = L^2$.

To now prove that $\lim_{x \to a}(f(x)g(x)) = LM$, we write $f(x)g(x)$ as

$$f(x)g(x) = \frac{1}{4}\left[(f(x)+g(x))^2 - (f(x)-g(x))^2\right]$$

Using the foregoing limit laws we know that

$$\lim_{x \to a}(f(x)+g(x)) = L+M$$
$$\lim_{x \to a}(f(x)+g(x))^2 = (L+M)^2$$
$$\lim_{x \to a}(f(x)-g(x)) = L-M$$
$$\lim_{x \to a}(f(x)-g(x))^2 = (L-M)^2$$

Therefore,

$$\lim_{x \to a}(f(x)g(x)) = \lim_{x \to a}\left\{\frac{1}{4}\left[(f(x)+g(x))^2 - (f(x)-g(x)^2)\right]\right\}$$
$$= \lim_{x \to a}\frac{1}{4}(f(x)+g(x))^2 - \lim_{x \to a}\frac{1}{4}(f(x)-g(x))^2$$
$$= \frac{1}{4}(L+M)^2 - \frac{1}{4}(L-M)^2 = LM$$

Using the definition of continuity we can conclude that if the functions $f(x)$ and $g(x)$ are continuous at $x = a$ then the function $f(x)g(x)$ is also continuous at $x = a$.

According to the **quotient rule for limits**, if $\lim_{x \to a} f(x) = L$ and $\lim_{x \to a} g(x) = M$, then $\lim_{x \to a} \dfrac{f(x)}{g(x)} = \dfrac{L}{M}$ for $M \neq 0$.

Proof: We will first prove that the limit of the reciprocal of a function is the reciprocal of its limit; i.e., $\lim_{x \to a} \dfrac{1}{g(x)} = \dfrac{1}{M}$ for $M \neq 0$.

We first consider the case where $M = 1$. Then, we have to show that $\left| \dfrac{1}{g(x)} - 1 \right| < \varepsilon$ or $\left| \dfrac{1 - g(x)}{g(x)} \right| < \varepsilon$. To ensure that the denominator $g(x)$ is not too small we can choose $\varepsilon > 0$ such that

$$\frac{1}{2} < 1 - \frac{\varepsilon}{2} < g(x) < 1 + \frac{\varepsilon}{2} < \frac{3}{2}.$$

Then,

$$\frac{|g(x) - 1|}{|g(x)|} < \frac{\varepsilon}{2} \left(\frac{1}{2} \right)^{-1} \quad \text{or} \quad \frac{|g(x) - 1|}{|g(x)|} < \varepsilon$$

Thus, we have proven that the limit of the reciprocal of a function is the reciprocal of its limit.

For the case where M is not equal to 1, we can use the constant multiple rule to write

$$\lim_{x \to a} \frac{g(x)}{M} = 1 \quad M \neq 0$$

Then, using the reciprocal rule for $M = 1$, we can write

$$\lim_{x \to a} \frac{M}{g(x)} = 1 \quad \text{or} \quad \lim_{x \to a} \frac{1}{g(x)} = \frac{1}{M} \quad M \neq 0$$

The quotient rule can now be proven using the product and reciprocal rules.

$$\lim_{x \to a} \frac{f(x)}{g(x)} = \lim_{x \to a} f(x) \lim_{x \to a} \frac{1}{g(x)} = \frac{L}{M} \quad M \neq 0$$

We can conclude that if the functions $f(x)$ and $g(x)$ are continuous at $x = a$ then the function $f(x)/g(x)$ is also continuous at $x = a$, provided $g(a)$ is not equal to zero.

To find a limit there are two points to remember.

1. Factor the expression completely and cancel all common factors in fractions.

2. Substitute the number to which the variable is approaching. In most cases this produces the value of the limit.

If the variable in the limit approaches ∞, factor and simplify first; then examine the result. If the result does not involve a fraction with the variable in the denominator, the limit is usually also equal to ∞. If the variable is in the denominator of the fraction, the denominator is getting larger which makes the entire fraction smaller. In other words, the limit is zero.

Example: Evaluate the following limits.

1. $\lim\limits_{x \to -3} \left(\dfrac{x^2 + 5x + 6}{x + 3} + 4x \right)$

First, factor the numerator. Then cancel the common factors.

$$\lim\limits_{x \to -3} \left(\dfrac{(x+3)(x+2)}{x+3} + 4x \right)$$

$$\lim\limits_{x \to -3} (x + 2 + 4x) = \lim\limits_{x \to -3} (5x + 2)$$

$$5(-3) + 2 = -15 + 2 = -13$$

2. $\lim\limits_{x \to \infty} \dfrac{2x^2}{x^5}$

Cancel the common factors and take the constant outside the limit.

$$2 \lim\limits_{x \to \infty} \dfrac{1}{x^3}$$

Evaluate the limit.

$$2 \dfrac{1}{\infty^3} = 0$$

5.2b. **Show that a polynomial function is continuous at a point**

The **continuity of a function** is easily understood graphically as the absence of any missing points or any breaks in the plot of the function. A more rigorous definition can be formulated, however. A function $f(x)$ is continuous at a point c if all of the following apply:

1. The function $f(x)$ is defined at $x = c$.
2. The limit $\lim_{x \to c} f(x)$ exists.
3. The limit can be found by substitution: $\lim_{x \to c} f(x) = f(c)$.

A function can then be called **continuous** for an open interval (a, b) if the above definition applies to the function for every point c in the interval. The function is also continuous at the points $x = a$ and $x = b$ if $\lim_{x \to a^+} f(x) = f(a)$ and $\lim_{x \to b^-} f(x) = f(b)$ both exist. (The +/– notation simply signifies approaching the limiting value from either the right or left, respectively.) If both of these conditions apply, then the function is continuous for the closed interval $[a, b]$.

To check whether the limit of the function exists, make sure that

$$\lim_{x \to c^+} f(x) = \lim_{x \to c^-} f(x)$$

That is, the limit as x approaches c from the left must be equal to the limit as x approaches c from the right.

To demonstrate that a function is continuous at a point, check to see that all of the three points given above apply. First, make sure that the function is defined at the point, then determine if the limit exists. If the limit does exist and is equal to the value of the function evaluated at the point, then the function is continuous at that point.

If it is necessary to determine whether a function is continuous over an open or closed interval, the above approach must be shown to generally apply to every point in that interval (excluding the endpoints for an open interval, but including the endpoints for a closed interval). It is often helpful to look at the graph of the function to help determine if there are any discontinuities. The graph can, at least, reveal any points that must be checked specifically.

<u>Example:</u> Determine whether the function ln x is continuous over the closed interval [0, 1].

One approach is to look at a plot of the function.

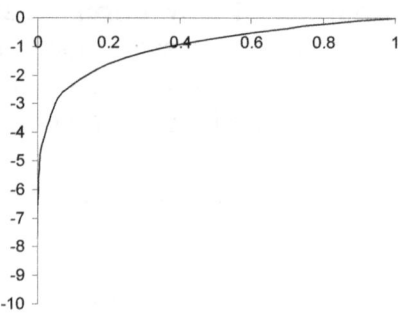

The limit of the function as x approaches zero from the right does not exist. Algebraically, this can be seen by noting that the equation $\ln x = L$ is the same as the equation $e^L = x$. For $x = 0$, the only possible value of L that satisfies this equation is $-\infty$. In other words,

$$\lim_{x \to 0} \ln x = -\infty$$

The limit does not exist, therefore, and the function is not continuous on the closed interval [0, 1]. The function is continuous on the open interval (0, 1), however. (It is also continuous on the half-open interval (0, 1].) Note that, for all $x > 0$, x is defined, and for $c > 0$,

$$\lim_{x \to c} \ln x = \ln c$$

Thus, $\ln x$ is continuous over $(0, \infty)$.

Example: Determine if the function shown in the graph is continuous at $x = 2$.

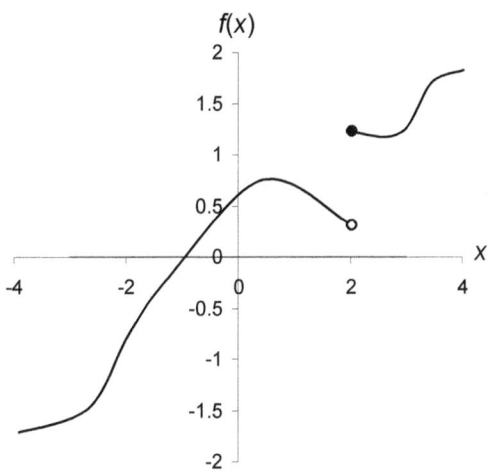

By inspection, it can be seen that the limits of the function as x approaches 2 from the right and left are not equal.

$$\lim_{x \to 2^+} f(x) \neq \lim_{x \to 2^-} f(x)$$

As a result, the function does not meet all of the criteria for continuity at x = 2 and is therefore discontinuous.

Example: Determine whether the following function is continuous at $x = 1$: $f(x) = \begin{cases} x^2 & x \neq 1 \\ 0 & x = 1 \end{cases}$.

The plot of this piecewise function is shown below.

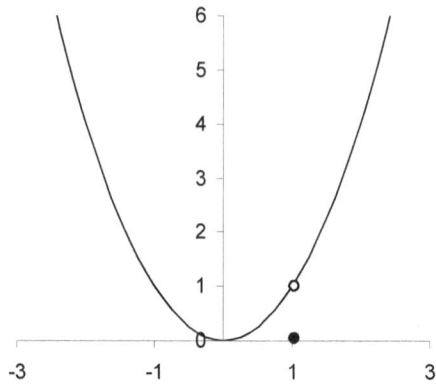

In this case, the function is defined at $x = 1$, and the limits of $f(x)$ as x approaches 1 from both the right and from the left are both equal to 1. Nevertheless, it is not the case that $\lim_{x \to 1} f(x) = f(1)$, since $\lim_{x \to 1} f(x) = 1$ and $f(1) = 0$. Thus, the function is not continuous at $x = 1$.

5.2c. Know and apply the Intermediate Value Theorem, using the geometric implications of continuity

The Intermediate Value Theorem states that if $f(x)$ is a continuous function on the interval $[a,b]$, then for every d between $f(a)$ and $f(b)$ there exists c between a and b such that $f(c) = d$.

More intuitively, this means that if the function $f(x)$ is continuous at every point of an interval $x = a$ to $x = b$, then it will take on each value between $f(a)$ and $f(b)$ for some value of x between $x = a$ and $x = b$.

Restated in geometric terms, the Intermediate Value Theorem requires that if a horizontal line is drawn on a graph of the function $f(x)$ somewhere between $f(a)$ and $f(b)$, the line will intersect the graph for at least one point that has an x coordinate between a and b.

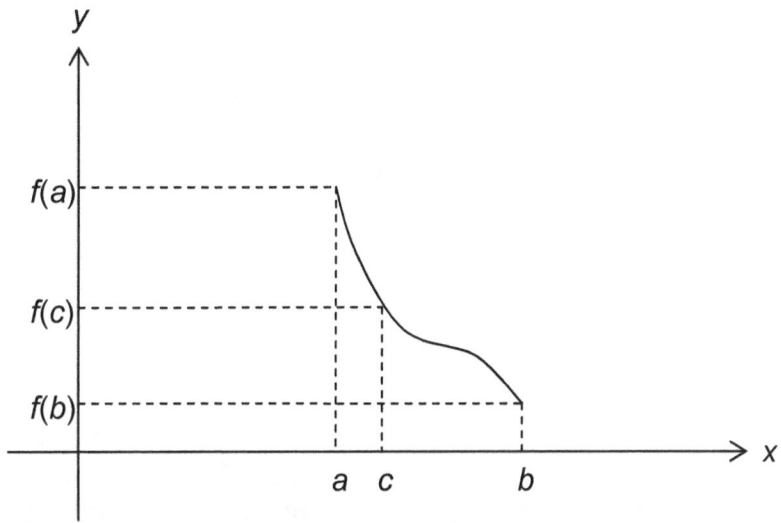

The Intermediate Value Theorem can be used to determine certain characteristics of the behavior of functions and their solutions.

<u>Example</u>: Show that the equation $x^3 - 9x + 5 = 0$ has a solution in the interval [0, 1].

Since $f(x) = x^3 - 9x + 5$ is a polynomial, it is continuous from $x = -\infty$ to $x = \infty$ including within the given interval [0, 1].

Evaluating the function at the end points of the interval we get $f(0) = 5$ and $f(1) = -3$.

Since 0 lies between 5 and −3, the Intermediate Value Theorem tells us that there must be a value c between 0 and 1 such that f(c)=0. (This essentially means that, since the function is continuous, it cannot go from 5 to −3 without passing through 0.)

Hence the equation $x^3 - 9x + 5 = 0$ must have a solution in the interval [0, 1].

Example: Show that the function $f(x) = x^3 - 3x + 1$ has at least 3 zeroes in the interval [−2, 2].

Evaluating the function at several points in the interval we see that,

$$f(-2) = -8 + 6 + 1 = -1$$
$$f(0) = 1$$
$$f(1) = 1 - 3 + 1 = -1$$
$$f(2) = 8 - 6 + 1 = 3$$

From the Intermediate Value Theorem, we know that every time a polynomial function goes from a negative value to a positive value (or vice versa) it must pass through the value zero (explained in the above example); i.e., if the value of the function has opposite signs at the two ends of an interval, it must have a zero in that interval. Applying this conclusion to the values of f(x) evaluated above, we see that $f(x) = x^3 - 3x + 1$ must have at least one zero in each of the following intervals:

[−2, 0]   (Since f(−2) = −1 and f(0) = 1)
[0, 1]   (Since f(0) = 1 and f(1) = −1)
[1, 2]   (Since f(1) = −1 and f(2) = 3)

SKILL 5.3 DERIVATICES AND APPLICATIONS

5.3a. **Derive the rules of differentiation for polynomial, trigonometric, and logarithmic functions using the formal definition of derivative**

The following properties of the derivative allow for differentiation of a wide range of functions (although the process of differentiation may be more or less difficult, depending on the complexity of the function). For illustration, consider to arbitrary functions $f(x)$ and $g(x)$ and arbitrary constant c.

Rule for multiplicative constants:

$$\frac{d}{dx}(cf) = cf'$$

Sum and difference rules:

$$\frac{d}{dx}(f+g) = f'+g'$$

$$\frac{d}{dx}(f-g) = f'-g'$$

Product rule:

$$\frac{d}{dx}(fg) = fg' + gf'$$

Quotient rule:

$$\frac{d}{dx}\left(\frac{f}{g}\right) = \frac{gf'-fg'}{g^2}$$

Another useful rule is the **chain rule**. The chain rule, as expressed below, allows differentiation of composite functions. The variable u can be an independent variable or it can be a function (of x). Note that, in the rule below, the differential elements du in the numerator of the first factor and the denominator of the second factor can otherwise cancel, making the right side of the equation identical to the left side.

$$\frac{df}{dx} = \frac{df}{du}\frac{du}{dx}$$

Derivation of rules of differentiation for algebraic functions

The formal definition of the derivative is expressed in terms of the limit of a difference quotient, as given below.

$$f'(x) = \lim_{\Delta x \to 0} \frac{f(x + \Delta x) - f(x)}{\Delta x}$$

Using this definition, the derivatives of algebraic functions (including, for instance, polynomial, trigonometric and logarithmic functions) can be derived. In addition, the general differentiation rules above can also be derived by applying in each case the properties of limits to the definition given above.

Polynomial functions

Note that the sum and difference rules for differentiation, along with the multiplicative constant rule, allow polynomials to be differentiated on a term-by-term basis. Thus, it suffices to simply derive the rule for differentiating the generic term x^n, where n is a constant and x is the variable of the function. Use the formal definition of the derivative given above and substitute this algebraic term for $f(x)$ (that is, use $f(x) = x^n$).

$$f'(x) = \lim_{\Delta x \to 0} \frac{(x + \Delta x)^n - (x)^n}{\Delta x}$$

Simplify the expression and apply the binomial expansion to the result.

$$f'(x) = \lim_{\Delta x \to 0} \frac{1}{\Delta x} \left[(x + \Delta x)^n - x^n \right]$$

$$f'(x) = \lim_{\Delta x \to 0} \frac{1}{\Delta x} \left[\binom{n}{0} x^n + \binom{n}{1} x^{n-1} \Delta x + \binom{n}{2} x^{n-2} (\Delta x)^2 + \ldots + \binom{n}{n} (\Delta x)^n - x^n \right]$$

In the above expression, the combinatorial form $\binom{n}{k}$ represents the number of combinations of n objects taken k at a time, or $\frac{n!}{k!(n-k)!}$.

$$f'(x) = \lim_{\Delta x \to 0} \frac{1}{\Delta x} \left[x^n + nx^{n-1}\Delta x + \binom{n}{2} x^{n-2}(\Delta x)^2 + \ldots + (\Delta x)^n - x^n \right]$$

$$f'(x) = \lim_{\Delta x \to 0} \frac{1}{\Delta x} \left[nx^{n-1}\Delta x + \binom{n}{2} x^{n-2}(\Delta x)^2 + \ldots + (\Delta x)^n \right]$$

$$f'(x) = \lim_{\Delta x \to 0} \left[nx^{n-1} + \binom{n}{2} x^{n-2}\Delta x + \ldots + (\Delta x)^{n-1} \right]$$

Note that, with the exception of the first term, all the terms in the brackets have a factor Δx. Thus, when the limit is applied, these terms all become zero, leaving the result of the differentiation.

$$f'(x) = nx^{n-1}$$

This is the well-known rule for differentiating polynomial terms with exponent n.

<u>Example:</u> Find the first derivative of the function $y = 5x^4$.

$$\frac{dy}{dx} = (5)(4)x^{4-1}$$
$$\frac{dy}{dx} = 20x^3$$

<u>Example:</u> Find y' where $y = \frac{1}{4x^3}$.

First, rewrite the function using a negative exponent, then apply the differentiation rule.

$$y' = \frac{1}{4}x^{-3}$$
$$y' = \frac{1}{4}(-3)x^{-3-1}$$
$$y' = -\frac{3}{4}x^{-4} = -\frac{3}{4x^4}$$

<u>Example:</u> Find the first derivative of $y = 3\sqrt{x^5}$.

Rewrite using $\sqrt[z]{x^n} = x^{n/z}$, then take the derivative.

$$y = 3x^{5/2}$$
$$\frac{dy}{dx} = (3)\left(\frac{5}{2}\right)x^{5/2-1}$$
$$\frac{dy}{dx} = \left(\frac{15}{2}\right)x^{3/2}$$
$$\frac{dy}{dx} = 7.5\sqrt{x^3} = 7.5x\sqrt{x}$$

Trigonometric functions

The same approach can be used for trigonometric functions. Only the example of the sine function is presented fully below, but the same logic and method applies to all trigonometric functions (cosine, tangent, cosecant, secant and cotangent) as well. Define $f(x) = \sin x$ and apply the formal definition of the derivative.

$$f'(x) = \lim_{\Delta x \to 0} \frac{\sin(x + \Delta x) - \sin(x)}{\Delta x}$$

Use the addition formula for sine functions.

$$f'(x) = \lim_{\Delta x \to 0} \frac{[\sin x \cos \Delta x + \cos x \sin \Delta x] - \sin x}{\Delta x}$$
$$f'(x) = \lim_{\Delta x \to 0} \frac{\cos x \sin \Delta x - \sin x (1 - \cos \Delta x)}{\Delta x}$$
$$f'(x) = \cos x \lim_{\Delta x \to 0} \frac{\sin \Delta x}{\Delta x} - \sin x \lim_{\Delta x \to 0} \frac{1 - \cos \Delta x}{\Delta x}$$

Evaluating these limits yields values of one and zero, respectively.

$$f'(x) = \cos x (1) - \sin x (0)$$
$$f'(x) = \cos x$$

Thus, the derivative of the sine function is the cosine function. Again, the same type of approach can be used to derive the derivatives of the other trigonometric functions. All that is needed is an understanding of the properties of the functions and of limits.

Example: Find the first derivative of the function $y = \pi \sin x$.

Use the multiplicative constant rule and then perform the differentiation.

$$\frac{dy}{dx} = \pi \cos x$$

Example: Find the first derivative of the function $y = 4\tan(5x^3)$.

Use the chain rule, where $u = 5x^3$.

$$\frac{dy}{dx} = 4\left[\frac{d}{du}\tan u\right]\left[\frac{d}{dx}5x^3\right]$$
$$\frac{dy}{dx} = 4\left[\sec^2 u\right]\left[15x^2\right]$$
$$\frac{dy}{dx} = 60x^2 \sec^2(5x^3)$$

Logarithmic functions

For logarithmic functions, the same formal definition of the derivative can hypothetically be used to derive the correct differentiation rule.

$$f'(x) = \lim_{\Delta x \to 0} \frac{\ln(x + \Delta x) - \ln(x)}{\Delta x}$$

For other logarithms (that is, logarithms of different bases), a change of base can be used to convert to a natural logarithm:

$$\log_a c = \frac{\ln c}{\ln a}$$

The derivative of the natural logarithmic function can be extremely tedious to derive in the above manner. The result is best memorized:

$$\frac{d}{dx}\ln x = \frac{1}{x}$$

Another method of deriving this result involves using the Fundamental Theorem of Calculus, where the function ln x is found as the antiderivative of $\frac{1}{x}$.

Example: Find the first derivative of $y = 3\ln(x^{-2})$

Use the chain rule and apply the above rules for differentiation.

$$\frac{dy}{dx} = 3\left[\frac{d}{du}\ln u\right]\left[\frac{d}{dx}x^{-2}\right]$$

$$\frac{dy}{dx} = 3\frac{1}{x^{-2}}\left[-2x^{-3}\right]$$

$$\frac{dy}{dx} = -6\frac{x^2}{x^3} = -\frac{6}{x}$$

Example: Find the derivative of the function $y = \log_5(\tan x)$.

First, convert to a natural logarithm and then find the derivative using the chain rule.

$$y = \frac{\ln(\tan x)}{\ln 5}$$

$$\frac{dy}{dx} = \frac{1}{\ln 5}\left[\frac{d}{du}\ln u\right]\left[\frac{d}{dx}\tan x\right]$$

$$\frac{dy}{dx} = \frac{1}{\ln 5}\left[\frac{1}{\tan x}\right]\left[\sec^2 x\right]$$

$$\frac{dy}{dx} = \frac{1}{\ln 5}\sec^2 x \cot x$$

Exponential functions

Based on the result for the natural logarithm, the rule for differentiating an exponential function can be derived using the chain rule. First, differentiate the function $\ln(e^x)$.

$$\frac{d}{dx}\ln(e^x) = \frac{1}{e^x}\frac{d}{dx}e^x$$

But, by the rules of logarithms, $\ln(e^x)$ is simply x. Rearrange the above expression to solve for the derivative of e^x.

$$\frac{d}{dx}\ln(e^x) = \frac{d}{dx}x = 1 = \frac{1}{e^x}\frac{d}{dx}e^x$$

$$\frac{d}{dx}e^x = e^x$$

Thus, the rule for differentiating exponential functions is known.

Summary of differentiation rules for transcendental functions

$$\frac{d}{dx}\sin x = \cos x \qquad \frac{d}{dx}\csc x = -\csc x \cot x$$

$$\frac{d}{dx}\cos x = -\sin x \qquad \frac{d}{dx}\sec x = \sec x \tan x$$

$$\frac{d}{dx}\tan x = \sec^2 x \qquad \frac{d}{dx}\cot x = -\csc^2 x$$

$$\frac{d}{dx}\arcsin x = \frac{1}{\sqrt{1-x^2}} \qquad \frac{d}{dx}\operatorname{arccsc} x = -\frac{1}{|x|\sqrt{x^2-1}}$$

$$\frac{d}{dx}\arccos x = -\frac{1}{\sqrt{1-x^2}} \qquad \frac{d}{dx}\operatorname{arcsec} x = \frac{1}{|x|\sqrt{x^2-1}}$$

$$\frac{d}{dx}\arctan x = \frac{1}{1+x^2} \qquad \frac{d}{dx}\operatorname{arccot} x = -\frac{1}{1+x^2}$$

$$\frac{d}{dx}\ln x = \frac{1}{x} \qquad \frac{d}{dx}e^x = e^x$$

Example: Find the derivative of the function $y = 4e^{x^2}\sin x$.

Apply the appropriate rules (product and chain rules) to the function.

$$\frac{dy}{dx} = 4\left(\sin x \frac{d}{dx}e^{x^2} + e^{x^2}\frac{d}{dx}\sin x\right)$$

$$\frac{dy}{dx} = 4\left(\sin x \left[2xe^{x^2}\right] + e^{x^2}\cos x\right)$$

$$\frac{dy}{dx} = 8xe^{x^2}\sin x + 4e^{x^2}\cos x$$

Example: Find the derivative of the function $y = \dfrac{5}{e^{\sin x}}$.

Rewrite the function with a negative exponent and use the chain rule.

$$y = 5e^{-\sin x}$$
$$\frac{dy}{dx} = 5\frac{d}{dx}e^{-\sin x}$$
$$\frac{dy}{dx} = 5e^{-\sin x}[-\cos x]$$
$$\frac{dy}{dx} = -5e^{-\sin x}\cos x = -\frac{5\cos x}{e^{\sin x}}$$

5.3b.   Interpret the concept of derivative geometrically, numerically, and analytically (i.e., slope of the tangent, limit of difference quotients, extrema, Newton's method, and instantaneous rate of change)

The **derivative of a function** has two basic interpretations:

I.   Instantaneous rate of change
II. Slope of a tangent line at a given point

The following is a list summarizing some of the more common quantities referred to in rate of change problems.

area	height	profit
decay	population growth	sales
distance	position	temperature
frequency	pressure	volume

The slope of a line is simply the change in the vertical (positive y) direction divided by the change in the horizontal (positive x) direction. Since the slope of a line is constant over the entire domain of the function, any two points can be used to calculate the slope.

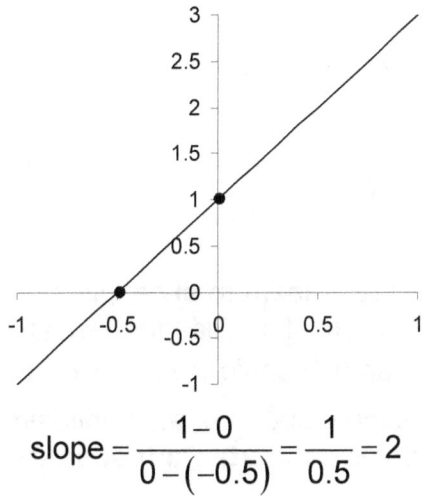

$$\text{slope} = \frac{1-0}{0-(-0.5)} = \frac{1}{0.5} = 2$$

Although the specific approach used for lines cannot be used for curves, it can be used in the general sense if the distance between the points (along the x-axis) becomes zero.

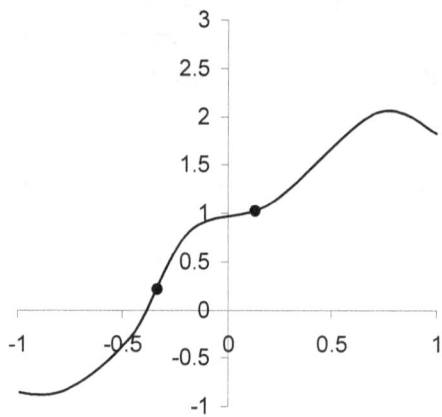

The equation for slope can be written as follows.

$$\text{slope} = \frac{f(x+\Delta x)-f(x)}{\Delta x}$$

This is also known as the difference quotient. For a curve defined by the function f, the difference quotient computes the slope of the secant line through the two points with x-coordinates x and x + h. The difference quotient is used in the definition of the derivative.

Take the limit as Δx goes to zero. This is the definition of the derivative, which is written as either $f'(x)$ or as $\frac{df(x)}{dx}$.

$$f'(x) = \lim_{\Delta x \to 0} \frac{f(x+\Delta x)-f(x)}{\Delta x}$$

This is the fundamental definition of the derivative, and it can be used to derive formulas for derivatives of specific types of functions. For instance, consider $f(x) = x^2$. Based on this formula, which defines the slope over an infinitesimal width Δx, the derivative can be seen as the **instantaneous rate of change** of the function.

$$f'(x) = \lim_{\Delta x \to 0} \frac{(x+\Delta x)^2 - x^2}{\Delta x} = \lim_{\Delta x \to 0} \frac{x^2 + 2x\Delta x + \Delta x^2 - x^2}{\Delta x}$$

$$f'(x) = \lim_{\Delta x \to 0} \frac{2x\Delta x + \Delta x^2}{\Delta x} = \lim_{\Delta x \to 0} (2x + \Delta x) = 2x$$

The same approach can be used to show generally, for instance, that $f'(x) = nx^{n-1}$ for $f(x) = x^n$.

The derivative of a function at a point can likewise be interpreted as the **slope of a line tangent to the function** at that same point. Pick a point (for instance, at $x = -3$) on the graph of a function and draw a tangent line at that point. Find the derivative of the function and substitute the value $x = -3$. This result will be the slope of the tangent line.

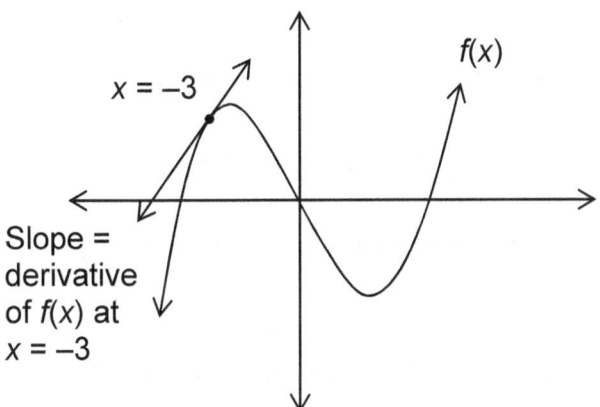

Example: Find the slope of the tangent line for the given function at the given point: $y = \dfrac{1}{x-2}$ at (3, 1).

Find the derivative of the function.

$$y' = \frac{d}{dx}(x-2)^{-1}$$
$$y' = (-1)(x-2)^{-2}(1) = -\frac{1}{(x-2)^2}$$

Evaluate the derivative at $x = 3$:

$$y' = -\frac{1}{(3-2)^2} = -1$$

Thus, the slope of the function at the point is -1.

Example: Find the points where the tangent to the curve $f(x) = 2x^2 + 3x$ is parallel to the line $y = 11x - 5$.

For the tangent line to be parallel to the given line, the only condition is that the slopes are equal. Thus, find the derivative of f, set the result equal to 11 and solve for x.

$$f'(x) = 4x + 3 = 11$$
$$4x = 8$$
$$x = 2$$

To find the y value of the point, simply substitute 2 into f.

$$f(2) = 2(2)^2 + 3(2) = 8 + 6 = 14$$

Thus, the tangent to f is parallel to $y = 11x - 5$ at the point (2, 14) only.

Example: Find the equation of the tangent line to $f(x) = 2e^{x^2}$ at $x = -1$.

To find the tangent line, a point and a slope are needed. The x value of the point is given; the y value can be found by substituting $x = -1$ into f.

$$f(-1) = 2e^{(-1)^2} = 2e$$

Thus, the point is (−1, 2e). The slope is found by substituting −1 into the derivative of f.

$$f'(x) = 2e^{x^2}(2x) = 4xe^{x^2}$$
$$f'(-1) = 4(-1)e^{(-1)^2} = -4e$$

Use the point-slope form of the line to determine the correct equation.

$$y - 2e = -4e(x - [-1])$$
$$y = 2e - 4ex - 4e = -4ex - 2e$$

Thus, the equation of the line tangent to f at $x = -1$ is $y = -4ex - 2e$.

When the slope of the tangent line is zero (that is, the tangent line is horizontal), then the instantaneous rate of change of the function at that point is also zero. This can occur in three cases: a maximum value, where the slope changes from positive to negative (going left to right); a minimum value, where the slope changes from negative to positive; or neither a maximum or minimum, where the sign of the slope does not change. The graph below illustrates the points where these **extrema** exist.

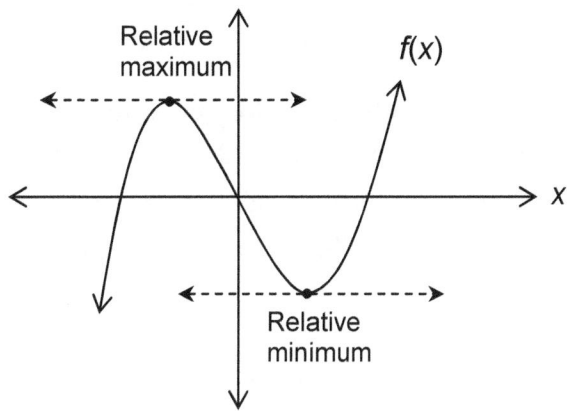

A non-extreme value where the slope of the tangent line is zero can also exist, as shown in the following graph.

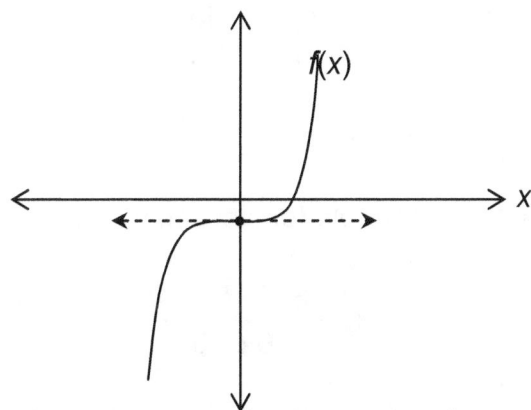

Newton's method is an approach to numerically determining the value of a particular root (or zero) of a function. Newton's method is based on the assumption that the function and the line tangent to the function at the root both cross the x-axis at approximately the same point. Consider the slope of a tangent line to $f(x)$ at a root $x = x_1$.

$$y - y_1 = m(x - x_1) = y - f(x_1) = f'(x_1)(x - x_1)$$

If x_1 corresponds to a root, the value of y must be zero. Thus,

$$0 - f(x_1) = xf'(x_1) - x_1 f'(x_1)$$

Solving for x yields the following:

$$xf'(x_1) = x_1 f'(x_1) - f(x_1)$$
$$x = x_1 - \frac{f(x_1)}{f'(x_1)}$$

Newton's method applies this formula iteratively: the value of x is found first with a guess for x_1. This new value of x is then placed back into the formula as x_1. The process is repeated until the result converges. The iterative formula is given below.

$$x_{n+1} = x_n - \frac{f(x_n)}{f'(x_n)} \text{ where } x_1 \text{ is an approximate guess}$$

<u>Example:</u> Calculate the positive root of the function $f(x) = 3x^2 - 5x - 1$ numerically using Newton's method.

From the question, it is clear we are looking for a single positive root of the function. First, determine the derivative of f.

$$f'(x) = 6x - 5$$

Write the formula for Newton's method.

$$x_{n+1} = x_n - \frac{3x^2 - 5x - 1}{6x - 5}$$

Choose a guess value. Try x = 1.

$$x_2 = 1 - \frac{3(1)^2 - 5(1) - 1}{6(1) - 5} = 1 - \left(\frac{-3}{1}\right) = 4$$

Continue the process. The table below shows the results.

x_2	4
x_3	2.579
x_4	2.001
x_5	1.857
x_6	1.847
x_7	1.847
x_8	1.847

The above results are of intentionally limited precision. Newton's method can, theoretically, produce a result of arbitrary precision as long as the precision is maintained throughout the process. Test the result:

$$f(1.847) = 3(1.847)^2 - 5(1.847) - 1 \approx 0$$

Although this result is not precisely zero, it is sufficiently close. The difference is due to numerical error.

5.3c. Interpret both continuous and differentiable functions geometrically and analytically and apply Rolle's Theorem, the Mean Value Theorem, and L'Hopital's rule

If the derivative of a function exists at x, then the function is said to be **differentiable at x**. Further, if the function is differentiable at every point in an open interval (a, b), then the function is said to be differentiable on (a, b).

For a function to be differentiable at x, the limit of the difference quotient at x must exist. That is to say,

$$\lim_{\Delta x \to 0} \frac{f(x+\Delta x)-f(x)}{\Delta x}$$

must exist. A test of the existence of this limit is examination of the one-sided limits on either side of x. Consider the function at $x = c$; to determine whether the function is differentiable, determine if the following equation is valid:

$$\lim_{x \to c^+} \frac{f(x)-f(c)}{x-c} = \lim_{x \to c^-} \frac{f(c)-f(x)}{c-x}$$

The left side of the equation is the limit as x approaches c from the right. The right side of the equation is the limit as x approaches c from the left. Only if these two limits exist and are equal is the function differentiable at c.

Consider the following function. Although the limits of the difference quotients both exist, they are different on either side of the point at $x = -1$. As a result, the function is not differentiable at $x = -1$.

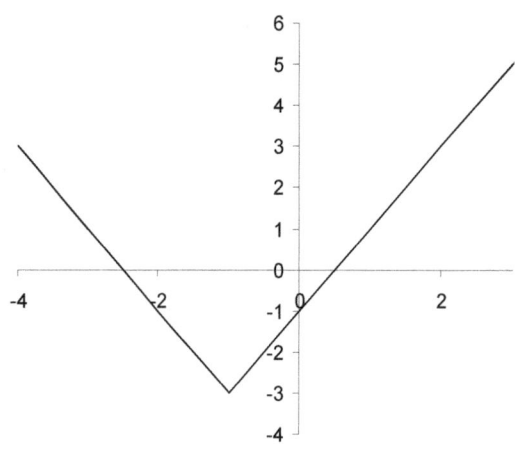

In addition to the existence of both one-sided limits, a function must also be continuous at a point to be differentiable. In the above case, the function is continuous at $x = -1$, but the limits do not exist. In the following case, the function is not continuous at $x = 1$, and, therefore, is not differentiable at this point.

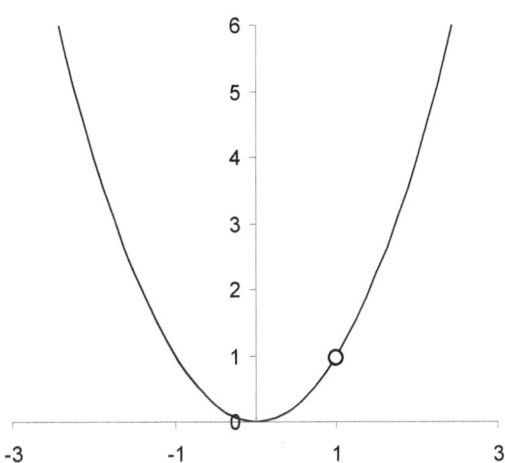

A function is continuous at a point if the function is defined at the point, the limit of the function as x approaches the corresponding value exists and the limit is equal to the function evaluated at the point. The function depicted in the above graph is not defined at $x = 1$. Nevertheless, even if the function is defined, as shown below, it can still be discontinuous.

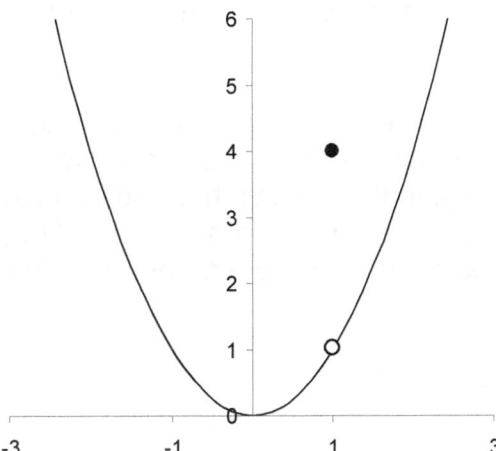

The function above would still not be differentiable at $x = 1$.

Rolle's Theorem states that if there are two values *a* and *b* such that $f(a) = f(b)$, then there is some number *c* between *a* and *b* such that the derivative of the function evaluated at *c* equals zero. In other words, there is a point somewhere between *x* = *a* and *x* = *b* where the graph reaches a maximum or a minimum. Consider the following graph.

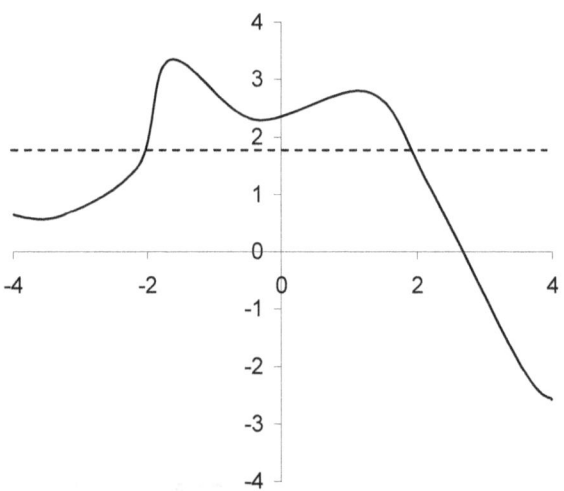

The dashed line corresponds to a fixed *y* value. Note that, regardless of the position of the line, as long as the line intersects the curve of the function at least twice, the portion of the curve between the intersection points includes at least one maximum or minimum. (This is an intuitive result.) At these extreme values, the line tangent to the curve has a slope of zero, meaning that the derivative is also zero. This is a graphical way of considering Rolle's Theorem.

Rolle's Theorem can be helpful in identifying the existence of an extreme value (maximum or minimum). If it is known, or can be shown, that a function has two equivalent values on either end of some interval [*a*, *b*] (that is, *f*(*a*) = *f*(*b*)), then it is known that there is at least one maximum or minimum in that interval.

Example: Determine whether the derivative of the following function has any roots between 0 and π: $f(x) = 3\cos(2x)$.

Rolle's Theorem states that if a function has an equal value at two separate points, there is at least one maximum or minimum between those points (meaning that the derivative is zero for at least one point in this domain).

$$f(0) = 3\cos(0) = 3$$
$$f(\pi) = 3\cos(2\pi) = 3$$

Thus, there is at least one point between $x = 0$ and $x = \pi$ such that $f'(x) = 0$, meaning that the derivative of f has at least one root in this domain.

The Mean Value Theorem states that there is some point c on the curve of any function f between $x = a$ and $x = b$ where the derivative of f is also equal to the slope of the secant line defined by these points. The slope m of the secant line is expressed as follows.

$$m = \frac{f(b) - f(a)}{b - a}$$

Set the derivative equal to this slope value and solve; To find the point or points where the tangent line is parallel to the secant line formed by connecting points $(a, f(a))$ and $(b, f(b))$, set the derivative of f equal to m and solve for c. The Mean Value Theorem is thus expressed mathematically as follows.

$$f'(c) = \frac{f(b) - f(a)}{b - a}$$

The Mean Value Theorem is useful in instances where, for example, a problem refers to average rates of change.

Example: Prove that if the rate of change of a function is zero over an interval, the function is also constant over the interval.

Let the function be defined as $f(x)$, where the first derivative is $f'(x)$. If the rate of change of the function is zero over the interval, then $f'(x) = 0$ for all x on the interval. Apply the Mean Value Theorem for some $x = c$ between $x = a$ and $x = b$ for any values a and b in the interval:

$$f'(c) = 0 = \frac{f(b) - f(a)}{b - a}$$

Simplify:

$$0 = f(b) - f(a)$$
$$f(a) = f(b)$$

Thus, for any two values a and b in the interval where the derivative of the function is zero, the function is constant. In other words, by the Mean Value Theorem, the function is constant over the interval.

L'Hopital's rule states that a limit can be evaluated by taking the derivative of the numerator and the derivative of the denominator and then finding the limit of the resulting quotient. This rule is extremely helpful in cases where simple evaluation of a limit leads to an undefined value (positive or negative infinity). Thus, L'Hopital's rule can be expressed as follows.

$$\lim_{x \to a} \frac{f(x)}{g(x)} = \lim_{x \to a} \frac{f'(x)}{g'(x)}$$

Example: Evaluate the limit of the function $f(x) = \frac{3x - 1}{x^2 + 2x + 3}$ as x approaches infinite.

The limit cannot be evaluated using simple substitution.

$$\lim_{x \to \infty} \frac{3x - 1}{x^2 + 2x + 3} = \frac{3\infty - 1}{\infty^2 + 2\infty + 3} = \frac{\infty}{\infty}$$

Apply L'Hopital's rule by taking the derivative of the numerator and denominator individually.

$$\lim_{x \to \infty} \frac{3x-1}{x^2+2x+3} = \lim_{x \to \infty} \frac{3}{2x+2}$$

$$\lim_{x \to \infty} \frac{3}{2x+2} = \frac{3}{2\infty+2} = 0$$

Example: Evaluate the following limit: $\lim_{x \to 1} \frac{\ln x}{x-1}$.

For $x = 1$, the denominator of the function becomes zero, as does the numerator. Therefore, apply L'Hopital's rule to simplify the limit.

$$\lim_{x \to 1} \frac{\ln x}{x-1} = \lim_{x \to 1} \frac{\frac{1}{x}}{1}$$

$$\lim_{x \to 1} \frac{\ln x}{x-1} = \lim_{x \to 1} \frac{1}{x} = \frac{1}{1} = 1$$

5.3d. **Use the derivative to solve rectilinear motion, related rate, and optimization problems**

Extreme value problems, also known as max-min problems or **optimization problems**, entail using the first derivative to find values that either maximize or minimize some quantity, such as area, profit or volume. The derivative is a critical tool in solving these types of problems. Follow these steps to solve an extreme value (optimization) problem.

1. Write an equation for the quantity to be maximized or minimized.
2. Use the other information in the problem to write secondary equations.
3. Use the secondary equations for substitutions, and rewrite the original equation in terms of only one variable.
4. Find the derivative of the primary equation (step 1) and the critical numbers of this derivative.
5. Substitute these critical numbers into the primary equation.

The value that produces either the largest or smallest result can be used to find the solution.

Example: A manufacturer wishes to construct an open box from a square piece of metal by cutting squares from each corner and folding up the sides. The metal is 12 feet on each side. What are the dimensions of the squares to be cut out such that the volume of the box is maximized?

First, draw a figure that represents the situation. Assume that the squares to be cut from the metal have sides of length x. Noting that the metal has sides of length 12 feet, this leaves $12 - 2x$ feet remaining on each side after the squares are cut out.

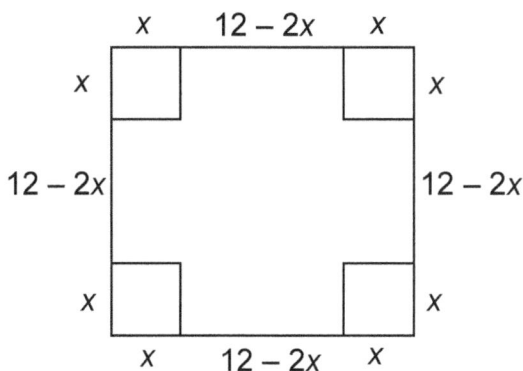

The volume $V(x)$ of the box formed when the sides are folded up is the following:

$$V(x) = x(12-2x)^2$$

Simplify and take the first derivative of the result.

$$V(x) = x(144 - 48x + 4x^2) = 4x^3 - 48x^2 + 144x$$
$$V'(x) = 12x^2 - 96x + 144$$

Set the first derivative to zero and solve by factoring.

$$V'(x) = 12x^2 - 96x + 144 = 0$$
$$(x-6)(x-2) = 0$$

The solutions are then $x = 2$ feet and $x = 6$ feet. Note that, if $x = 6$ feet, the sides of the box become zero in width. This, therefore, is not a legitimate solution. Choose $x = 2$ feet as the solution that leads to the largest volume of the box.

Problems involving rectilinear motion

If a particle (such as a car, bullet or other object) is moving along a line, then the position of the particle can be expressed as a function of time.

The rate of change of position with respect to time is the velocity of the object; thus, the first derivative of the distance function yields the velocity function for the particle. Substituting a value for time into this expression provides the instantaneous velocity of the particle at that time. The absolute value of the derivative is the speed (magnitude of the velocity) of the particle. A positive value for the velocity indicates that the particle is moving forward (that is, in the positive x direction); a negative value indicates the particle is moving backward (that is, in the negative x direction).

The acceleration of the particle is the rate of change of the velocity. The second derivative of the position function (which is also the first derivative of the velocity function) yields the acceleration function. If a value for time produces a positive acceleration, the particle's velocity is increasing; if it produces a negative value, the particle's velocity is decreasing. If the acceleration is zero, the particle is moving at a constant speed.

Example: The motion of a particle moving along a line is according to the equation $s(t) = 20 + 3t - 5t^2$, where s is in meters and t is in seconds. Find the position, velocity and acceleration of the particle at $t = 2$ seconds.

To find the position, simply use $t = 2$ in the given position function. Note that the initial position of the particle is $s(0) = 20$ meters.

$$s(2) = 20 + 3(2) - 5(2)^2$$
$$s(2) = 20 + 6 - 20 = 6\,\text{m}$$

To find the velocity of the particle, calculate the first derivative of $s(t)$ and then evaluate the result for $t = 2$ seconds.

$$s'(t) = v(t) = 3 - 10t$$
$$v(2) = 3 - 10(2) = 3 - 20 = -17\,\text{m/s}$$

Finally, for the acceleration of the particle, calculate the second derivative of $s(t)$ (also equal to the first derivative of $v(t)$) and evaluate for $t = 2$ seconds.

$$s''(t) = v'(t) = a(t) = -10\,\text{m/s}^2$$

Since the acceleration function $a(t)$ is a constant, the acceleration is always -10 m/s² (the velocity of the particle decreases every second by 10 meters per second).

Related rate problems

Some rate problems may involve functions with different parameters that are each dependent on time. In such a case, implicit differentiation may be required. Often times, related rate problems give certain rates in the description, thus eliminating the need to have specific functions of time for every parameter. Related rate problems are otherwise solved in the same manner as other similar problems.

Example: A spherical balloon is inflated such that its radius is increasing at a constant rate of 1 inch per second. What is the rate of increase of the volume of the balloon when the radius is 10 inches?

First, write the equation for the volume of a sphere in terms of the radius, r.

$$V(r) = \frac{4}{3}\pi r^3$$

Differentiate the function implicitly with respect to time, t, by using the chain rule.

$$\frac{dV(r)}{dt} = \frac{4}{3}\pi \frac{d}{dt}(r^3)$$

$$\frac{dV(r)}{dt} = \frac{4}{3}\pi (3r^2)\frac{dr}{dt} = 4\pi r^2 \frac{dr}{dt}$$

To find the solution to the problem, use the radius value $r = 10$ inches and the rate of increase of the radius $\frac{dr}{dt} = 1$ in/sec. Calculate the resulting rate of increase of the volume, $\frac{dV(r)}{dt}$.

$$\frac{dV(10)}{dt} = 4\pi (10\,\text{in})^2 \, 1\,\text{in/sec} = 400\pi \,\text{in}^3/\text{sec} \approx 1257\,\text{in}^3/\text{sec}$$

The problem is thus solved.

5.3e. Use the derivative to analyze functions and planar curves (e.g., maxima, minima, inflection points, concavity)

Differential calculus can be a helpful tool in analyzing functions and the graphs of functions. Derivatives deal with the slope (or rate of change) of a function, and this information can be used to calculate the locations and values of extrema (maxima and minima) and inflection points, as well as to determine information concerning concavity.

The concept of extrema (maxima and minima) can be differentiated into local (or relative) and global (or absolute) extrema. For instance, consider the following function:

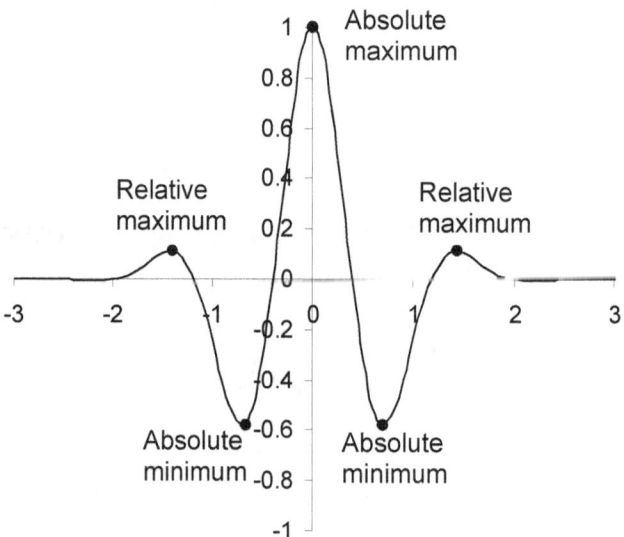

It is apparent that there are a number of peaks and valleys, each of which could, in some sense, be called a maximum or minimum. To allow greater clarity, local and global extrema can be specified. For instance, the peak at $x = 0$ is the maximum for the entire function. Additionally, the valleys at about $x = \pm 0.7$ both correspond to an (equivalent) minimum for the entire function. These are absolute extrema. On the other hand, the peaks at about $x = \pm 1.4$ are each a maximum for the function within a specific area; thus, they are relative maxima. Relative extrema are extreme values of the function over some limited interval. The points at which the derivative of a function is equal to zero are called **critical points** (the x values are called **critical numbers**).

By inspection of any graph, it is apparent that all extrema (where the function is continuous on either side of the maximum or minimum point) are located at points where the slope of the function is zero. This is to say that the derivative of the function at an extremum is zero. It is not necessarily the case, however, that all points where the derivative of the function is zero correspond to extrema. Consider the function $y = x^3$, whose graph is shown below.

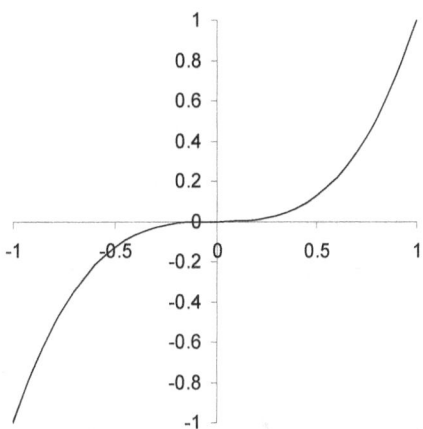

The derivative of y is $3x^2$, and the function is equal to zero only at $x = 0$. Nevertheless, the function y does not have an extremum at $x = 0$. The only cases where critical points correspond to extrema are when the derivative of the function actually crosses the x-axis. These cases correspond to the function having a positive slope on one side of the critical point and a negative slope on the other. This is a requirement for an extremum. (Notice that, for the plot of $y = x^3$, the function has a positive slope on both sides of the critical point.)

A positive slope on the left side of a critical point and a negative slope on the right side indicate that the critical point is a maximum. If the slope is negative on the left and positive on the right, then the critical point corresponds to a minimum. If the slopes on either side are both positive or both negative, then there is no extremum at the critical point.

Whether a critical point is an extremum can be determined using the second derivative. A critical point corresponds to the function f having zero slope. Thus, f' is zero at these points. As noted above, f has a maximum at the critical point only if f' is positive on one side of the critical point and negative on the other. This is to say that f' must cross the x-axis. If f' does not cross the x-axis, however, then it is either a maximum or minimum. As a result, if the critical number of f is also a critical number of f', then the critical point does not correspond to an extremum of f. The procedure for finding extrema for $f(x)$ is thus the following.

1. Calculate $f'(x)$.
2. Solve $f'(x) = 0$; the solutions of this equation are the critical numbers.
3. Calculate $f''(x)$.
4. Evaluate $f''(x)$ for each critical number c. If:
    a. $f''(c) = 0$, the critical point is not an extremum of f.
    b. $f''(c) > 0$, the critical point is a minimum of f.
    c. $f''(c) < 0$, the critical point is a maximum of f.

Example: Find the maxima and minima of $f(x) = 2x^4 - 4x^2$ on the closed interval [–2, 1].

First, differentiate the function and set the result equal to zero.

$$\frac{df}{dx} = 8x^3 - 8x = 0$$

Next, solve by factoring to find the critical numbers.

$$8x(x^2 - 1) = 0$$
$$x(x-1)(x+1) = 0$$

The solutions for this equation, which are also the critical numbers, are $x = -1$, 0 and 1. For each critical number, it is necessary to determine whether the point corresponds to a maximum, minimum or neither.

$$\frac{d^2f}{dx^2} = 24x^2 - 8$$

MATHEMATICS

Test each critical point by substituting into the result above.

$$f''(-1) = 24(-1)^2 - 8 = 24 - 8 = 16 \rightarrow \text{minimum}$$
$$f''(0) = 24(0)^2 - 8 = -8 \rightarrow \text{maximum}$$
$$f''(1) = 24(1)^2 - 8 = 24 - 8 = 16 \rightarrow \text{minimum}$$

The critical numbers correspond to the minima (–1, –2) and (1, –2) and to the maximum (0, 0). The endpoint of the closed interval at $x = -2$ should also be tested to determine if it constitutes an extremum, as such may not be detectable using derivatives (the minimum at the endpoint $x = 1$ was detected, however). This endpoint corresponds to (–2, 16), which is the absolute maximum. Absolute minima exist at (–1, –2) and (1, –2), and a relative maximum exists at (0, 0).

The second derivative of a function can also be viewed in terms of concavity. The first derivative reveals whether a curve is increasing or decreasing (increasing or decreasing) from the left to the right. In much the same way, the second derivative relates whether the curve is concave up (slope increasing) or concave down (slope decreasing). Curves that are concave can be viewed as "collecting water"; curves that are concave down can be viewed as "dumping water."

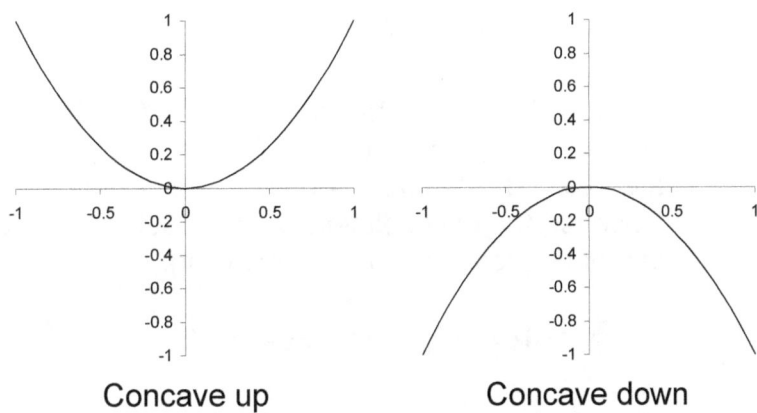

Concave up   Concave down

A **point of inflection** is a point where a curve changes from being concave up to concave down (or vice versa). To find these points, find the critical numbers of the first derivative of the function (that is, solve the equation for which the second derivative of the function is set equal to zero). A critical number is coincides with an inflection point if the curve is concave up on one side of the value and concave down on the other. The critical number is the x coordinate of the inflection point. To get the y coordinate, plug the critical number into the **original** function.

Example: Find the inflection points of $f(x) = 2x - \tan x$ over the interval $-\frac{\pi}{2} < x < \frac{\pi}{2}$.

First, calculate the second derivative of f.

$$f''(x) = \frac{d^2 f(x)}{dx^2} = \frac{d}{dx}\left[\frac{d}{dx}(2x - \tan x)\right]$$

$$f''(x) = \frac{d}{dx}\left[2 - \sec^2 x\right] = -2\sec x \frac{d}{dx}\sec x$$

$$f''(x) = -2\sec x (\sec x \tan x) = -2\sec^2 x \tan x$$

Set the second derivative equal to zero and solve.

$$f''(x) = -2\sec^2 x \tan x = 0$$

The function is zero for either sec x = 0 or tan x = 0. Only tan x = 0, however, has real solutions. This means that the inflection points are at $x = n\pi$, where n = 0, 1, 2, etc. Within the given interval, however, the only solution is x = 0. Substituting this value into the original equation yields the following:

$$f(0) = 2(0) - \tan 0 = 0 - 0 = 0$$

Thus, the inflection point for this function on the interval $-\frac{\pi}{2} < x < \frac{\pi}{2}$ is (0, 0). The plot of the function is shown below, along with the associated inflection point. As hinted earlier, the inflection point can be seen graphically as the point at which the slope changes from an increasing value to a decreasing value (or vice versa).

TEACHER CERTIFICATION STUDY GUIDE

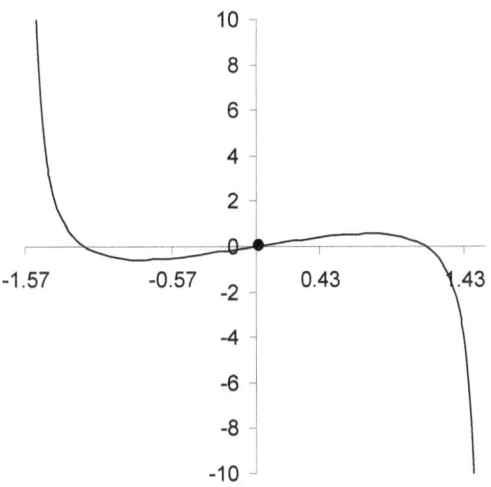

Example: Identify approximately the locations of the extrema (excluding the endpoints) and inflection points for the following graph.

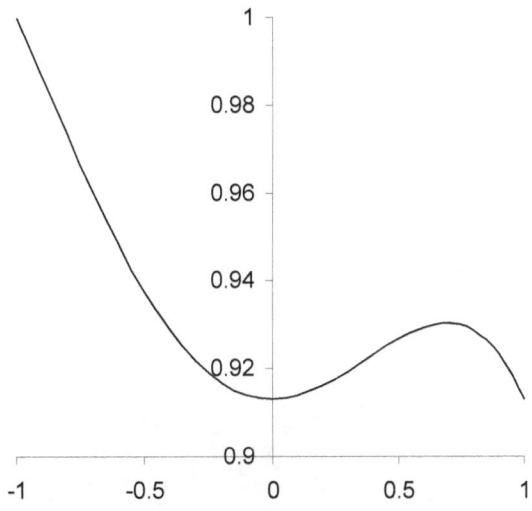

There are two obvious extrema in the graph: a minimum at about (0, .915) and a maximum at about (0.7, 0.93). These extrema are evidently relative extrema, since the function (at least apparently) has both larger and smaller values elsewhere. There is also an obvious concavity shift between the maximum and minimum. The inflection point is at about (0.35, 0.92). The extrema and inflection points are shown marked below.

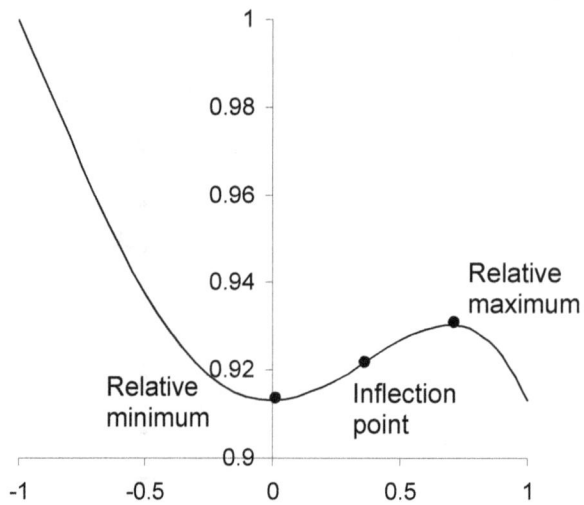

5.3f. Solve separable first-order differential equations and apply them to growth and decay problems

Separable first-order differential equations

A **differential equation** is an equation that involves both a function and some number of derivatives of that function. For instance, a differential equation involving the function y(x) might be the following:

$$y''(x) + y(x) = 1$$

This equation can be written alternatively in a slightly different form:

$$\frac{d^2 y(x)}{dx^2} + y(x) = 1$$

A **first-order** differential equation involves only the unknown function (y, for instance) and its first derivative. The following is a first-order differential equation.

$$\frac{dy(x)}{dx} + y(x) = 1$$

For a differential equation to be **separable**, it must be possible to collect all the terms involving y (including dy) and all the terms involving x (including dx) separately. Thus, it must be possible to move all terms involving y to one side of the equation and all terms involving x to the other side. Thus, a separable, first-order differential equation can be written in the following form.

$$A(y)dy = B(x)dx$$

Here, A is some function of y and B is some function of x.

Solving this type of differential equations involves three basic steps:

1. Separation of variables
2. Integration to find general solution
3. Invocation of boundary conditions to find particular solution

Solving separable first-order differential equations

Differential equations can often be solved using the method of **separation of variables**. Obviously, for separation of variables to be applicable, the differential equation must be separable (that is, it must be of the form specified above). Once the variables are isolated, each side of the equation can then be integrated.

$$\int A(y)\,dy = \int B(x)\,dx + C$$

Here, C is the constant of integration. Evaluation of the integrals yields a **general solution** that can be expressed in terms of y and x. If the problem provides additional data such as initial conditions or other function values corresponding to specific times, locations or other parameters, then these **boundary conditions** can be invoked to find a **particular solution** to the problem. Consider the following examples, which illustrate the procedure for solving separable first-order differential equations.

<u>Example:</u> Find the general solution to the following differential equation: $\dfrac{dy}{dx} = ky$.

To apply separation of variables, move the occurrence of y to the left side of the equation and move dx to the right side.

$$\frac{1}{y}\,dy = k\,dx$$

Thus, the equation is now in the appropriate form:

$$A(y)\,dy = B(x)\,dx$$

Integrate both sides and simplify.

$$\int \frac{1}{y}\,dy = \int k\,dx + C$$
$$\ln y = kx + C$$
$$e^{\ln y} = e^{kx+C}$$
$$y = e^C e^{kx}$$

Note that e^C is simply a constant, so redefine the value C.

$$y = Ce^{kx}$$

This is the solution to the equation.

Example: The velocity of an experimental automobile for time $t = 0$ seconds to $t = 10$ seconds is $t^2 + 2t + 15$. If the automobile is initially located at a position of 1,000 meters beyond a start line and is traveling away from it, what is its position at any given time, with respect to the start line, between 0 and 10 seconds?

The speed of a vehicle is the derivative of its position with respect to time. Thus, write the differential equation for position $s(t)$ as follows.

$$\frac{ds(t)}{dt} = t^2 + 2t + 15$$

Perform separation of variables and integrate the result.

$$ds(t) = \left(t^2 + 2t + 15\right)dt$$
$$\int ds(t) = \int \left(t^2 + 2t + 15\right)dt + C$$

Evaluate the integrals using the standard rules of integration.

$$\int ds(t) = s(t) = \int \left(t^2 + 2t + 15\right)dt + C = \frac{t^3}{3} + \frac{2t^2}{2} + 15t + C$$
$$s(t) = \frac{t^3}{3} + t^2 + 15t + C$$

A particular solution to this problem can be found by applying the initial condition that the position of the automobile at $t = 0$ is 1,000 meters beyond a start line.

$$s(0) = 1{,}000\text{m} = \frac{0^3}{3} + 0^2 + 15(0) + C = C$$
$$C = 1{,}000\text{m}$$

The particular solution to the differential equation for this problem, expressed in meters beyond the start line is then given below.

$$s(t) = \frac{t^3}{3} + t^2 + 15t + 1000$$

The technique discussed above for solving separable first-order differential equations can also be applied to growth and decay problems. Examples of such problems include situations that involve radioactive decay (with a so-called half life), population growth and continuously compounded interest. In each of these cases, the rate of growth or decay depends on the current value of the parameter. For instance, the rate of radioactive decay depends on the amount of material at any given time. Likewise, interest accrues in accordance with the balance. The differential equation can then be written as follows, where y corresponds to mass (for radioactive decay), population, balance or some other parameter.

$$\frac{dy}{dt} = f(y)$$

If $f(y)$ is simply the product of y and some constant k, then the equation becomes

$$\frac{dy}{dt} = ky$$

But this equation was solved in the first example above. The result is then

$$y = Ce^{kt}$$

It is apparent that k is a proportionality constant for the rate of growth and decay, and C is an initial condition (starting balance, population or mass, for instance). If the problem involves decay, then k must be a negative number (so that y decreases as t increases). If the problem involves growth, then k must be positive (so that y increases as t increases).

Thus, solving problems that involve simple **exponential growth or decay** require using this equation.

Example: A 10-gram sample of Einsteinium-254 decays radioactively with a half-life of about 276 days. What is the remaining mass of Einsteinium-254 after 5 years (assume each year is 365 days).

Use the exponential decay formula derived above, where $m(t)$ is the mass of Einsteinium in the sample at time t.

$$m(t) = Ce^{kt}$$

TEACHER CERTIFICATION STUDY GUIDE

The initial mass of Einsteinium-254 is 10 grams. Use this to find the value of C.

$$m(0) = 10g = Ce^{k(0)} = C$$

Thus, C is 10 grams. To find k, note that after 276 days, the amount of remaining Einsteinium-254 must be half the initial amount.

$$m(276d) = (10g)e^{k(276d)} = 5g$$
$$e^{k(276d)} = \frac{1}{2}$$

Solve for k. Note that, to make the argument of the exponential dimensionless, the units of k should be inverse days.

$$\ln\left[e^{k(276d)}\right] = \ln\frac{1}{2}$$
$$(276d)k = \ln\frac{1}{2}$$
$$k = \frac{1}{276d}\ln\frac{1}{2}$$
$$k \approx -0.00251\frac{1}{d}$$

The complete expression for m is then the following, where t is in days.

$$m(t) \approx (10g)e^{-0.00251t}$$

Finally, calculate the amount of Einsteinium remaining after 5 years (1,825 days).

$$m(1825) \approx (10g)e^{-0.00251(1825)}$$
$$m(1825) \approx 0.102g$$

Thus, after 5 years, only about 0.102 grams of the initial sample remain.

Example: Calculate the balance after 20 years for a savings account with an initial balance of $1,000 and an annual interest rate of 3%. Assume that the interest is compounded continuously.

In this case, the exponential growth formula can be used, where $A(t)$ is the amount of money in the account after t years. The equation is expressed using the standard "Pert" form.

$$A(t) = Pe^{rt}$$

The initial balance ($t = 0$) is $1,000.

$$A(0) = \$1{,}000 = Pe^{r(0)} = P$$
$$A(t) = \$1{,}000e^{rt}$$

The annual interest rate is 3%, or 0.03. Thus, after 1 year, the balance in the account must be 3% higher than the initial balance, or $1,030.

$$A(1) = \$1{,}030 = \$1{,}000e^{r(1)}$$
$$e^r = \frac{1030}{1000} = 1.03$$
$$\ln(e^r) = \ln 1.03$$
$$r = \ln 1.03 \approx 0.0296$$
$$A(t) = \$1{,}000e^{0.0296t}$$

The balance after 20 years is then

$$A(20) = \$1{,}000e^{0.0296(20)} = \$1807.60$$

The balance in the account after 20 years is then $1,807.60.

TEACHER CERTIFICATION STUDY GUIDE

SKILL 5.4 INTEGRALS AND APPLICATIONS

5.4a. Derive definite integrals of standard algebraic functions using the formal definition of integral

The formal definition of an integral is based on the **Riemann sum**. A Riemann sum is the sum of the areas of a set rectangles that is used to approximate the area under the curve of a function. Given a function f defined over some closed interval $[a, b]$, the interval can be divided into a set of n arbitrary partitions, each of length Δx_i. Within the limits of each partition, some value $x = c_i$ can be chosen such that Δx_i and $f(c_i)$ define the width and height (respectively) of a rectangle. The sum of the aggregate of all the rectangles defined in this manner over the interval $[a, b]$ is the Riemann sum.

Consider, for example, the function $f(x) = x^2 + 1$ over the interval $[0,1]$. The plot of the function is shown below.

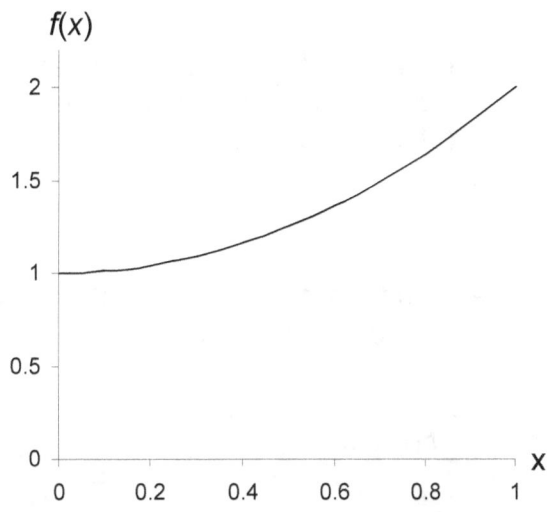

Partition the interval into segments of width 0.2 along the x-axis, and choose the function value $f(c_i)$ at the center of each interval. This function value is the height of the respective rectangle.

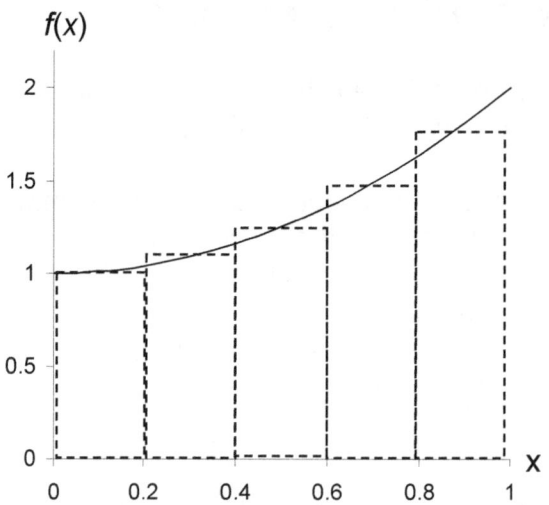

The Riemann sum for this case is expressed below.

$$\sum_{i=1}^{5} 0.2f(0.2i - 0.1) = 1.33$$

This expression is the sum of the areas of all the rectangles shown above. This is an approximation of the area under the curve of the function (and a reasonably accurate one, as well—the actual area is $\frac{4}{3}$).

Generally, the Riemann sum for arbitrary partitioning and selection of the values c_i is the following:

$$\sum_{i=1}^{n} f(c_i) \Delta x_i$$

where c_i is within the closed interval defined by the partition Δx_i.

The **definite integral** is defined as the limit of the Riemann sum as the widths of the partitions Δx_i go to zero (and, consequently, n goes to infinity). Thus, the definite integral can be expressed mathematically as follows:

$$\int_a^b f(x)\,dx = \lim_{\Delta x_m \to 0} \sum_{i=1}^{n} f(c_i)\,\Delta x_i$$

where Δx_m is the width of the largest partition. If the partitioning of the interval is such that each partition has the same width, then the definition can be written as follows:

$$\int_a^b f(x)\,dx = \lim_{\Delta x \to 0} \sum_{i=1}^{n} f(c_i)\,\Delta x$$

Note that $n = \dfrac{b-a}{\Delta x}$ in this case.

The definite integral, therefore, is the area under the curve of $f(x)$ over the interval $[a, b]$. By taking the limit of the Riemann sum, the number of rectangles used to find the area under the curve becomes infinite and, therefore, the error in the result goes to zero since the width of each rectangle becomes infinitesimal.

Since this is the formal definition of a definite integral, it is helpful to understand the process of deriving the **integrals of algebraic functions** based on this definition. The following example illustrates this process using the Riemann sum. The process can be summarized with the following basic steps.

1. Partition the interval into n segments of equal width.
2. Substitute the value of the function into the Riemann sum using the x value at the center of each subinterval.
3. Write the sum in closed form.
4. Take the limit of the result as n approaches infinity.

Example: For $f(x) = x^2$, find the values of the Riemann sum over the interval [0, 1] using n subintervals of equal width, each evaluated at the right endpoint of each subinterval. Find the limit of the Riemann sum.

Take the interval [0, 1] and subdivide it into n subintervals each of length $\frac{1}{n}$.

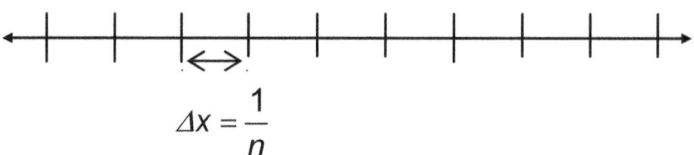

$$\Delta x = \frac{1}{n}$$

The endpoints of the ith subinterval are

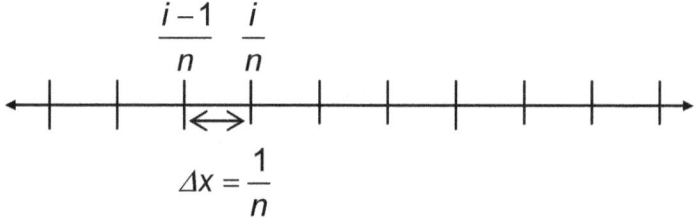

$$\Delta x = \frac{1}{n}$$

Let $x_i = \frac{i}{n}$ be the right endpoint. Draw a line of length $f(x_i) = \left(\frac{i}{n}\right)^2$ at the right-hand endpoint.

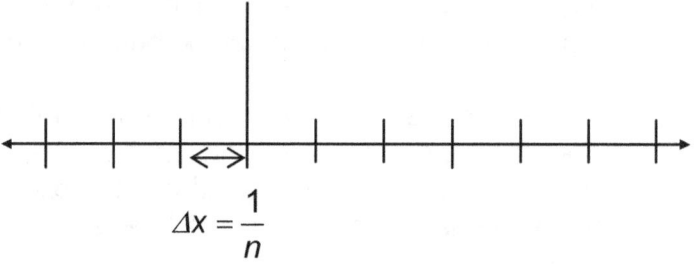

$$\Delta x = \frac{1}{n}$$

Draw a rectangle.

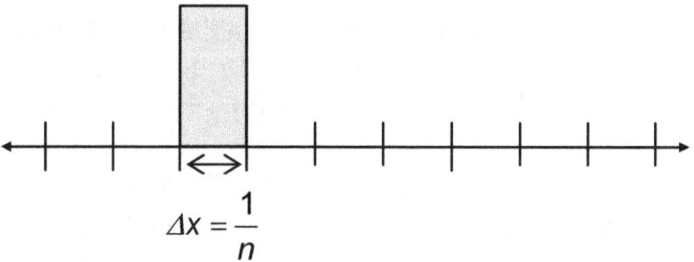

$$\Delta x = \frac{1}{n}$$

The area of this rectangle is $f(x)\Delta x$.

$$f(x)\Delta x = \left(\frac{i}{n}\right)^2 \frac{1}{n} = \frac{i^2}{n^3}$$

Now draw all *n* rectangles (drawing below not to scale).

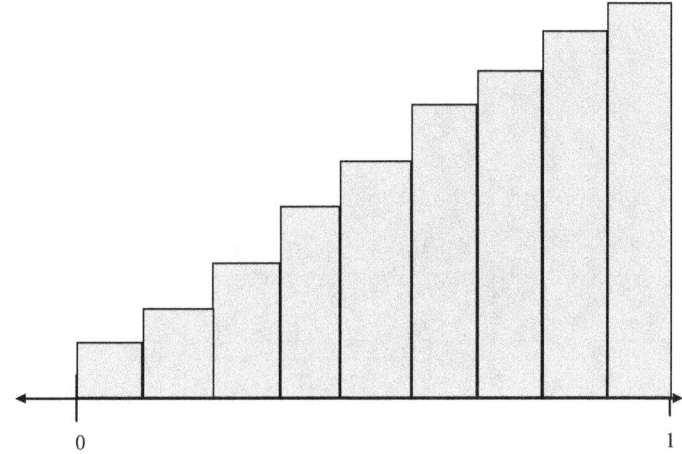

The sum of the area of these rectangles is the following.

$$\sum_{i=1}^{n} \frac{i^2}{n^3} = \frac{1}{n^3} \sum_{i=1}^{n} i^2$$

The sum can be evaluated as follows.

$$\frac{1}{n^3} \sum_{i=1}^{n} i^2 = \frac{1}{n^3} \frac{n(n+1)(2n+1)}{6}$$

This is the Riemann sum for *n* subdivisions of the interval [0, 1].

Finally, to evaluate the integral, take the limit as *n* approaches infinity.

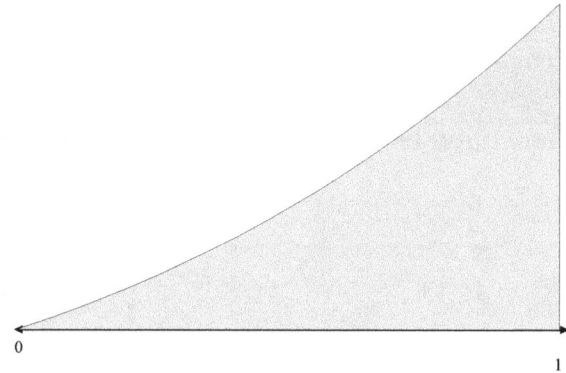

$$\lim_{n\to\infty}\frac{1}{n^3}\frac{n(n+1)(2n+1)}{6} = \frac{1}{6}\lim_{n\to\infty}\frac{2n^3+3n^2+n}{n^3}$$
$$= \frac{1}{6}\lim_{n\to\infty}\left(2+\frac{3}{n}+\frac{1}{n^2}\right) = \frac{1}{3}$$

This is the correct answer. Thus,

$$\int_0^1 x^2 dx = \frac{1}{3}$$

5.4b. Interpret the concept of a definite integral geometrically, numerically, and analytically (e.g., limit of Riemann sums)

Geometrically, the definite integral is the area between the curve of the function $f(x)$ and the x-axis over some specified interval. Since, in general, $f(x)$ is not piecewise linear, the use of rectangles, trapezoids or other polygons (in finite numbers) is not sufficient to accurately calculate this area (unless additional mathematical machinery is brought to bear). For instance, although two triangles can approximate the area under the curve of the function shown in the graph below, they do not do so exactly.

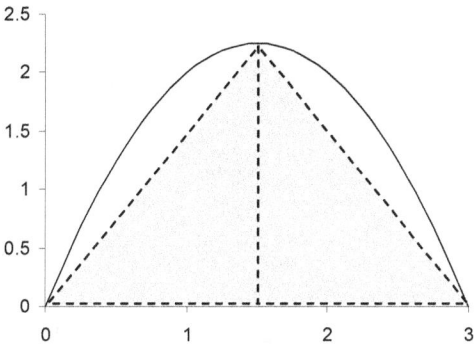

Numerically, the definite integral is an area of a region defined by the product of a height and a width.

$$\int_a^b f(x)\,dx$$

In this case, the height is $f(x)$, and the width is dx. The height is continuously changing, so the width dx is infinitesimally small. Thus, the integral is a calculation of the product of the variable height and the constant width over the interval $[a, b]$.

Analytically, as seen in the previous section, a definite integral is the limit of the Riemann sum as the number of subintervals (n) of a specific width (Δx) approaches infinity. Since it is apparent that larger rectangles generally provide less accuracy in the Riemann sum than do smaller rectangles, taking the limit as n approaches infinity in fact is a matter of increasing the accuracy of the result. In the limit, the Riemann sum is perfectly accurate. This concept is illustrated in the graphs below, where the increasing accuracy of the Riemann sum as n increases is apparent.

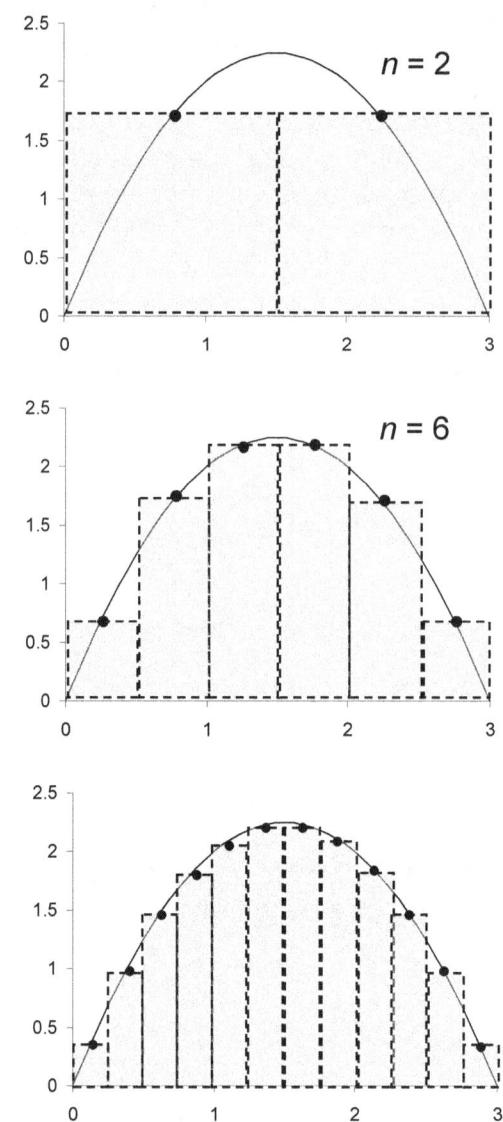

Again, notice how the accuracy of the area estimate using rectangles increases as *n* increases. This is the rationale behind the use of the limit for the Riemann sum, which yields the definite integral.

Thus, the limit of the Riemann sum increases the accuracy of the approximation to the area of a curve. In the limit, the accuracy is infinite. This is to say that the result is equal to the definite integral, which is the exact area under the curve on the specified interval.

$$\int_a^b f(x)\,dx = \lim_{\Delta x_m \to 0} \sum_{i=1}^n f(c_i)\,\Delta x_i$$

5.4c. **Prove the Fundamental Theorem of Calculus, and use it to interpret definite integrals as antiderivatives**

The Fundamental Theorem of Calculus

The Fundamental Theorem of Calculus relates differentiation with definite integration, which is fundamentally defined in terms of the Riemann sum. According to the theorem, definite integration is the inverse of differentiation. The theorem is expressed below for the function $F(x)$, where $f(x) = F'(x)$ and where $f(x)$ is continuous on the interval $[a, b]$.

$$\int_a^b f(x)\,dx = F(b) - F(a)$$

The function $F(x)$ is also called an **antiderivative** of $f(x)$, because the derivative of $F(x)$ is $f(x)$. Based on this theorem, it is clear that integrals can be evaluated without the need of finding the limit of a Riemann sum as long as the antiderivative of a function can be determined. Thus, the key to evaluating definite integrals is knowledge of how to find the antiderivative of a function.

To prove the Fundamental Theoreom of Calculus, it is necessary to look at the integral as a Riemann sum. Divide the interval $[a, b]$ into n equivalent partitions of width Δx, where

$$\Delta x = \frac{b-a}{n}$$

Let the boundaries of each subdivision of the interval be labeled x_i, according to the following definition.

$$a = x_0 < x_1 < x_2 < x_3 < \ldots < x_{n-1} < x_n = b$$

Note that $x_{i+1} - x_i = \Delta x$ for all i. Next, rewrite $F(b) - F(a)$ as follows, by adding and subtracting like terms.

$$F(b) - F(a) = F(x_n) - F(x_{n-1}) + F(x_{n-1}) - F(x_{n-2}) +$$
$$+ F(x_{n-2}) - \ldots - F(x_1) + F(x_1) - F(x_0)$$

This series can be written in the form of a summation.

$$F(b) - F(a) = \sum_{i=1}^{n} \{F(x_i) - F(x_{i-1})\}$$

The Mean Value Theorem can then be applied. There exists some value c_i on the interval (x_{i-1}, x_i) such that

$$F'(c_i) = \frac{F(x_i) - F(x_{i-1})}{x_i - x_{i-1}}$$

(See 5.3 Skill c for more information on the Mean Value Theorem.) But, $F'(c_i)$ is simply f(x) evaluated at c_i and $x_i - x_{i-1}$ is Δx, so

$$f(c_i) = \frac{F(x_i) - F(x_{i-1})}{\Delta x}$$
$$F(x_i) - F(x_{i-1}) = f(c_i)\Delta x$$

Substitute this result into the summation above.

$$F(b) - F(a) = \sum_{i=1}^{n} f(c_i)\Delta x$$

This summation, then, is just a Riemann sum. If the limit as *n* approaches infinity is taken, then this sum becomes a definite integral from *a* to *b*.

$$\lim_{n \to \infty} \{F(b) - F(a)\} = \lim_{n \to \infty} \left\{ \sum_{i=1}^{n} f(c_i)\Delta x \right\}$$
$$F(b) - F(a) = \int_{a}^{b} f(x)dx$$

This proves the Fundamental Theorem of Calculus.

The definite integral can thus be interpreted in terms of antiderivatives. Note that the definite integral for the interval [a, b] is the area under the curve f(x) between x = a and x = b. The antiderivative, F(c), is then the cumulative area under f(x) between x = 0 and x = c. Thus, the difference between the antiderivative evaluated at *b* and the antiderivative evaluated at *a* is the definite integral of f(x) between *a* and *b*.

The example graph below shows a function $f(x)$. The antiderivative $F(x)$ evaluated at $x = 1$ is the solid shaded area; the antiderivative evaluated at $x = 2$ is the striped area. The difference $F(2) - F(1)$ is the difference between the two areas (the non-overlapping striped region).

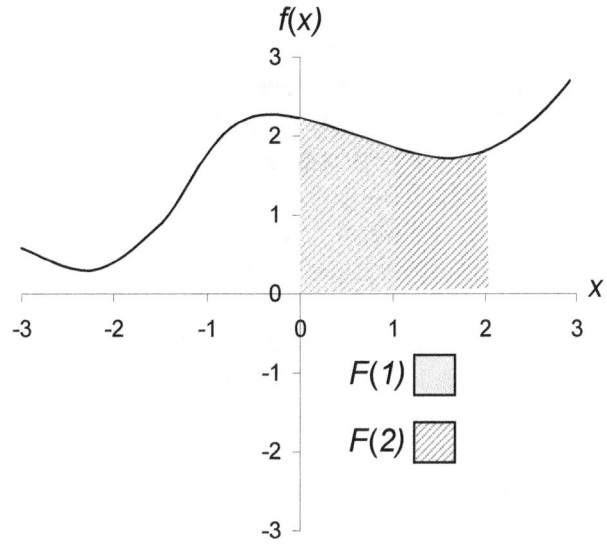

5.4d. **Apply the concept of integrals to compute the length of curves and the areas and volumes of geometric figures**

Taking the integral of a function and evaluating it over some interval on x provides the total **area under the curve** (or, more formally, the **area bounded by the curve and the x-axis**). Thus, the area of geometric figures can be determined when the figure can be cast as a function or set of functions in the coordinate plane. Remember, though, that regions above the x-axis have "positive" area and regions below the x-axis have "negative" area. It is necessary to account for these positive and negative values when finding the area under curves. The boundaries between positive and negative regions are delineated by the roots of the function. Follow these steps to find the total area under the curve.

1. Determine the interval or intervals on which the area under the curve is to be found. If portions of the function are negative, a given interval may need to be divided appropriately if all areas are to be considered positive.
2. Integrate the function.
3. Evaluate the integral once for each interval.
4. If any of the intervals evaluates to a negative number, reverse the sign (equivalently, take the absolute value of each integral).
5. Add the value of all the integral to get the area under the curve.

Example: Find the area under the following function on the given interval: $f(x) = \sin x$; $[0, 2\pi]$.

First, find the roots of the function on the interval.

$$f(x) = \sin x = 0$$
$$x = 0, \pi$$

The function sin x is positive over [0, π] (since $\sin \frac{\pi}{2} = 1$) and negative over [π, 2π] (since $\sin \frac{3\pi}{2} = -1$). Use these intervals for the integration to find the area A under the curve.

$$A = \int_0^{2\pi} |\sin x| dx = \left| \int_0^{\pi} \sin x \, dx \right| + \left| \int_{\pi}^{2\pi} \sin x \, dx \right|$$

$$A = \left| -\cos x \Big|_0^{\pi} \right| + \left| -\cos x \Big|_{\pi}^{2\pi} \right| = \left| -\cos \pi + \cos 0 \right| + \left| -\cos 2\pi + \cos \pi \right|$$

$$A = |1 + 1| + |-1 - 1| = 2 + 2 = 4$$

Thus, the total area under the curve of $f(x) = \sin x$ on the interval $[0, 2\pi]$ is 4 square units.

Finding the **area between two curves** is similar to finding the area under one curve. The general process involves integrating the absolute value of the difference between the two functions over the interval of interest. In some instances, it is necessary to find the intervals over which the difference is positive and over which the difference is negative. For the former, the integral can simply be taken with no modifications; for the latter, however, the result of the integral must be negated. To find the points where the difference between the functions changes from positive to negative (or vice versa), simply set the functions equal to each other and solve. Take the absolute value of each portion of the integral (that is, each integral over a portion of the interval) and add all the parts. This yields the total area between the curves.

Example: Find the area of the regions bounded by the two functions on the indicated interval: $f(x) = x + 2$ and $g(x) = x^2$ on [–2, 3].

The integral of interest is the following:

$$\int_{-2}^{3} |f(x) - g(x)| \, dx$$

To eliminate the need to use the absolute value notation inside the integral, find the values for which $f(x) = g(x)$.

$$f(x) = x + 2 = g(x) = x^2$$
$$x^2 - x - 2 = 0 = (x-2)(x+1)$$

The functions are then equal at $x = -1$ and $x = 2$. Perform the integration over the intervals defined by these values.

$$\int_{-2}^{3} |f(x) - g(x)| \, dx = \left| \int_{-2}^{-1} f(x) - g(x) \, dx \right| + \left| \int_{-1}^{2} f(x) - g(x) \, dx \right| + \left| \int_{2}^{3} f(x) - g(x) \, dx \right|$$

The antiderivative of $f(x)-g(x)$ is the following (ignoring the constant of integration).

$$\int [f(x)-g(x)]dx = \int (x+2-x^2)dx = \frac{x^2}{2}+2x-\frac{x^3}{3}$$

Evaluate over the intervals above.

$$\int_{-2}^{3}|f(x)-g(x)|dx = \left|\left[\frac{x^2}{2}+2x-\frac{x^3}{3}\right]_{-2}^{-1}\right| + \left|\left[\frac{x^2}{2}+2x-\frac{x^3}{3}\right]_{-1}^{2}\right| + \left|\left[\frac{x^2}{2}+2x-\frac{x^3}{3}\right]_{2}^{3}\right|$$

$$\left|\left[\frac{x^2}{2}+2x-\frac{x^3}{3}\right]_{-2}^{-1}\right| = \left|\left(\frac{1}{2}-2+\frac{1}{3}\right)-\left(\frac{4}{2}-4+\frac{8}{3}\right)\right| = \left|-\frac{7}{6}-\frac{2}{3}\right| = \frac{11}{6}$$

$$\left|\left[\frac{x^2}{2}+2x-\frac{x^3}{3}\right]_{-1}^{2}\right| = \left|\left(\frac{4}{2}+4-\frac{8}{3}\right)-\left(\frac{1}{2}-2+\frac{1}{3}\right)\right| = \left|\frac{10}{3}+\frac{7}{6}\right| = \frac{27}{6}$$

$$\left|\left[\frac{x^2}{2}+2x-\frac{x^3}{3}\right]_{2}^{3}\right| = \left|\left(\frac{9}{2}+6-\frac{27}{3}\right)-\left(\frac{4}{2}+4-\frac{8}{3}\right)\right| = \left|\frac{3}{2}-\frac{10}{3}\right| = \frac{11}{6}$$

The sum of these individual parts is $\frac{49}{6}$.

An area, bounded by a curve (or curves), that is revolved about a line is called a **solid of revolution**. To find the volume of such a solid, the **disc method** (called the **washer method** if the solid has an empty interior of some form) works in most instances. Imagine slicing through the solid perpendicular to the line of revolution. The cross section should resemble either a disc or a washer. The washer method involves finding the sum of the volumes of all "washers" that compose the solid, using the following general formula:

$$V = \pi(r_1^2 - r_2^2)t$$

where V is the volume of the washer, r_1 and r_2 are the interior and exterior radii and t is the thickness of the washer.

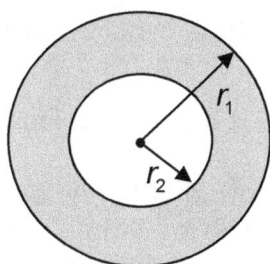

Depending on the situation, the radius is the distance from the line of revolution to the curve; or if there are two curves involved, the radius is the difference between the two functions. The thickness is dx if the line of revolution is parallel to the x-axis and dy if the line of revolution is parallel to the y-axis. The integral is then the following, where dV is the differential volume of a washer.

$$\int dV = \int \pi \left(r_1^2 - r_2^2 \right) dt$$
$$V = \pi \int \left(r_1^2 - r_2^2 \right) dt$$

It is assumed here that r_1 is the outer radius and r_2 is the inner radius. For the disc method, where only one radius is needed, $r_2 = 0$.

Example: Find the volume of the solid of revolution made by revolving $f(x) = 9 - x^2$ about the x axis on the interval $[0, 4]$.

This problem can be solved using the disc method. First, note that the radius is $9 - x^2$ and the thickness of the disc is dx. Write the appropriate integral as follows.

$$V = \pi \int_0^4 (9 - x^2)^2 \, dx$$

Next, expand the radius term and evaluate the integral.

$$V = \pi \int_0^4 \left(81 - 18x^2 + x^4 \right) dx$$

$$V = \pi \left[81x - \frac{18}{3}x^3 + \frac{1}{5}x^5 \right]_0^4$$

$$V = \pi \left[81(4) - \frac{18}{3}(4)^3 + \frac{1}{5}(4)^5 \right]$$

$$V = \pi[324 - 384 + 204.8] = 144.8\pi \approx 454.9$$

The volume is thus approximately 454.9 cubic units.

The **arc length** of a curve is another useful application of integration. The arc length is the distance traversed by a curve over a given interval. Geometrically, the distance d between two points (x_1, y_1) and (x_2, y_2) is given by the following formula.

$$d = \sqrt{(x_2 - x_1)^2 + (y_2 - y_1)^2}$$

If the points are only an infinitesimal distance apart (ds, which is the differential arc length), then the above expression can be written as follows in differential form.

$$ds = \sqrt{dx^2 + dy^2}$$

Factor out the dx term:

$$ds = \sqrt{1 + \left(\frac{dy}{dx}\right)^2} \, dx$$

But $\frac{dy}{dx}$ is simply the derivative of a function $y(x)$ (which can be expressed as $f(x)$ instead). Thus, the integral of the above expression over the interval $[a, b]$ yields the formula for the arc length.

$$\int ds = s = \int_a^b \sqrt{1 + [f'(x)]^2} \, dx$$

TEACHER CERTIFICATION STUDY GUIDE

Example: Find the distance traversed by the function $f(x) = \ln(\cos x)$ on the interval $\left[-\dfrac{\pi}{4}, \dfrac{\pi}{4}\right]$.

Use the formula for arc length s, applying trigonometric identities as appropriate.

$$s = \int \sqrt{1 + \left[\dfrac{d}{dx}\ln(\cos x)\right]^2} = \int \sqrt{1 + \left[\dfrac{\sin x}{\cos x}\right]^2}\, dx$$

$$s = \int \sqrt{1 + [\tan x]^2}\, dx = \int \sqrt{1 + \tan^2 x}\, dx = \int \sqrt{\sec^2 x}\, dx$$

$$s = \int \sqrt{1 + [\tan x]^2}\, dx = \int \sqrt{1 + \tan^2 x}\, dx = \int \sec x\, dx$$

Evaluate the integral over the limits of integration.

$$s = \int_{-\pi/4}^{\pi/4} \sec x\, dx = \ln(\sec x + \tan x)\Big|_{-\pi/4}^{\pi/4}$$

$$s = \ln\left(\sec\dfrac{\pi}{4} + \tan\dfrac{\pi}{4}\right) - \ln\left(\sec\left[-\dfrac{\pi}{4}\right] + \tan\left[\dfrac{\pi}{4}\right]\right)$$

$$s = \ln(\sqrt{2} + 1) - \ln(\sqrt{2} - 1) \approx 1.763$$

The result is approximately 1.763 units.

SKILL 5.5 SEQUENCES AND SERIES

5.5a. Derive and apply the formulas for the sums of finite arithmetic series and finite and infinite geometric series (e.g., express repeating decimals as a rational number)

A finite series of numbers where the difference between successive terms is constant is called an **arithmetic series**. An arithmetic series with n terms can be expressed as follows, where a and d are constants. (The constant a is the first term, and d is the difference between successive terms.)

$$a+(a+d)+(a+2d)+(a+3d)+\ldots(a+[n-1]d)$$

To derive the general formula, examine the series sum for several small values of n.

n	Sum
1	a
2	$2a + d$
3	$3a + 3d$
4	$4a + 6d$
5	$5a + 10d$
6	$6a + 15d$
$\vdots$	$\vdots$
n	$na + d \sum_{i=1}^{n-1} i$

The result in the table for n terms is found by examining the pattern of the previous series. All that is necessary, then, is to determine a closed expression for the summation. By inspection, it can be seen that the product of n and $(n-1)$, divided by 2, is the expression for the sum of $1 + 2 + 3 + 4 + 5 + \ldots + n$. Then:

$$\sum_{i=1}^{n} i = \frac{1}{2}n(n+1)$$

Often times, closed formulas for series such as the arithmetic series must be found by inspection in this manner, as a more rigorous derivation is difficult. The result can be proven using mathematical induction, however, as is shown in Section 3.1, Skill b.

Substitute this result into the arithmetic series expression.

$$na + d\sum_{i=1}^{n-1} i = na + d\frac{1}{2}(n-1)(n)$$

Simplify the result.

$$na + d\sum_{i=1}^{n-1} i = na + n\frac{d}{2}(n-1)$$

$$na + d\sum_{i=1}^{n-1} i = n\left[a + \frac{d}{2}(n-1)\right]$$

$$na + d\sum_{i=1}^{n-1} i = \frac{1}{2}n\left[2a + d(n-1)\right]$$

Thus,

$$a + (a+d) + (a+2d) + \ldots (a + [n-1]d) = \frac{1}{2}n\left[2a + d(n-1)\right]$$

This is the closed expression for an arithmetic series.

<u>Example</u>: Calculate the sum of the series 1 + 5 + 9 + ... + 57.

This is an arithmetic series, as the difference between successive terms, d, is constant ($d = 4$). Determine the total number of terms by subtracting the first term from the last term, dividing by d and adding 1.

$$n = \frac{57-1}{4} + 1 = \frac{56}{4} + 1 = 14 + 1 = 15$$

That this approach works can be seen by testing simple examples. For instance, if the series is 1 + 5 + 9, then

$$n = \frac{9-1}{4} + 1 = \frac{8}{4} + 1 = 2 + 1 = 3$$

There are indeed 3 terms in this simple series. Next, apply the formula, noting that $a = 1$.

$$\frac{1}{2}n\left[2a + d(n-1)\right] = \frac{1}{2}(15)\left[2(1) + (4)(15-1)\right]$$

$$= \frac{15}{2}[2+4(14)] = \frac{15}{2}(58) = 435$$

Thus, the answer is 435.

A **geometric series** is a series whose successive terms are related by a common factor (rather than the common difference of the arithmetic series). Assuming a is the first term of the series and r is the common factor, the general n-term geometric series can be written as follows.

$$a + ar + ar^2 + ar^3 + \ldots + ar^{n-1}$$

The geometric series can also be written using sum notation.

$$a + ar + ar^2 + \ldots + ar^{n-1} = \sum_{i=0}^{n-1} ar^i$$

To derive the closed-form expression for this finite series, let the sum for n terms be defined as S_n. Multiply S_n by r.

$$S_n = a + ar + ar^2 + \ldots + ar^{n-1}$$
$$rS_n = ar + ar^2 + ar^3 + \ldots + ar^n$$

Note that if a is added to this new series, the result is the sum S_{n+1}, which has $n + 1$ terms.

$$a + rS_n = a + ar + ar^2 + ar^3 + \ldots + ar^n = S_{n+1}$$

But S_{n+1} is simply $S_n + ar^n$, so the above expression can be written solely in terms of S_n.

$$a + rS_n = S_{n+1} = S_n + ar^n$$

Rearrange the result to obtain a simple formula for the geometric series.

$$a + rS_n = S_n + ar^n$$
$$a - ar^n = S_n - rS_n$$
$$a(1 - r^n) = S_n(1 - r)$$

$$S_n = a\frac{1-r^n}{1-r}$$

The infinite geometric series is the limit of S_n as n approaches infinity.

$$a + ar + ar^2 + \ldots = \lim_{n \to \infty} a\frac{1-r^n}{1-r}$$

Three cases are of interest: $r \geq 1$, $r \leq -1$ and $-1 < r < 1$. To determine the limit in each case, first apply L'Hopital's rule.

$$\lim_{n \to \infty} a\frac{1-r^n}{1-r} = a \lim_{n \to \infty} \frac{\frac{d}{dr}(1-r^n)}{\frac{d}{dr}(1-r)} = a \lim_{n \to \infty} \frac{-nr^{n-1}}{-1}$$

$$\lim_{n \to \infty} a\frac{1-r^n}{1-r} = a \lim_{n \to \infty} nr^{n-1}$$

Thus, it can be seen that if r is either 1 or –1, the limit goes to infinity due to the factor n. The same reasoning applies if r is greater than 1 or less than –1. For $-1 < r < 1$, rearrange the original form of the limit.

$$\lim_{n \to \infty} a\frac{1-r^n}{1-r} = a\frac{1-r^\infty}{1-r}$$

Since the magnitude of r is less than 1, r^∞ must be zero. This yields a closed form for the infinite geometric series, which converges only if $-1 < r < 1$.

$$a + ar + ar^2 + \ldots = \frac{a}{1-r}$$

Example: Evaluate the following series: $1 + \frac{1}{2} + \frac{1}{4} + \frac{1}{8} + \ldots$

Note that this series is an infinite geometric series with $a = 1$ and $r = \frac{1}{2}$ (or 0.5). Use the formula to evaluate the series.

$$1 + \frac{1}{2} + \frac{1}{4} + \frac{1}{8} + \ldots = \frac{a}{1-r} = \frac{1}{1-0.5} = \frac{1}{0.5} = 2$$

The answer is thus 2.

The infinite geometric series can be used to **express repeating decimals as a rational number**. Consider some repeating decimal D where a particular sequence of numbers, d, repeats continually.

$$D = 0.dddddddd\ldots$$

Here, d could be a single digit (such as 4) or a string of several digits (such as 9392). Thus, D might be 0.4444… or it might be 0.939293929392…. Next, write the decimal as the sum of decimals involving just one instance of d. The number of necessary zeros depends on the number of digits in d. Thus, if d has one digit (for instance, if d is 4),

$$D = 0.d + 0.0d + 0.00d + \ldots$$

If d has two digits, however, then

$$D = 0.d + 0.00d + 0.0000d + \ldots$$

The same pattern applies for values of d with more digits. Note that D can be expressed as an infinite geometric series.

$$D = \frac{d}{10} + \frac{d}{10^2} + \frac{d}{10^3} + \ldots$$

$$D = d\left[\frac{1}{10} + \frac{1}{10^2} + \frac{1}{10^3} + \ldots\right]$$

$$D = \frac{d}{10}\left[1 + \left(\frac{1}{10}\right) + \left(\frac{1}{10}\right)^2 + \ldots\right]$$

This is simply the geometric series with $a = \frac{d}{10}$ and $r = \frac{1}{10}$ (or 0.1). Use the formula to find a simple expression for the infinite series.

$$D = \frac{d}{10}\left[1 + \left(\frac{1}{10}\right) + \left(\frac{1}{10}\right)^2 + \ldots\right] = \frac{d}{10}\left(\frac{1}{1-0.1}\right)$$

$$D = \frac{d}{10}\left(\frac{1}{0.9}\right) = \frac{d}{9}$$

MATHEMATICS

Thus, the following decimals can be simplified to rational numbers:

$$0.111... = \frac{1}{9}$$
$$0.222... = \frac{2}{9}$$

and so on.

The process of writing a repeating decimal as a rational number is summarized in the following steps.

1. Find the smallest repeating unit.
2. Write the decimal as the sum of decimals that include a single instance of the repeating unit.
3. Write the sum as an infinite geometric series.
4. Use the formula to evaluate the series.
5. Write the resulting fraction in simplest form.

Example: Write $0.\overline{132}$ as a rational number.

The fundamental repeating unit for this decimal is 132. Write the decimal as a sum of decimals that each contain a single instance of this unit.

$$0.132132\overline{132} = 0.132 + 0.000132 + 0.000000132 + ...$$

Write this series in a more familiar form.

$$0.\overline{132} = \frac{132}{1000} + \frac{132}{1000^2} + \frac{132}{1000^3} + ...$$

This is simply a geometric series with $a = 0.132$ and $r = 0.001$. Use the formula to evaluate the series.

$$0.\overline{132} = \frac{132}{1000}\left[1 + \left(\frac{1}{1000}\right) + \left(\frac{1}{1000}\right)^2 + \ldots\right]$$

$$0.\overline{132} = 0.132\left(\frac{1}{1-0.001}\right) = \frac{0.132}{0.999} = \frac{132}{999}$$

Finally, write the fraction in simplest form.

$$0.\overline{132} = \frac{132}{999} = \frac{44}{333}$$

This is the final result.

5.5b. **Determine convergence of a given sequence or series using standard techniques (e.g., Ratio, Comparison, Integral Tests)**

Convergence of sequences

Sequences and series may converge to a finite number or they may diverge, either through approaching infinity or through oscillation. Determining the convergence of a sequence or series con be accomplished through several means.

Let a sequence of numbers be expressed as $\{a_n\}$, where a_n is the nth term of the sequence. The limit L of the sequence is then the following:

$$\lim_{n \to \infty} a_n = L$$

If L is a finite value, then the sequence $\{a_n\}$ converges; otherwise, the sequence diverges. The limit L exists (and the sequence converges) if, for every number $\varepsilon > 0$, there is a value C such that $|a_n - L| < \varepsilon$ for all $n > C$.

The convergence of a sequence can be determined using the Squeeze Theorem. This theorem states that if the limit of two sequences $\{a_n\}$ and $\{b_n\}$ is L, or

$$\lim_{n \to \infty} a_n = \lim_{n \to \infty} b_n = L$$

then the convergence of a sequence $\{c_n\}$ can be determined if it is the case that

$$a_n \leq c_n \leq b_n$$

for all $n > N$. (Here, N is some integer.) In such a case, the term c_n must (for $n > N$) be between the terms a_n and b_n. As a result, the limit of the sequence $\{c_n\}$ is "squeezed" to L by the sequences $\{a_n\}$ and $\{b_n\}$.

Example: Determine the limit of the sequence $\{c_n\} = \left(4e^{-2n} \sin n\right)$, if it exists.

In this case, take the limit of the expression for $\{c_n\}$ as n approaches infinity.

$$\lim_{n \to \infty} c_n = \lim_{n \to \infty} 4e^{-2n} \sin n$$

$$\lim_{n \to \infty} c_n = \left(\lim_{n \to \infty} 4e^{-2n}\right)\left(\lim_{n \to \infty} \sin n\right)$$

$$\lim_{n \to \infty} c_n = \left(4e^{-\infty}\right)\left(\lim_{n \to \infty} \sin n\right) = 0\left(\lim_{n \to \infty} \sin n\right)$$

Although the second factor cannot be evaluated in any definite sense, it is clear that the range of the sine function is [−1, 1]. Thus, the limit of sin n cannot exceed either of these boundary values. The limit, then, is simply zero.

$$\lim_{n \to \infty} c_n = 0$$

Convergence of series

The same type of approach can be applied to series. A series S_n is defined as the sum $a_1 + a_2 + a_3 + \ldots a_n$. If the series is infinite (that is, $n = \infty$), then it is simply denoted as S and is equal to the sum $a_1 + a_2 + a_3 + \ldots$. The determination of convergence or divergence for a series is slightly more complex than that for a sequence, but it is the case that the sequence $\{a_n\}$ must have a limit of zero if the series S_n is to converge. This preliminary test does not ensure that a series converges, but it can be used to prove that a series diverges (if $\lim_{n \to \infty} a_n = 0$, then S_n diverges).

Several tests can be used to determine whether a particular series converges or diverges. These tests include the integral test, the direct comparison test and the ratio test.

Integral test

Suppose that $f(x)$ is a positive, continuous, decreasing function for $x \geq 1$ and that $f(n) = a_n$. Then:

1. If $\int_1^\infty f(x)\,dx$ is convergent, so is $\sum_{n=1}^{\infty} a_n$
2. If $\int_1^\infty f(x)\,dx$ is divergent, so is $\sum_{n=1}^{\infty} a_n$

Thus, if a function can be found to "bound" the series in the above manner, an integral can be used to determine the convergence of the series.

Direct comparison test

Given two sequences a_n and b_n such that $0 \leq a_n \leq b_n$ for all n, then the following conclusions can be drawn:

1. $\sum_{n=1}^{\infty} a_n$ converges if $\sum_{n=1}^{\infty} b_n$ converges
2. $\sum_{n=1}^{\infty} b_n$ diverges if $\sum_{n=1}^{\infty} a_n$ diverges

Ratio test

For a series $\sum a_n$ where a_n are nonzero terms, the following conclusions can be drawn:

1. If $\lim_{n \to \infty} \left| \frac{a_{n+1}}{a_n} \right| > 1$, then the series diverges
2. If $\lim_{n \to \infty} \left| \frac{a_{n+1}}{a_n} \right| < 1$, then the series converges
3. If $\lim_{n \to \infty} \left| \frac{a_{n+1}}{a_n} \right| = 1$, then no conclusion can be drawn

Example: Determine if the series $\sum_{n=1}^{\infty} \frac{1}{n^2}$ converges.

Use the integral test, where $f(x) = \frac{1}{x^2}$. Calculate the integral:

$$\int_1^{\infty} \frac{1}{x^2} dx = -\frac{1}{x}\Big|_1^{\infty} = \left(-\frac{1}{\infty}\right) - \left(-\frac{1}{1}\right) = 0 + 1 = 1$$

Therefore, since the integral converges, so does the series $\sum_{n=1}^{\infty} \frac{1}{n^2}$.

5.5c. **Calculate Taylor series and Taylor polynomials of basic functions**

Given a function $f(x)$ whose first n derivatives exist, the **Taylor polynomial** $P_n(x)$ of degree n is defined for the function $f(x)$ about the value c as the following:

$$P_n(x) = f(c) + f'(c)(x-c) + \frac{f''(c)(x-c)^2}{2!} + \ldots + \frac{f^{(n)}(c)(x-c)^n}{n!}$$

where $f^{(n)}(c)$ denotes the nth derivative of the function f evaluated at $x = c$. The value c is chosen arbitrarily (subject to the constraint that the necessary derivatives exist at this point), and simply signifies the x value of a point at which the function f and the Taylor polynomial P_n intersect.

The **Taylor series** associated with f about c is simply the Taylor polynomial $P_n(x)$ for f about c where $n \to \infty$. More precisely, the Taylor series expansion is the following:

$$f(x) = \sum_{n=0}^{\infty} \frac{f^{(n)}(c)(x-c)^n}{n!}$$

It is assumed that the Taylor series only exists if all n derivatives of f exist (that is, an infinite number of derivatives of f exist).

If $c = 0$, then the Taylor polynomial and Taylor series are known respectively as the Maclaurin polynomial and Maclaurin series.

The Taylor (or Maclaurin) series and polynomial are useful for approximating functions or for writing them in a form that may be more amenable to manipulation in certain circumstances. For instance, the Taylor polynomial of a small number of terms may be useful for approximating highly complex functions in order to assist with analytical problem solving.

Example: Calculate the Taylor polynomial of order 3 for the function $f(x) = e^x$ about $x = 2$. Also write the corresponding Maclaurin polynomial.

First, determine the first three derivatives of f. In this case, they are all equal to e^x. Then, write the Taylor polynomial.

$$P_3(x) = e^2 + e^2(x-2) + \frac{e^2(x-2)^2}{2!} + \frac{e^2(x-2)^3}{3!}$$

Simplify the result.

$$P_3(x) = e^2 + e^2(x-2) + \frac{1}{2}e^2(x-2)^2 + \frac{1}{6}e^2(x-2)^3$$

$$P_3(x) = e^2\left[1 + (x-2) + \frac{1}{2}(x-2)^2 + \frac{1}{6}(x-2)^3\right]$$

The corresponding Maclaurin polynomial can be found by writing the Taylor polynomial for $c = 0$. The result is shown below.

$$P_3(x) = 1 + x + \frac{x^2}{2} + \frac{x^3}{6}$$

<u>Example</u>: Write the Taylor series for the function $f(x) = \sin x$ about $x = \pi$.

The Taylor series can be expressed succinctly as follows.

$$f(x) = \sum_{n=0}^{\infty} \frac{f^{(n)}(c)(x-\pi)^n}{n!}$$

Note the following pattern in the derivatives of f.

$$f^{(1)}(x) = \cos x$$
$$f^{(2)}(x) = -\sin x$$
$$f^{(3)}(x) = -\cos x$$
$$f^{(4)}(x) = \sin x$$

The pattern then repeats from this point. Note, however, that the nth derivative (for even n) evaluated at $x = \pi$ is zero. For odd n, the nth derivative evaluated at $x = \pi$ alternates between -1 and 1.

$$f^{(1)}(\pi) = -1$$
$$f^{(2)}(\pi) = 0$$
$$f^{(3)}(\pi) = 1$$
$$f^{(4)}(\pi) = 0$$

Then, rewrite the Taylor series to include only odd n values.

$$f(x) = \sum_{n=0}^{\infty} \frac{f^{(2n+1)}(c)(x-\pi)^{2n+1}}{(2n+1)!}$$

The derivatives can be written in terms of a power of -1.

$$f(x) = \sum_{n=0}^{\infty} \frac{(-1)^{n+1}(x-\pi)^{2n+1}}{(2n+1)!}$$

This can also be expanded to illustrate the first few terms.

$$f(x) = -(x-\pi) + \frac{1}{3!}(x-\pi)^3 - \frac{1}{5!}(x-\pi)^5 + \ldots$$

COMPETENCY 6.0 HISTORY OF MATHEMATICS

SKILL 6.1 CHRONOLOGICAL AND TOPICAL DEVELOPMENT OF MATHEMATICS

6.1a. Demonstrate understanding of the development of mathematics, its cultural connections, and its contributions to society

The development of mathematics has been ongoing throughout history. The primary early uses of mathematics were for astronomy, architecture, trading and taxation. The early history of mathematics originated in Mesopotamia (Sumeria and Babylon), Egypt, Greece and Rome. Throughout the history of humanity, every culture, ethnicity and gender has contributed to the field of mathematics (see Skill 6.1b) and, thereby, to society in general.

The contributions of mathematics to society are too numerous to mention in totality. Its contributions to such diverse fields as economics, physics, sociology, management, medicine, astronomy and psychology are manifold. Present-day contributions include development of algorithms that can ease Internet traffic congestion while increasing the rate at which data is transmitted, development of graph theory for applications in expanding the Internet, robotic vision systems and communication networks. High-level mathematics has revolutionized economics with set theory and axiomatic proofs. The documentation of a mathematical model of gasoline spray has been used to cut back on car emissions. For psychologists, mathematics (particularly statistics) has been and still is a crucial tool for quantifying and analyzing findings. Mathematics was also a crucial tool in creating the breakthrough in human genome research through the development of computational analysis.

6.1b. **Demonstrate understanding of the historical development of mathematics, including the contributions of diverse populations as determined by race, ethnicity, culture, geography, and gender**

Noted mathematicians from early times include Pythagoras (born 580 B.C.) and Theano (the wife of Pythagoras who was born 546 B.C.), who was a mathematician and physician who wrote the significant piece on the principle of the "Golden Mean." Euclid (300 B.C.) is considered the father of geometry; Archimedes (born 287 B.C.) made the first real progress on the estimation of π, and Apollonius and Ptolemy (85 A.D.) also made significant contributions to the development of mathematics.

During the 3rd century in China, Tsu Ch'ung-Chih estimated π as Archimedes did, using circumscribed and inscribed polygons. In India, Brahmagupta made valuable contributions to geometry during the 6th century A.D., and Arabs played an important role in preserving the work of the Greeks through translations and expanding that knowledge.

Archeological digs in Babylonia and Greece have uncovered counting boards. These include the Chinese abacus, whose current form dates from approximately 1200 AD. Prior to the development of the concept of zero, a counting board or abacus was the common method used for all types of calculations. In fact, the abacus is still taught in Asian schools and is used by some Asian proprietors. Blind children learn to use the abacus, which is an equivalent method of learning basic mathematical calculations.

Islamic culture from the 6th through 12th centuries drew knowledge from areas ranging from Africa and Spain to India. Al-Khowarizmi introduced Hindu numerals to the West for the first time during the 9th century, and wrote a significant article on algebra. At the beginning of the 15th century, notable Muslim mathematician Al-Kashi wrote the book Key to Arithmetic, in which he used decimals instead of fractions. Fibonacci made important contributions to algebra and geometry during the 1200's.

It was after the Renaissance era, however, that some of the most significant contributions were made (during the 17th century). Newton, along with Leibniz, developed calculus, and Descartes formulated analytical geometry. Maria Gaetana Agnesi is known for the "Witch of Agnesi": the modern version of the curve called the Cartesian equation. Also during this period, John Napier developed a theory of logarithms and Pascal and Fermat broadened knowledge of number theory. The 18th century saw contributions by Gauss in arithmetic, algebra and number theory. Gauss insisted that every area of mathematics must apply rigorous proofs, and this influenced Cauchy in the 19th century to develop a more comprehensible theory of limits, the definitive integral, continuity and the derivative. David Hilbert laid the foundations of geometry in the 19th century.

During the 20th century, increased abstract mathematics broadened the definitions of the operations of systems so that areas of topology, algebra and geometry are connected. There are present-day individuals who have made significant contributions to the field of mathematics. David Blackwell was the first African-American to be named to the National Academy of Sciences, and he won the von Neumann Theory Prize in 1979 for his contributions to the field of statistics. African-American Etta Falconer (1933 – 2002) received numerous awards and recognitions (from 1967 to 1995) during her lifetime for her contributions to furthering the opportunities for minorities and women in the fields of mathematics and science. Margaret Wright is well known in such fields as linear algebra and numerical and scientific computing. She has received several awards recognizing her contributions to mathematics. Sijue Wu received two awards in 2001 for her part in finding a solution to a long-standing problem in the water-wave equation.

This mix of cultures, gender and ethnicities have culminated in substantial developments in many areas of mathematics, including algebra, our current numbering system, geometry, trigonometry, calculus, statistics and discrete mathematics.

TEACHER CERTIFICATION STUDY GUIDE

CONSTRUCTED-RESPONSE EXAMPLES

Exercise: Interpreting Slope as a Rate of Change
Connection: Social Sciences/Geography

Real-life Application: Slope is often used to describe a constant or average rate of change. These problems usually involve units of measure such as miles per hour or dollars per year.

Problem:

The town of Verdant Slopes has been experiencing a boom in population growth. By the year 2000, the population had grown to 45,000, and by 2005, the population had reached 60,000.

Communicating about Algebra:

a. Using the formula for slope as a model, find the average rate of change in population growth, expressing your answer in people per year.

Extension:

b. Using the average rate of change determined in a., predict the population of Verdant Slopes in the year 2010.

Solution:

a. *Let t represent the time and p represent population growth. The two observances are represented by (t_1, p_1) and (t_2, p_2).*

1st observance = (t_1, p_1) = (2000, 45000)
2nd observance = (t_2, p_2) = (2005, 60000)

Use the formula for slope to find the average rate of change.

$$\text{Rate of change} = \frac{p_2 - p_1}{t_2 - t_1}$$

Substitute values.

$$= \frac{60000 - 45000}{2005 - 2000}$$

Simplify.

$$=\frac{15000}{5}=3000\,people/year$$

The average rate of change in population growth for Verdant Slopes between the years 2000 and 2005 was 3000 people/year.

b.
$$3000\,people/year \times 5\,years = 15000\,people$$
$$60000\,people + 15000\,people = 75000\,people$$

At a continuing average rate of growth of 3000 people/year, the population of Verdant Slopes could be expected to reach 75,000 by the year 2010.

Exercise:

(a) Find the midpoint between (5, 2) and (-13, 4).

Using the Midpoint Formula:

$$\left(\frac{x_1+x_2}{2},\frac{y_1+y_2}{2}\right)=\left(\frac{5+(-13)}{2},\frac{2+4}{2}\right)=\left(\frac{-8}{2},\frac{6}{2}\right)=(-4,3)$$

(b) Find the value of x_1 so that (-3, 5) is the midpoint between (x_1, 6) and (-2, 4)

Using the Midpoint Formula:

$$(-3, 5) = \left(\frac{x_1+x_2}{2},\frac{y_1+y_2}{2}\right)$$

$$=\left(\frac{x_1+(-2)}{2},\frac{6+4}{2}\right)$$

$$=\left(\frac{x_1-2}{2},\frac{10}{2}\right)$$

$$=\left(\frac{x_1-2}{2},5\right)$$

Separate out the x value to determine x_1.

$$-3 = \frac{x_1 - 2}{2}$$
$$-6 = x_1 - 2$$
$$-4 = x_1$$

c) **Is $y = 3x - 6$ a bisector of the line segment with endpoints at (2, 4) and (8, -1)?**

Find the midpoint of the line segment and then see if the midpoint is a point on the given line. Using the Midpoint Formula:

$$P = \left(\frac{2+8}{2}, \frac{4+(-1)}{2}\right) = \left(\frac{10}{2}, \frac{4-1}{2}\right) = \left(5, \frac{3}{2}\right) = (5, 1.5)$$

Check to see if this point is on the line:

$$y = 3x - 6$$
$$y = 3(5) - 6 = 15 - 6 = 9$$

In order for this line to be a bisector, y must equal 1.5. However, since $y = 9$, the answer to the question is "No, this is not a bisector."

Exercise:

a) **One line passes through the points (-4, -6) and (4, 6); another line passes through the points (-5, -4) and (3, 8). Are these lines parallel, perpendicular or neither?**

Find the slopes.

$$m = \frac{y_2 - y_1}{x_2 - x_1}$$

$$m_1 = \frac{6 - (-6)}{4 - (-4)} = \frac{6 + 6}{4 + 4} = \frac{12}{8} = \frac{3}{2}$$

MATHEMATICS

$$m_2 = \frac{8-(-4)}{3-(-5)} = \frac{8+4}{3+5} = \frac{12}{8} = \frac{3}{2}$$

Since the slopes are the same, the lines are parallel.

b) One line passes through the points (1, -3) and (0, -6); another line passes through the points (4, 1) and (-2, 3). Are these lines parallel, perpendicular or neither?

Find the slopes.

$$m = \frac{y_2 - y_1}{x_2 - x_1}$$

$$m_1 = \frac{-6-(-3)}{0-1} = \frac{-6+3}{-1} = \frac{-3}{-1} = 3$$

$$m_2 = \frac{3-1}{-2-4} = \frac{2}{-6} = -\frac{1}{3}$$

The slopes are negative reciprocals, so the lines are perpendicular.

c) One line passes through the points (-2, 4) and (2, 5); another line passes through the points (-1, 0) and (5, 4). Are these lines parallel, perpendicular or neither?

Find the slopes.

$$m = \frac{y_2 - y_1}{x_2 - x_1}$$

$$m_1 = \frac{5-4}{2-(-2)} = \frac{1}{2+2} = \frac{1}{4}$$

$$m_2 = \frac{4-0}{5-(-1)} = \frac{4}{5+1} = \frac{4}{6} = \frac{2}{3}$$

Since the slopes are not the same, the lines are not parallel. Since they are not negative reciprocals, they are not perpendicular, either. Therefore, the answer is "neither."

TEACHER CERTIFICATION STUDY GUIDE

Exercise:

For 2000 through 2005, the consumption of a certain product sweetened with sugar, as a percent, $f(t)$, of the total consumption of the product, can be modeled by:

$$f(t) = 75 + 37.25(0.615)^t$$

where $t = 2$ represents 2000.

(a) Find a model for the consumption of the product sweetened with non-sugar sweeteners as a percent, $g(t)$, of the total consumption of the product.

Since 100% represents the total consumption of the product, the model can be found by subtracting the model for sugar-sweetened product from 100:

$$g(t) = 100 - (75 + 37.25(0.615)^t$$
$$= 100 - 75 - 37.25(0.615)^t$$
$$= 25 - 37.25(0.615)^t$$

(b) Sketch the graphs of f and g. Does the consumption of one type of product seem to be stabilizing compared to the other product? Explain.

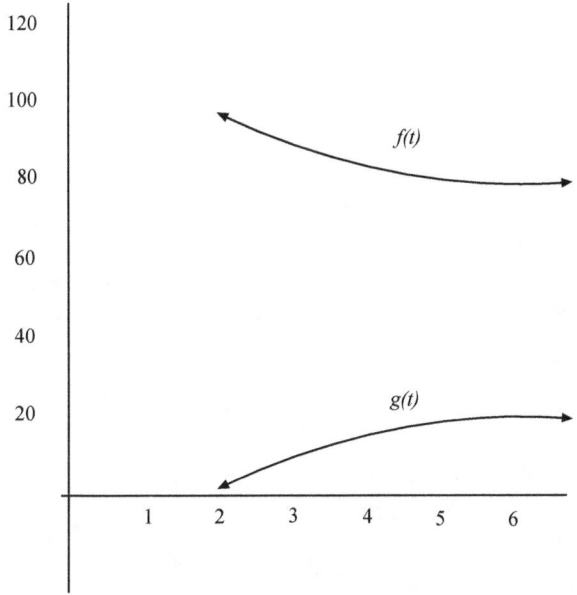

Yes, the consumption of the product sweetened with sugar (represented by $f(t)$) is decreasing less and less each year.

(c) Sketch the graph of $f(x) = 2^x$. Does it have an x-intercept? What does this tell you about the number of solutions of the equation $2^x = 0$? Explain.

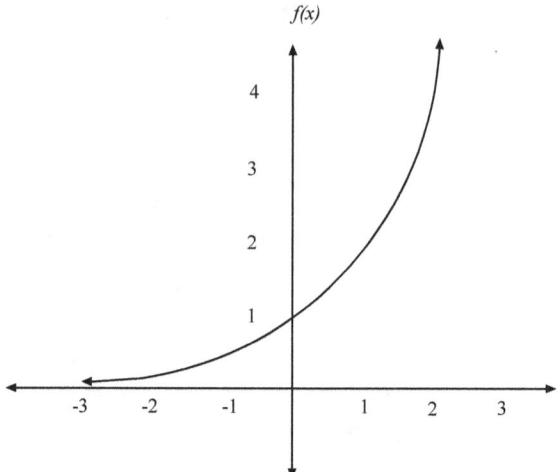

No, there is no solution. The solutions of $2^x = 0$ are the x-intercepts of $y = 2^x$.

CURRICULUM AND INSTRUCTION

The National Council of Teachers of Mathematics standards emphasize the teacher's obligation to make mathematics relevant to the students and applicable to the real world. The mathematics need in our technological society is different from that need in the past; we need thinking skills rather than computational. Mathematics needs to connect to other subjects, as well as other areas of math.

ERROR ANALYSIS

A simple method for analyzing student errors is to ask how the answer was obtained. The teacher can then determine if a common error pattern has resulted in the wrong answer. There is a value to having the students explain how the arrived at the correct as well as the incorrect answers.

Many errors are due to simple **carelessness**. Students need to be encouraged to work slowly and carefully. They should check their calculations by redoing the problem on another paper, not merely looking at the work. Addition and subtraction problems need to be written neatly so the numbers line up. Students need to be careful regrouping in subtraction. Students must write clearly and legibly, including erasing fully. Use estimation to ensure that answers make sense.

Many students computational skills exceed their **reading** level. Although they can understand basic operations, they fail to grasp the concept or completely understand the question. Students must read directions slowly.

Fractions are often a source of many errors. Students need to be reminded to use common denominators when adding and subtracting and to always express answers in simplest terms. Again, it is helpful to check by estimating.

The most common error that is made when working with **decimals** is failure to line up the decimal points when adding or subtracting or not moving the decimal point when multiplying or dividing. Students also need to be reminded to add zeroes when necessary. Reading aloud may also be beneficial. Estimation, as always, is especially important.

Students need to know that it is okay to make mistakes. The teacher must keep a positive attitude, so they do not feel defeated or frustrated.

REPRESENTATIONS OF CONCEPTS

Mathematical operations can be shown using manipulatives or drawings. Multiplication can be shown using arrays.

3×4
```
☐ ☐ ☐ ☐
☐ ☐ ☐ ☐
☐ ☐ ☐ ☐
```

Addition and subtractions can be demonstrated with symbols.

ψ ψ ψ ξ ξ ξ ξ
3 + 4 = 7
7 − 3 = 4

Fractions can be clarified using pattern blocks, fraction bars, or paper folding.

CONCEPT DEVELOPMENT

Manipulatives can foster learning for all students. Mathematics needs to be derived from something that is real to the learner. If he can "touch" it, he will understand and remember. Students can use fingers, ice cream sticks, tiles and paper folding, as well as those commercially available manipulatives to visualize operations and concepts. The teacher needs to solidify the concrete examples into abstract mathematics.

PROBLEM SOLVING

Problem solving strategies are simply plans of attack. Student often panic when confronted with word problems. If they have a "list" of ideas, ways to attempt a solution, they will be able to approach the problems more calmly and confidently. Some methods include, but are not limited to, draw a diagram, work backwards, guess and check, and solve a simpler problem.

It is helpful to have students work in groups. Mathematics does not have to be solitary activity. Cooperative learning fosters enthusiasm. Creating their own problems is another useful tool. Also, encourage students to find more than one way to solve a problem. Thinking about problem solving after the solution has been discovered encourages understanding and creativity. The more they practice problems, the more comfortable and positive students will feel.

MATHEMATICAL LANGUAGE

Students need to use the proper mathematical terms and expressions. When reading decimals, they need to read 0.4 as "four tenths" to promote better understanding of the concepts. They should do their work in a neat and organized manner. Students need to be encouraged to verbalize their strategies, both in computation and word problems. Additionally, writing original word problems fosters understanding of math language. Another idea is requiring students to develop their own mathematical terms. Knowing the answers and being able to communicate them are equally important.

MANIPULATIVES

Example:
Using tiles to demonstrate both geometric ideas and number theory.

Give each group of students 12 tiles and instruct them to build rectangles. Students draw their rectangles on paper.

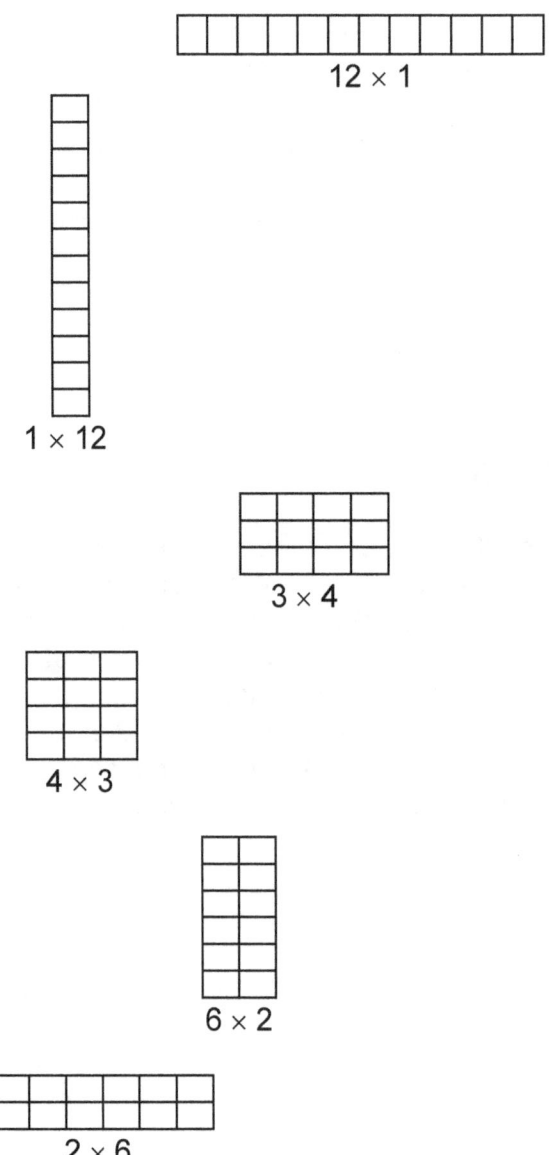

Encourage students to describe their reactions. Extend to 16 tiles. Ask students to form additional problems.

CALCULATORS

Calculators are an important tool. They should be encouraged in the classroom and at home. They do not replace basic knowledge but they can relieve the tedium of mathematical computations, allowing students to explore more challenging mathematical directions. Students will be able to use calculators more intelligently if they are taught how. Students need to always check their work by estimating. The goal of mathematics is to prepare the child to survive in the real world. Technology is a reality in today's society.

CHILD DEVELOPMENT

Means of instruction need to be varied to reach children of different skill levels and learning styles. In addition to directed instruction, students should work cooperatively, explore hands-on activities and do projects.

COMPUTERS

Computers can not replace teachers. However, they can be used to enhance the curriculum. They may be used cautiously to help students practice basic skills. Many excellent programs exist to encourage higher-order thinking skills, creativity and problem solving. Learning to use technology appropriately is an important preparation for adulthood. Computers can also show the connections between mathematics and the real world.

QUESTIONING TECHNIQUES

As the teacher's role in the classroom changes from lecturer to facilitator, the questions need to further stimulate students in various ways.

- Helping students work together

What do you think about what John said?
Do you agree? Disagree?
Can anyone explain that differently?

- Helping students determine for themselves if an answer is correct

What do you think that is true?
How did you get that answer?
Do you think that is reasonable? Why?

- Helping students learn to reason mathematically

Will that method always work?
Can you think of a case where it is not true?
How can you prove that?
Is that answer true in all cases?

- Helping student brainstorm and problem solve

Is there a pattern?
What else can you do?
Can you predict the answer?
What if...?

- Helping students connect mathematical ideas

What did we learn before that is like this?
Can you give an example?
What math did you see on television last night? in the newspaper?

SAMPLE TEST

DIRECTIONS: Read each item and select the best response.

1. Change $.\overline{63}$ into a fraction in simplest form.
   (Easy) (Skill 1.1)

   A) 63/100
   B) 7/11
   C) 6 3/10
   D) 2/3

2. Which of the following sets is closed under division?
   (Average Rigor) (Skill 1.1)

   I) {½, 1, 2, 4}
   II) {-1, 1}
   III) {-1, 0, 1}

   A) I only
   B) II only
   C) III only
   D) I and II

3. Which of the following illustrates an inverse property?
   (Easy) (Skill 1.1)

   A) a + b = a - b
   B) a + b = b + a
   C) a + 0 = a
   D) a + (-a) = 0

4. Which of the following sets is not a ring?
   (Average Rigor) (Skill 1.1)

   A) the complex numbers
   B) the rational numbers
   C) the integers
   D) the natural numbers

5. Choose the correct statement:
   (Average Rigor) (Skill 1.1)

   A) Rational and irrational numbers are both proper subsets of the real numbers.
   B) The set of whole numbers is a proper subset of the set of natural numbers.
   C) The set of integers is a proper subset of the set of irrational numbers.
   D) The set of real numbers is a proper subset of the natural, whole, integers, rational, and irrational numbers.

6. Which of the following statements demonstrates that the complex numbers are not an ordered field?
   (Average Rigor) (Skill 1.1)

   A) $\exists a : a = 0$
   B) $1 > -1$
   C) $i^2 < 0$
   D) $0 \cdot i = 0$

7. Which of the following sets is not a field?
   (Average Rigor) (Skill 1.1)

   A) the integers
   B) the rational numbers
   C) the real numbers
   D) the complex numbers

MATHEMATICS

8. Simplify: $\dfrac{10}{1+3i}$
   (Average Rigor) (Skill 1.1)

   A) $-1.25(1-3i)$
   B) $1.25(1+3i)$
   C) $1+3i$
   D) $1-3i$

9. Which of the following is a factor of $6+48m^3$
   (Rigorous) (Skill 1.2)

   A) (1 + 2m)
   B) (1 - 8m)
   C) (1 + m - 2m)
   D) (1 - m + 2m)

10. Which graph represents the equation of $y = x^2 + 3x$?
    (Average Rigor) (Skill 1.2)

    A) B)

    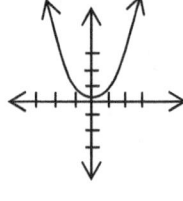

    C) D)

    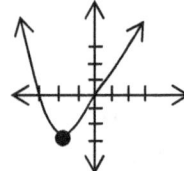 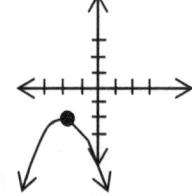

11. Given $K(-4, y)$ and $M(2, -3)$ with midpoint $L(x, 1)$, determine the values of x and y.
    (Rigorous) (Skill 1.2)

    A) $x = -1,\ y = 5$
    B) $x = 3,\ y = 2$
    C) $x = 5,\ y = -1$
    D) $x = -1,\ y = -1$

12. Solve the system of equations for x, y and z.
    (Rigorous) (Skill 1.2)

    $3x + 2y - z = 0$
    $2x + 5y = 8z$
    $x + 3y + 2z = 7$

    A) (−1, 2, 1)
    B) (1, 2, −1)
    C) (−3, 4, −1)
    D) (0, 1, 2)

13. Solve for x: $18 = 4 + |2x|$
    (Rigorous) (Skill 1.2)

    A) $\{-11, 7\}$
    B) $\{-7, 0, 7\}$
    C) $\{-7, 7\}$
    D) $\{-11, 11\}$

14. Find the zeroes of $f(x) = x^3 + x^2 - 14x - 24$
    (Rigorous) (Skill 1.2)

    A) 4, 3, 2
    B) 3, -8
    C) 7, -2, -1
    D) 4, -3, -2

15. Solve for x by factoring
    $2x^2 - 3x - 2 = 0$.
    (Average Rigor) (Skill 1.2)

    A) x = (-1,2)
    B) x = (0.5,-2)
    C) x = (-0.5,2)
    D) x = (1,-2)

16. Which graph represents the solution set for $x^2 - 5x > -6$?
    (Average Rigor) (Skill 1.2)

    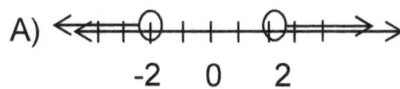

    A) number line with open circles at -2, 0, 2
    B) number line with open circles at -3, 0
    C) number line with open circles at -2, 0, 2
    D) number line with open circles at -3, 0, 2, 3

17. What would be the seventh term of the expanded binomial $(2a+b)^8$?
    (Rigorous) (Skill 1.2)

    A) $2ab^7$
    B) $41a^4b^4$
    C) $112a^2b^6$
    D) $16ab^7$

18. What would be the shortest method of solution for the system of equations below?
    (Easy) (Skill 1.2)

    $3x + 2y = 38$
    $4x + 8 = y$

    A) linear combination
    B) additive inverse
    C) substitution
    D) graphing

19. Identify the correct sequence of subskills required for solving and graphing inequalities involving absolute value in one variable, such as $|x+1| \le 6$.
    (Average Rigor) (Skill 1.2)

    A) understanding absolute value, graphing inequalities, solving systems of equations
    B) graphing inequalities on a Cartesian plane, solving systems of equations, simplifying expressions with absolute value
    C) plotting points, graphing equations, graphing inequalities
    D) solving equations with absolute value, solving inequalities, graphing conjunctions and disjunctions

20. The volume of water flowing through a pipe varies directly with the square of the radius of the pipe. If the water flows at a rate of 80 liters per minute through a pipe with a radius of 4 cm, at what rate would water flow through a pipe with a radius of 3 cm?
    (Rigorous) (Skill 1.3)

    A) 45 liters per minute
    B) 6.67 liters per minute
    C) 60 liters per minute
    D) 4.5 liters per minute

21. Evaluate $3^{1/2}(9^{1/3})$
    (Rigorous) (Skill 1.3)

    A) $27^{5/6}$
    B) $9^{7/12}$
    C) $3^{5/6}$
    D) $3^{6/7}$

22. Simplify: $\sqrt{27} + \sqrt{75}$
    (Rigorous) (Skill 1.3)

    A) $8\sqrt{3}$
    B) 34
    C) $34\sqrt{3}$
    D) $15\sqrt{3}$

23. $f(x) = 3x - 2;\ f^{-1}(x) =$
    (Average Rigor) (Skill 1.3)

    A) $3x + 2$
    B) $x/6$
    C) $2x - 3$
    D) $(x+2)/3$

24. State the domain of the function $f(x) = \dfrac{3x-6}{x^2 - 25}$
    (Average Rigor) (Skill 1.3)

    A) $x \neq 2$
    B) $x \neq 5, -5$
    C) $x \neq 2, -2$
    D) $x \neq 5$

25. Given $f(x) = 3x - 2$ and $g(x) = x^2$, **determine** $g(f(x))$.
    (Average Rigor) (Skill 1.3)

    A) $3x^2 - 2$
    B) $9x^2 + 4$
    C) $9x^2 - 12x + 4$
    D) $3x^3 - 2$

26. Which equation corresponds to the logarithmic statement: $\log_x k = m$?
    (Rigorous) (Skill 1.3)

    A) $x^m = k$
    B) $k^m = x$
    C) $x^k = m$
    D) $m^x = k$

27. Find the value of the determinant of the matrix.
    (Average Rigor) (Skill 1.4)

    $$\begin{vmatrix} 2 & 1 & -1 \\ 4 & -1 & 4 \\ 0 & -3 & 2 \end{vmatrix}$$

    A) 0
    B) 23
    C) 24
    D) 40

28. Given a vector with horizontal component 5 and vertical component 6, determine the length of the vector.
    (Average Rigor) (Skill 1.4)

    A) 61
    B) $\sqrt{61}$
    C) 30
    D) $\sqrt{30}$

29. Find the determinant of the following matrix.
    (Easy) (Skill 1.4)

    $$\begin{vmatrix} a & b \\ c & d \end{vmatrix}$$

    A) ab − cd
    B) ad + bc
    C) ad − bc
    D) ac − bd

30. Which term most accurately describes two coplanar lines without any common points?
    (Easy) (Skill 2.1)

    A) perpendicular
    B) parallel
    C) intersecting
    D) skew

31. If the two marked angles in the following figure are congruent, what can be said about lines L and M?
    (Easy) (Skill 2.1)

    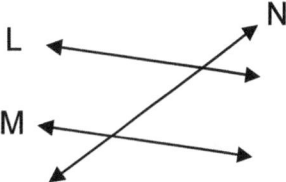

    A) L and M are perpendicular.
    B) L and M intersect at a point.
    C) L and M are parallel.
    D) Nothing can be said about L and M.

32. What is the sum of the interior angles of the following triangle?
    (Easy) (Skill 2.2)

    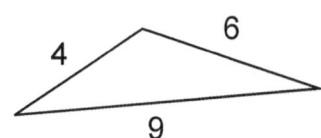

    A) 90°
    B) 180°
    C) 270°
    D) 360°

33. Compute the area of the shaded region, given a radius of 5 meters. 0 is the center.
    (Rigorous) (Skill 2.2)

    A) 7.13 cm²
    B) 7.13 m²
    C) 78.5 m²
    D) 19.63 m²

    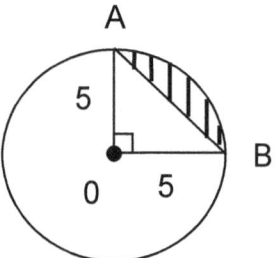

34. What is the degree measure of an interior angle of a regular 10 sided polygon?
    (Rigorous) (Skill 2.2)

    A) 18°
    B) 36°
    C) 144°
    D) 54°

35. If a ship sails due south 6 miles, then due west 8 miles, how far was it from the starting point?
    (Average Rigor) (Skill 2.2)

    A) 100 miles
    B) 10 miles
    C) 14 miles
    D) 48 miles

36. Choose the diagram which illustrates the construction of a perpendicular to the line at a given point on the line.
    (Rigorous) (Skill 2.2)

    A)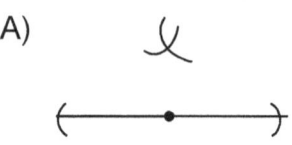

    B)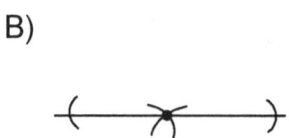

    C)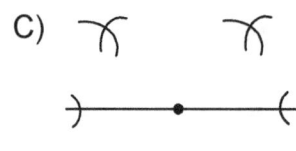

    D)

37. Given a 30 meter x 60 meter garden with a circular fountain with a 5 meter radius, calculate the area of the portion of the garden not occupied by the fountain.
(Average Rigor) (Skill 2.2)

   A) 1721 m²
   B) 1879 m²
   C) 2585 m²
   D) 1015 m²

38. When you begin by assuming the conclusion of a theorem is false, then show that through a sequence of logically correct steps you contradict an accepted fact, this is known as
(Easy) (Skill 2.2)

   A) inductive reasoning
   B) direct proof
   C) indirect proof
   D) exhaustive proof

39. Compute the distance from (-2,7) to the line $x = 5$.
(Average Rigor) (Skill 2.2)

   A) -9
   B) -7
   C) 5
   D) 7

40. What is the measure of minor arc AD, given measure of arc PS is 40° and $m < K = 10°$?
(Rigorous) (Skill 2.2)

   A) 50°
   B) 20°
   C) 30°
   D) 25°

41. Which theorem can be used to prove $\triangle BAK \cong \triangle MKA$?
(Average Rigor) (Skill 2.2)

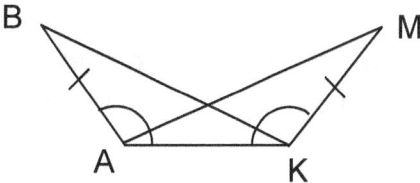

   A) SSS
   B) ASA
   C) SAS
   D) AAS

42. Given that QO⊥NP and QO=NP, quadrilateral NOPQ can most accurately be described as a
(Easy) (Skill 2.2)

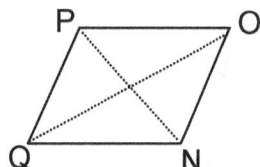

   A) parallelogram
   B) rectangle
   C) square
   D) rhombus

43. Choose the correct statement concerning the median and altitude in a triangle.
    (Average Rigor) (Skill 2.2)

    A) The median and altitude of a triangle may be the same segment.
    B) The median and altitude of a triangle are always different segments.
    C) The median and altitude of a right triangle are always the same segment.
    D) The median and altitude of an isosceles triangle are always the same segment.

44. Which equation represents a circle with a diameter whose endpoints are $(0,7)$ and $(0,3)$?
    (Rigorous) (Skill 2.2)

    A) $x^2 + y^2 + 21 = 0$
    B) $x^2 + y^2 - 10y + 21 = 0$
    C) $x^2 + y^2 - 10y + 9 = 0$
    D) $x^2 - y^2 - 10y + 9 = 0$

45. Find the length of the major axis of $x^2 + 9y^2 = 36$.
    (Rigorous) (Skill 2.2)

    A) 4
    B) 6
    C) 12
    D) 8

46. Find the area of the figure pictured below.
    (Rigorous) (Skill 2.2)

    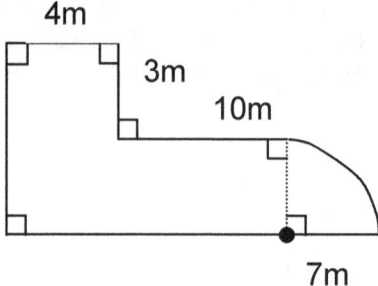

    A) 136.47 m²
    B) 148.48 m²
    C) 293.86 m²
    D) 178.47 m²

47. Determine the area of the shaded region of the trapezoid in terms of x and y.
    (Rigorous) (Skill 2.2)

    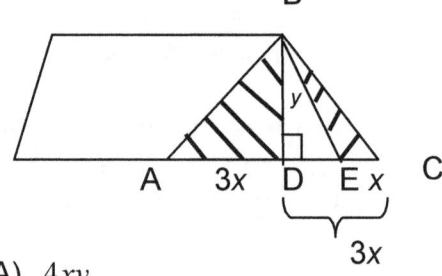

    A) $4xy$
    B) $2xy$
    C) $3x^2 y$
    D) There is not enough information given.

48. Determine the measures of angles A and B.
(Average Rigor) (Skill 2.2)

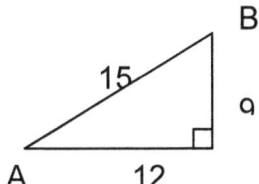

A) A = 30°, B = 60°
B) A = 60°, B = 30°
C) A = 53°, B = 37°
D) A = 37°, B = 53°

49. Which of the following statements about a trapezoid is incorrect?
(Average Rigor) (Skill 2.2)

A) It has one pair of parallel sides
B) The parallel sides are called bases
C) If the two bases are the same length, the trapezoid is called isosceles
D) The median is parallel to the bases

50. If the area of the base of a cone is tripled, the volume will be
(Rigorous) (Skill 2.3)

A) the same as the original
B) 9 times the original
C) 3 times the original
D) 3π times the original

51. Find the surface area of a box which is 3 feet wide, 5 feet tall, and 4 feet deep.
(Easy) (Skill 2.3)

A) 47 sq. ft.
B) 60 sq. ft.
C) 94 sq. ft
D) 188 sq. ft.

52. The coordinate transformation $T : (x,y) \rightarrow (x\cos\theta - y\sin\theta, x\sin\theta + y\cos\theta)$ corresponds to which of the following?
(Average Rigor) (Skill 2.4)

A) counterclockwise rotation
B) clockwise rotation
C) reflection
D) translation

53. Which of the following is always composite if *x* is odd, *y* is even, and both *x* and *y* are greater than or equal to 2?
(Average Rigor) (Skill 3.1)

A) $x+y$
B) $3x+2y$
C) $5xy$
D) $5x+3y$

54. What is the smallest number that is divisible by 3 and 5 and leaves a remainder of 3 when divided by 7?
(Average Rigor) (Skill 3.1)

A) 15
B) 18
C) 25
D) 45

55. Find the LCM of 27, 90 and 84.
    (Easy) (Skill 3.1)

    A) 90
    B) 3780
    C) 204120
    D) 1260

56. How many ways are there to choose a potato and two green vegetables from a choice of three potatoes and seven green vegetables?
    (Average Rigor) (Skill 4.1)

    A) 126
    B) 63
    C) 21
    D) 252

57. A jar contains 3 red marbles, 5 white marbles, 1 green marble and 15 blue marbles. If one marble is picked at random from the jar, what is the probability that it will be red?
    (Easy) (Skill 4.1)

    A) 1/3
    B) 1/8
    C) 3/8
    D) 1/24

58. If there are three people in a room, what is the probability that at least two of them will share a birthday? (Assume a year has 365 days)
    (Rigorous) (Skill 4.1)

    A) 0.67
    B) 0.05
    C) 0.008
    D) 0.33

59. Compute the median for the following data set:
    (Easy) (Skill 4.2)

    {12, 19, 13, 16, 17, 14}

    A) 14.5
    B) 15.17
    C) 15
    D) 16

60. Half the students in a class scored 80% on an exam, most of the rest scored 85% except for one student who scored 10%. Which would be the best measure of central tendency for the test scores?
    (Rigorous) (Skill 4.2)

    A) mean
    B) median
    C) mode
    D) either the median or the mode because they are equal

61. Compute the standard deviation for the following set of temperatures.
    (37, 38, 35, 37, 38, 40, 36, 39)
    (Easy) (Skill 4.2)

    A) 37.5
    B) 1.5
    C) 0.5
    D) 2.5

62. Determine the rectangular coordinates of the point with polar coordinates (5, 60°). *(Average Rigor) (Skill 5.1)*

   A) (0.5, 0.87)
   B) (-0.5, 0.87)
   C) (2.5, 4.33)
   D) (25, 150°)

63. Which expression is equivalent to $1-\sin^2 x$? *(Rigorous) (Skill 5.1)*

   A) $1-\cos^2 x$
   B) $1+\cos^2 x$
   C) $1/\sec x$
   D) $1/\sec^2 x$

64. Which expression is not equal to sinx? *(Average Rigor) (Skill 5.1)*

   A) $\sqrt{1-\cos^2 x}$
   B) $\tan x \cos x$
   C) $1/\csc x$
   D) $1/\sec x$

65. For an acute angle x, sinx = 3/5. What is cotx? *(Rigorous) (Skill 5.1)*

   A) 5/3
   B) 3/4
   C) 1.33
   D) 1

66. Find the following limit:
   $$\lim_{x \to 2} \frac{x^2 - 4}{x - 2}$$
   (Average Rigor) (Skill 5.2)

   A) 0
   B) Infinity
   C) 2
   D) 4

67. Find the following limit:
   $$\lim_{x \to 0} \frac{\sin 2x}{5x}$$
   (Rigorous) (Skill 5.2)

   A) Infinity
   B) 0
   C) 1.4
   D) 1

68. Find the first derivative of the function:
   $f(x) = x^3 - 6x^2 + 5x + 4$
   (Rigorous) (Skill 5.3)

   A) $3x^3 - 12x^2 + 5x = f'(x)$
   B) $3x^2 - 12x - 5 = f'(x)$
   C) $3x^2 - 12x + 9 = f'(x)$
   D) $3x^2 - 12x + 5 = f'(x)$

69. Differentiate: $y = e^{3x+2}$
   (Rigorous) (Skill 5.3)

   A) $3e^{3x+2} = y'$
   B) $3e^{3x} = y'$
   C) $6e^3 = y'$
   D) $(3x+2)e^{3x+1} = y'$

70. If the velocity of a body is given by v = 16 - t², find the distance traveled from t = 0 until the body comes to a complete stop.
    (Average Rigor) (Skill 5.3)

    A) 16
    B) 43
    C) 48
    D) 64

71. Find the slope of the line tangent to $y = 3x(\cos x)$ at $(\pi/2, \pi/2)$.
    (Rigorous) (Skill 5.3)

    A) $-3\pi/2$
    B) $3\pi/2$
    C) $\pi/2$
    D) $-\pi/2$

72. Find the equation of the line tangent to $y = 3x^2 - 5x$ at $(1,-2)$.
    (Rigorous) (Skill 5.3)

    A) $y = x - 3$
    B) $y = 1$
    C) $y = x + 2$
    D) $y = x$

73. The acceleration of a particle is dv/dt = 6 m/s². Find the velocity at t=10 given an initial velocity of 15 m/s.
    (Average Rigor) (Skill 5.3)

    A) 60 m/s
    B) 150 m/s
    C) 75 m/s
    D) 90 m/s

74. How does the function $y = x^3 + x^2 + 4$ behave from $x = 1$ to $x = 3$?
    (Average Rigor) (Skill 5.3)

    A) increasing, then decreasing
    B) increasing
    C) decreasing
    D) neither increasing nor decreasing

75. Find the absolute maximum obtained by the function $y = 2x^2 + 3x$ on the interval $x = 0$ to $x = 3$.
    (Rigorous) (Skill 5.3)

    A) $-3/4$
    B) $-4/3$
    C) 0
    D) 27

76. L'Hospital's rule provides a method to evaluate which of the following?
    (Easy) (Skill 5.3)

    A) Limit of a function
    B) Derivative of a function
    C) Sum of an arithmetic series
    D) Sum of a geometric series

77. Find the antiderivative for $4x^3 - 2x + 6 = y$.
    (Rigorous) (Skill 5.4)

    A) $x^4 - x^2 + 6x + C$
    B) $x^4 - 2/3x^3 + 6x + C$
    C) $12x^2 - 2 + C$
    D) $4/3x^4 - x^2 + 6x + C$

TEACHER CERTIFICATION STUDY GUIDE

78. Find the antiderivative for the function $y = e^{3x}$.
    (Rigorous) (Skill 5.4)

    A) $3x(e^{3x}) + C$
    B) $3(e^{3x}) + C$
    C) $1/3(e^x) + C$
    D) $1/3(e^{3x}) + C$

79. Evaluate: $\int (x^3 + 4x - 5) dx$
    (Rigorous) (Skill 5.4)

    A) $3x^2 + 4 + C$
    B) $\frac{1}{4}x^4 - 2/3x^3 + 6x + C$
    C) $x^{4/3} + 4x - 5x + C$
    D) $x^3 + 4x^2 - 5x + C$

80. Evaluate $\int_0^2 (x^2 + x - 1) dx$
    (Rigorous) (Skill 5.4)

    A) 11/3
    B) 8/3
    C) -8/3
    D) -11/3

81. Find the area under the function $y = x^2 + 4$ from $x = 3$ to $x = 6$.
    (Average Rigor) (Skill 5.4)

    A) 75
    B) 21
    C) 96
    D) 57

82. Find the sum of the first one hundred terms in the progression.
    (-6, -2, 2 . . .)
    (Rigorous) (Skill 5.5)

    A) 19,200
    B) 19,400
    C) -604
    D) 604

83. What is the sum of the first 20 terms of the geometric sequence (2,4,8,16,32,…)?
    (Average Rigor) (Skill 5.5)

    A) 2097150
    B) 1048575
    C) 524288
    D) 1048576

84. Which mathematician is best known for his work in developing non-Euclidean geometry?
    (Easy) (Skill 6.1)

    A) Descartes
    B) Riemann
    C) Pascal
    D) Pythagoras

85. Which of the following mathematicians is known for his work in developing calculus?
    (Easy) (Skill 6.1)

    A) Blaise Pascal
    B) Isaac Newton
    C) René Descartes
    D) Abraham de Moivre

ANSWER KEY

1) B	18) C	35) B	52) A	69) A
2) B	19) D	36) D	53) C	70) B
3) D	20) A	37) A	54) D	71) A
4) D	21) B	38) C	55) B	72) A
5) D	22) A	39) D	56) A	73) C
6) C	23) D	40) B	57) B	74) B
7) A	24) B	41) C	58) C	75) D
8) D	25) C	42) C	59) C	76) A
9) A	26) A	43) A	60) B	77) A
10) C	27) C	44) B	61) B	78) D
11) A	28) B	45) C	62) C	79) B
12) A	29) C	46) B	63) D	80) B
13) C	30) B	47) B	64) D	81) A
14) D	31) C	48) D	65) B	82) A
15) C	32) B	49) C	66) D	83) A
16) D	33) B	50) C	67) C	84) B
17) C	34) C	51) C	68) D	85) B

Rigor Table

	Easy %20	Average Rigor %40	Rigorous %40
Question #	1, 3, 18, 29, 30, 31, 32, 38, 42, 51, 55, 57, 59, 61, 76, 84, 85	2, 4, 5, 6, 7, 8, 10, 15, 16, 19, 23, 24, 25, 27, 28, 35, 37, 39, 41, 43, 48, 49, 52, 53, 54, 56, 62, 64, 66, 70, 73, 74, 81, 83	9, 11, 12, 13, 14, 17, 20, 21, 22, 26, 33, 34, 36, 40, 44, 45, 46, 47, 50, 58, 60, 63, 65, 67, 68, 69, 71, 72, 75, 77, 78, 79, 80, 82

TEACHER CERTIFICATION STUDY GUIDE

Rationales with Sample Questions

1. Change $.\overline{63}$ into a fraction in simplest form.
   (Easy) (Skill 1.1)

   A) 63/100
   B) 7/11
   C) 6 3/10
   D) 2/3

Answer: B

Let N = .636363…. Then multiplying both sides of the equation by 100 or 10^2 (because there are 2 repeated numbers), we get 100N = 63.636363… Then subtracting the two equations gives 99N = 63 or N = $\frac{63}{99} = \frac{7}{11}$.

2. Which of the following sets is closed under division?
   (Average Rigor) (Skill 1.1)

   I) {½, 1, 2, 4}
   II) {-1, 1}
   III) {-1, 0, 1}

   A) I only
   B) II only
   C) III only
   D) I and II

Answer: B

I is not closed because $\frac{4}{.5} = 8$ and 8 is not in the set.

III is not closed because $\frac{1}{0}$ is undefined.

II is closed because $\frac{-1}{1} = -1, \frac{1}{-1} = -1, \frac{1}{1} = 1, \frac{-1}{-1} = 1$ and all the answers are in the set.

MATHEMATICS

TEACHER CERTIFICATION STUDY GUIDE

3. **Which of the following illustrates an inverse property?**
   (Easy) (Skill 1.1)

   A) a + b = a - b
   B) a + b = b + a
   C) a + 0 = a
   D) a + (-a) = 0

   Answer: D

   Because a + (-a) = 0 is a statement of the Additive Inverse Property of Algebra.

4. **Which of the following sets is not a ring?**
   (Average Rigor) (Skill 1.1)

   A) the complex numbers
   B) the rational numbers
   C) the integers
   D) the natural numbers

   Answer: D

   No element of the set of natural numbers is invertible with respect to addition, thus the natural numbers do not form a ring. For instance, there is no additive inverse in the set of natural numbers for the number 3 (such that 3 + (-3) = 0).

5. **Choose the correct statement:**
   (Average Rigor) (Skill 1.1)

   A) Rational and irrational numbers are both proper subsets of the real numbers.
   B) The set of whole numbers is a proper subset of the set of natural numbers.
   C) The set of integers is a proper subset of the set of irrational numbers.
   D) The set of real numbers is a proper subset of the natural, whole, integers, rational, and irrational numbers.

   Answer: D

   A complex number is the square root of a negative number. The complex number is defined as the square root of –1. The exponent ½ represents a square root.

MATHEMATICS

TEACHER CERTIFICATION STUDY GUIDE

6. **Which of the following statements demonstrates that the complex numbers are not an ordered field?**
   (Average Rigor) (Skill 1.1)

   A) $\exists\, a : a = 0$
   B) $1 > -1$
   C) $i^2 < 0$
   D) $0 \cdot i = 0$

   Answer: C

   Since the square of *i* is negative, the complex numbers cannot form an ordered field. The other properties do not disqualify the complex numbers from being an ordered field.

7. **Which of the following sets is not a field?**
   (Average Rigor) (Skill 1.1)

   A) the integers
   B) the rational numbers
   C) the real numbers
   D) the complex numbers

   Answer: A

   Integers do not generally obey the property of multiplicative inverses; that is, there exists elements a of the set of integers such that the inverse of a, which satisfies $a \cdot (a)^{-1} \neq 1$, is not itself an integer. An example is the number 3. The inverse of 3, or 1/3, is not an integer.

MATHEMATICS

8. **Simplify:** $\dfrac{10}{1+3i}$

   (Average Rigor) (Skill 1.1)

   A) $-1.25(1-3i)$
   B) $1.25(1+3i)$
   C) $1+3i$
   D) $1-3i$

   Answer: D

   Multiplying numerator and denominator by the conjugate gives

   $$\dfrac{10}{1+3i} \times \dfrac{1-3i}{1-3i} = \dfrac{10(1-3i)}{1-9i^2} = \dfrac{10(1-3i)}{1-9(-1)} = \dfrac{10(1-3i)}{10} = 1-3i.$$

9. **Which of the following is a factor of** $6+48m^3$

   (Rigorous) (Skill 1.2)

   A) (1 + 2m)
   B) (1 - 8m)
   C) (1 + m - 2m)
   D) (1 - m + 2m)

   Answer: A

   Removing the common factor of 6 and then factoring the sum of two cubes gives
   $6 + 48m^3 = 6(1 + 8m^3) = 6(1 + 2m)(1^2 - 2m + (2m)^2)$.

10. Which graph represents the equation of $y = x^2 + 3x$?
    (Average Rigor) (Skill 1.2)

A)   B)

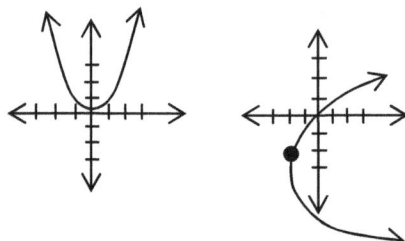

C)   D)

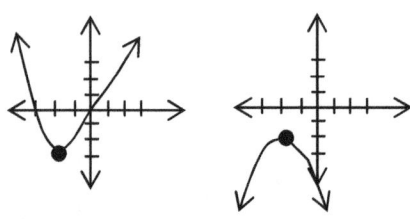

Answer: C

B is not the graph of a function. D is the graph of a parabola where the coefficient of x^2 is negative. A appears to be the graph of $y = x^2$. To find the x-intercepts of $y = x^2 + 3x$, set $y = 0$ and solve for x: $0 = x^2 + 3x = x(x + 3)$ to get $x = 0$ or $x = -3$. Therefore, the graph of the function intersects the x-axis at x=0 and x=-3.

TEACHER CERTIFICATION STUDY GUIDE

11. Given $K(-4, y)$ and $M(2, -3)$ with midpoint $L(x, 1)$, determine the values of x and y.
    (Rigorous) (Skill 1.2)

A) $x = -1, y = 5$
B) $x = 3, y = 2$
C) $x = 5, y = -1$
D) $x = -1, y = -1$

Answer: A

The formula for finding the midpoint (a,b) of a segment passing through the points (x_1, y_1) and (x_2, y_2) is $(a,b) = (\frac{x_1 + x_2}{2}, \frac{y_1 + y_2}{2})$. Setting up the corresponding equations from this information gives us $x = \frac{-4 + 2}{2}, and\, 1 = \frac{y - 3}{2}$. Solving for x and y gives x = -1 and y = 5.

12. Solve the system of equations for x, y and z.
    (Rigorous) (Skill 1.2)

$$3x + 2y - z = 0$$
$$2x + 5y = 8z$$
$$x + 3y + 2z = 7$$

A) $(-1, 2, 1)$
B) $(1, 2, -1)$
C) $(-3, 4, -1)$
D) $(0, 1, 2)$

Answer: A

Multiplying equation 1 by 2, and equation 2 by –3, and then adding together the two resulting equations gives -11y + 22z = 0. Solving for y gives y = 2z. In the meantime, multiplying equation 3 by –2 and adding it to equation 2 gives –y – 12z = -14. Then substituting 2z for y, yields the result z = 1. Subsequently, one can easily find that y = 2, and x = -1.

MATHEMATICS

TEACHER CERTIFICATION STUDY GUIDE

13. **Solve for** x: $18 = 4 + |2x|$
    (Rigorous) (Skill 1.2)

    A) $\{-11, 7\}$
    B) $\{-7, 0, 7\}$
    C) $\{-7, 7\}$
    D) $\{-11, 11\}$

    Answer: C

    Using the definition of absolute value, two equations are possible: 18 = 4 + 2x or 18 = 4 – 2x. Solving for x gives x = 7 or x = -7.

14. **Find the zeroes of** $f(x) = x^3 + x^2 - 14x - 24$
    (Rigorous) (Skill 1.2)

    A) 4, 3, 2
    B) 3, -8
    C) 7, -2, -1
    D) 4, -3, -2

    Answer: D

    Possible rational roots of the equation 0 = x³ + x² – 14x -24 are all the positive and negative factors of 24. By substituting into the equation, we find that –2 is a root, and therefore that x+2 is a factor. By performing the long division (x³ + x² – 14x – 24)/(x+2), we can find that another factor of the original equation is x² – x – 12 or (x-4)(x+3). Therefore the zeros of the original function are –2, -3, and 4.

TEACHER CERTIFICATION STUDY GUIDE

15. **Solve for x by factoring** $2x^2 - 3x - 2 = 0$.
    (Average Rigor) (Skill 1.2)

A) x = (-1,2)
B) x = (0.5,-2)
C) x = (-0.5,2)
D) x = (1,-2)

Answer: C

$2x^2 - 3x - 2 = 2x^2 - 4x + x - 2 = 2x(x-2) + (x-2) = (2x+1)(x-2) = 0$.
Thus x = -0.5 or 2.

16. **Which graph represents the solution set for** $x^2 - 5x > -6$?
    (Average Rigor) (Skill 1.2)

A)
```
   -2  0  2
```

B)
```
   -3  0
```

C)
```
   -2  0  2
```

D)
```
   -3  0  2 3
```

Answer: D

Rewriting the inequality gives $x^2 - 5x + 6 > 0$. Factoring gives $(x-2)(x-3) > 0$. The two cut-off points on the number line are now at x = 2 and x = 3. Choosing a random number in each of the three parts of the numberline, we test them to see if they produce a true statement. If x = 0 or x = 4, (x-2)(x-3)>0 is true. If x = 2.5, (x-2)(x-3)>0 is false. Therefore the solution set is all numbers smaller than 2 or greater than 3.

MATHEMATICS

17. What would be the seventh term of the expanded binomial $(2a+b)^8$?
    (Rigorous) (Skill 1.2)

    A) $2ab^7$
    B) $41a^4b^4$
    C) $112a^2b^6$
    D) $16ab^7$

Answer: C

The set-up for finding the seventh term is $\dfrac{8(7)(6)(5)(4)(3)}{6(5)(4)(3)(2)(1)}(2a)^{8-6}b^6$ which gives $28(4a^2b^6)$ or $112a^2b^6$.

18. What would be the shortest method of solution for the system of equations below?
    (Easy) (Skill 1.2)

    $$3x+2y=38$$
    $$4x+8=y$$

    A) linear combination
    B) additive inverse
    C) substitution
    D) graphing

Answer: C

Since the second equation is already solved for y, it would be easiest to use the substitution method.

19. **Identify the correct sequence of subskills required for solving and graphing inequalities involving absolute value in one variable, such as $|x+1| \leq 6$.**
(Average Rigor) (Skill 1.2)

A) understanding absolute value, graphing inequalities, solving systems of equations
B) graphing inequalities on a Cartesian plane, solving systems of equations, simplifying expressions with absolute value
C) plotting points, graphing equations, graphing inequalities
D) solving equations with absolute value, solving inequalities, graphing conjunctions and disjunctions

Answer: D

The steps listed in answer D would look like this for the given example:
If $|x+1| \leq 6$, then $-6 \leq x+1 \leq 6$, which means $-7 \leq x \leq 5$. Then the inequality would be graphed on a numberline and would show that the solution set is all real numbers between −7 and 5, including −7 and 5.

20. **The volume of water flowing through a pipe varies directly with the square of the radius of the pipe. If the water flows at a rate of 80 liters per minute through a pipe with a radius of 4 cm, at what rate would water flow through a pipe with a radius of 3 cm?**
(Rigorous) (Skill 1.3)

A) 45 liters per minute
B) 6.67 liters per minute
C) 60 liters per minute
D) 4.5 liters per minute

Answer: A

Set up the direct variation: $\frac{V}{r^2} = \frac{V}{r^2}$. Substituting gives $\frac{80}{16} = \frac{V}{9}$. Solving for V gives 45 liters per minute.

21. Evaluate $3^{1/2}(9^{1/3})$
    (Rigorous) (Skill 1.3)

    A) $27^{5/6}$
    B) $9^{7/12}$
    C) $3^{5/6}$
    D) $3^{6/7}$

Answer: B

Getting the bases the same gives us $3^{\frac{1}{2}}3^{\frac{2}{3}}$. Adding exponents gives $3^{\frac{7}{6}}$. Then some additional manipulation of exponents produces $3^{\frac{7}{6}} = 3^{\frac{14}{12}} = (3^2)^{\frac{7}{12}} = 9^{\frac{7}{12}}$.

22. Simplify: $\sqrt{27} + \sqrt{75}$
    (Rigorous) (Skill 1.3)

    A) $8\sqrt{3}$
    B) 34
    C) $34\sqrt{3}$
    D) $15\sqrt{3}$

Answer: A

Simplifying radicals gives $\sqrt{27} + \sqrt{75} = 3\sqrt{3} + 5\sqrt{3} = 8\sqrt{3}$.

23. $f(x) = 3x - 2;\ f^{-1}(x) =$
    (Average Rigor) (Skill 1.3)

    A) $3x + 2$
    B) $x/6$
    C) $2x - 3$
    D) $(x+2)/3$

Answer: D

To find the inverse, $f^{-1}(x)$, of the given function, reverse the variables in the given equation, y = 3x – 2, to get x = 3y – 2. Then solve for y as follows: x+2 = 3y, and y = $\frac{x+2}{3}$.

TEACHER CERTIFICATION STUDY GUIDE

24. State the domain of the function $f(x) = \dfrac{3x-6}{x^2-25}$

(Average Rigor) (Skill 1.3)

A) $x \neq 2$
B) $x \neq 5, -5$
C) $x \neq 2, -2$
D) $x \neq 5$

Answer: B

The values of 5 and –5 must be omitted from the domain of all real numbers because if x took on either of those values, the denominator of the fraction would have a value of 0, and therefore the fraction would be undefined.

25. Given $f(x) = 3x - 2$ **and** $g(x) = x^2$, **determine** $g(f(x))$.
(Average Rigor) (Skill 1.3)

A) $3x^2 - 2$
B) $9x^2 + 4$
C) $9x^2 - 12x + 4$
D) $3x^3 - 2$

Answer: C

The composite function g(f(x)) = (3x-2)² = 9x² – 12x + 4.

26. Which equation corresponds to the logarithmic statement: $\log_x k = m$?
(Rigorous) (Skill 1.3)

A) $x^m = k$
B) $k^m = x$
C) $x^k = m$
D) $m^x = k$

Answer: A

By definition of log form and exponential form, $\log_x k = m$ corresponds to $x^m = k$.

27. **Find the value of the determinant of the matrix.**
    (Average Rigor) (Skill 1.4)

$$\begin{vmatrix} 2 & 1 & -1 \\ 4 & -1 & 4 \\ 0 & -3 & 2 \end{vmatrix}$$

A) 0
B) 23
C) 24
D) 40

Answer: C

To find the determinant of a matrix without the use of a graphing calculator, repeat the first two columns as shown,

```
2    1    -1    2    1
4    -1    4    4    -1
0    -3    2    0    -3
```

Starting with the top left-most entry, 2, multiply the three numbers in the diagonal going down to the right: 2(-1)(2)=-4. Do the same starting with 1: 1(4)(0)=0. And starting with –1: -1(4)(-3) = 12. Adding these three numbers, we get 8. Repeat the same process starting with the top right-most entry, 1. That is, multiply the three numbers in the diagonal going down to the left: 1(4)(2) = 8. Do the same starting with 2: 2(4)(-3) = -24 and starting with –1: -1(-1)(0) = 0. Add these together to get -16. To find the determinant, subtract the second result from the first: 8-(-16)=24.

28. **Given a vector with horizontal component 5 and vertical component 6, determine the length of the vector.**
    (Average Rigor) (Skill 1.4)

A) 61
B) $\sqrt{61}$
C) 30
D) $\sqrt{30}$

Answer: B

Using the Pythagorean Theorem, we get v = $\sqrt{36 + 25} = \sqrt{61}$.

29. **Find the determinant of the following matrix.**
    (Easy) (Skill 1.4)

    $$\begin{vmatrix} a & b \\ c & d \end{vmatrix}$$

    A) ab − cd
    B) ad + bc
    C) ad − bc
    D) ac − bd

    Answer: C

    Simply use the formula for calculating the determinant of a 2 x 2 matrix.

30. **Which term most accurately describes two coplanar lines without any common points?**
    (Easy) (Skill 2.1)

    A) perpendicular
    B) parallel
    C) intersecting
    D) skew

    Answer: B

    By definition, parallel lines are coplanar lines without any common points.

31. If the two marked angles in the following figure are congruent, what can be said about lines L and M?
    (Easy) (Skill 2.1)

    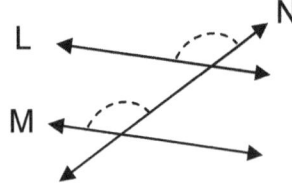

    A) L and M are perpendicular.
    B) L and M intersect at a point.
    C) L and M are parallel.
    D) Nothing can be said about L and M.

    Answer: C

    Because these corresponding angles are congruent, the lines L and M must be parallel.

32. What is the sum of the interior angles of the following triangle?
    (Easy) (Skill 2.2)

    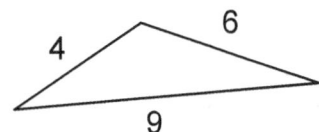

    A) 90°
    B) 180°
    C) 270°
    D) 360°

    Answer: B

    The sum of the interior angles of any Euclidean triangle is always 180°. Hence, the lengths of the sides of the triangle in the figure are irrelevant.

TEACHER CERTIFICATION STUDY GUIDE

33. Compute the area of the shaded region, given a radius of 5 meters. 0 is the center.
    (Rigorous) (Skill 2.2)

    A) 7.13 cm²
    B) 7.13 m²
    C) 78.5 m²
    D) 19.63 m²

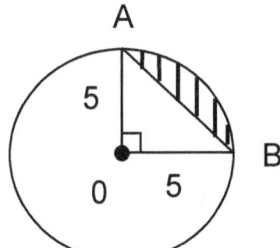

Answer: B

Area of triangle AOB is .5(5)(5) = 12.5 square meters. Since $\frac{90}{360} = .25$, the area of sector AOB (pie-shaped piece) is approximately $.25(\pi)5^2 = 19.63$. Subtracting the triangle area from the sector area to get the area of segment AB, we get approximately 19.63-12.5 = 7.13 square meters.

34. What is the degree measure of an interior angle of a regular 10 sided polygon?
    (Rigorous) (Skill 2.2)

    A) 18°
    B) 36°
    C) 144°
    D) 54°

Answer: C

Formula for finding the measure of each interior angle of a regular polygon with n sides is $\frac{(n-2)180}{n}$. For n=10, we get $\frac{8(180)}{10} = 144$.

TEACHER CERTIFICATION STUDY GUIDE

35. **If a ship sails due south 6 miles, then due west 8 miles, how far was it from the starting point?**
    (Average Rigor) (Skill 2.2)

   A) 100 miles
   B) 10 miles
   C) 14 miles
   D) 48 miles

Answer: B

Draw a right triangle with legs of 6 and 8. Find the hypotenuse using the Pythagorean Theorem. $6^2 + 8^2 = c^2$. Therefore, c = 10 miles.

36. Choose the diagram which illustrates the construction of a perpendicular to the line at a given point on the line.
(Rigorous) (Skill 2.2)

A)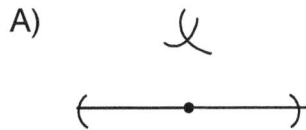

B)

C)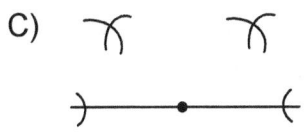

D)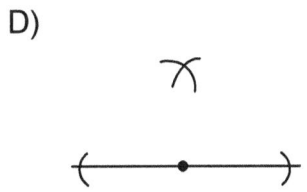

Answer: D

Given a point on a line, place the compass point there and draw two arcs intersecting the line in two points, one on either side of the given point. Then using any radius larger than half the new segment produced, and with the pointer at each end of the new segment, draw arcs which intersect above the line. Connect this new point with the given point.

TEACHER CERTIFICATION STUDY GUIDE

37. Given a 30 meter x 60 meter garden with a circular fountain with a 5 meter radius, calculate the area of the portion of the garden not occupied by the fountain.
    (Average Rigor) (Skill 2.2)

    A) 1721 m²
    B) 1879 m²
    C) 2585 m²
    D) 1015 m²

Answer: A

Find the area of the garden and then subtract the area of the fountain:
$30(60) - \pi(5)^2$ or approximately 1721 square meters.

38. When you begin by assuming the conclusion of a theorem is false, then show that through a sequence of logically correct steps you contradict an accepted fact, this is known as
    (Easy) (Skill 2.2)

    A) inductive reasoning
    B) direct proof
    C) indirect proof
    D) exhaustive proof

Answer: C

By definition this describes the procedure of an indirect proof.

39. Compute the distance from (-2,7) to the line $x = 5$.
    (Average Rigor) (Skill 2.2)

    A) -9
    B) -7
    C) 5
    D) 7

Answer: D

The line $x = 5$ is a vertical line passing through (5,0) on the Cartesian plane. By observation the distance along the horizontal line from the point (-2,7) to the line $x=5$ is 7 units.

MATHEMATICS

TEACHER CERTIFICATION STUDY GUIDE

40. **What is the measure of minor arc AD, given measure of arc PS is 40° and $m<K=10°$?**
    (Rigorous) (Skill 2.2)

    A) 50°
    B) 20°
    C) 30°
    D) 25°

    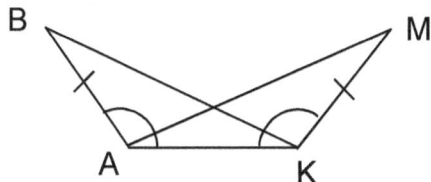

    Answer: B

    The formula relating the measure of angle K and the two arcs it intercepts is $m\angle K = \frac{1}{2}(mPS - mAD)$. Substituting the known values, we get $10 = \frac{1}{2}(40 - mAD)$. Solving for mAD gives an answer of 20 degrees.

41. **Which theorem can be used to prove $\triangle BAK \cong \triangle MKA$?**
    (Average Rigor) (Skill 2.2)

    A) SSS
    B) ASA
    C) SAS
    D) AAS

    Answer: C

    Since side AK is common to both triangles, the triangles can be proved congruent by using the Side-Angle-Side Postulate.

42. Given that QO⊥NP and QO=NP, quadrilateral NOPQ can most accurately be described as a
    (Easy) (Skill 2.2)

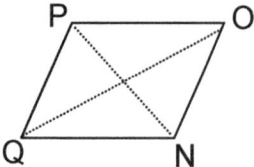

A) parallelogram
B) rectangle
C) square
D) rhombus

Answer: C

In an ordinary parallelogram, the diagonals are not perpendicular or equal in length. In a rectangle, the diagonals are not necessarily perpendicular. In a rhombus, the diagonals are not equal in length. In a square, the diagonals are both perpendicular and congruent.

43. Choose the correct statement concerning the median and altitude in a triangle.
    (Average Rigor) (Skill 2.2)

A) The median and altitude of a triangle may be the same segment.
B) The median and altitude of a triangle are always different segments.
C) The median and altitude of a right triangle are always the same segment.
D) The median and altitude of an isosceles triangle are always the same segment.

Answer: A

The most one can say with certainty is that the median (segment drawn to the midpoint of the opposite side) and the altitude (segment drawn perpendicular to the opposite side) of a triangle may coincide, but they more often do not. In an isosceles triangle, the median and the altitude to the base are the same segment.

44. Which equation represents a circle with a diameter whose endpoints are $(0,7)$ and $(0,3)$?
(Rigorous) (Skill 2.2)

A) $x^2 + y^2 + 21 = 0$
B) $x^2 + y^2 - 10y + 21 = 0$
C) $x^2 + y^2 - 10y + 9 = 0$
D) $x^2 - y^2 - 10y + 9 = 0$

Answer: B

With a diameter going from (0,7) to (0,3), the diameter of the circle must be 4, the radius must be 2, and the center of the circle must be at (0,5). Using the standard form for the equation of a circle, we get $(x-0)^2 + (y-5)^2 = 2^2$. Expanding, we get $x^2 + y^2 - 10y + 21 = 0$.

45. Find the length of the major axis of $x^2 + 9y^2 = 36$.
(Rigorous) (Skill 2.2)

A) 4
B) 6
C) 12
D) 8

Answer: C

Dividing by 36, we get $\frac{x^2}{36} + \frac{y^2}{4} = 1$, which tells us that the ellipse intersects the x-axis at 6 and –6, and therefore the length of the major axis is 12. (The ellipse intersects the y-axis at 2 and –2).

46. Find the area of the figure pictured below.
    (Rigorous) (Skill 2.2)

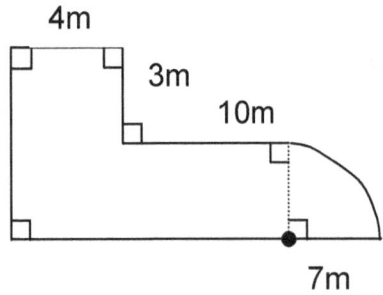

A) 136.47 m²
B) 148.48 m²
C) 293.86 m²
D) 178.47 m²

Answer: B

Divide the figure into 2 rectangles and one quarter circle. The tall rectangle on the left will have dimensions 10 by 4 and area 40. The rectangle in the center will have dimensions 7 by 10 and area 70. The quarter circle will have area $.25(\pi)7^2 = 38.48$.
The total area is therefore approximately 148.48.

47. Determine the area of the shaded region of the trapezoid in terms of x and y.
    (Rigorous) (Skill 2.2)

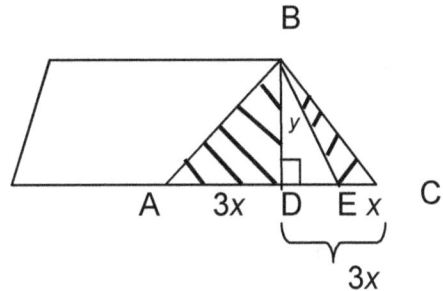

A) $4xy$
B) $2xy$
C) $3x^2 y$
D) There is not enough information given.

Answer: B

To find the area of the shaded region, find the area of triangle ABC and then subtract the area of triangle DBE. The area of triangle ABC is $.5(6x)(y) = 3xy$. The area of triangle DBE is $.5(2x)(y) = xy$. The difference is $2xy$.

48. Determine the measures of angles A and B.
    (Average Rigor) (Skill 2.2)

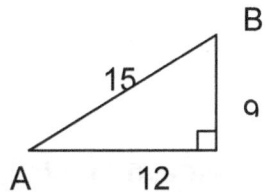

A) $A = 30°$, $B = 60°$
B) $A = 60°$, $B = 30°$
C) $A = 53°$, $B = 37°$
D) $A = 37°$, $B = 53°$

Answer: D

Tan A = 9/12 = .75 and $\tan^{-1} .75 = 37$ degrees. Since angle B is complementary to angle A, the measure of angle B is therefore 53 degrees.

TEACHER CERTIFICATION STUDY GUIDE

49. **Which of the following statements about a trapezoid is incorrect?**
    (Average Rigor) (Skill 2.2)

    A) It has one pair of parallel sides
    B) The parallel sides are called bases
    C) If the two bases are the same length, the trapezoid is called isosceles
    D) The median is parallel to the bases

Answer: C

A trapezoid is isosceles if the two legs (not bases) are the same length.

50. **If the area of the base of a cone is tripled, the volume will be**
    (Rigorous) (Skill 2.3)

    A) the same as the original
    B) 9 times the original
    C) 3 times the original
    D) 3π times the original

Answer: C

The formula for the volume of a cone is $V = \frac{1}{3}Bh$, where B is the area of the circular base and h is the height. If the area of the base is tripled, the volume becomes
$V = \frac{1}{3}(3B)h = Bh$, or three times the original area.

51. **Find the surface area of a box which is 3 feet wide, 5 feet tall, and 4 feet deep.**
    (Easy) (Skill 2.3)

    A) 47 sq. ft.
    B) 60 sq. ft.
    C) 94 sq. ft
    D) 188 sq. ft.

Answer: C

Let's assume the base of the rectangular solid (box) is 3 by 4, and the height is 5. Then the surface area of the top and bottom together is 2(12) = 24. The sum of the areas of the front and back are 2(15) = 30, while the sum of the areas of the sides are 2(20)=40. The total surface area is therefore 94 square feet.

TEACHER CERTIFICATION STUDY GUIDE

52. The coordinate transformation $T : (x,y) \rightarrow$
    $(x\cos\theta - y\sin\theta, x\sin\theta + y\cos\theta)$
    corresponds to which of the following?
    (Average Rigor) (Skill 2.4)

    A) counterclockwise rotation
    B) clockwise rotation
    C) reflection
    D) translation

    Answer: A

    By plugging in a few coordinates for basic points (such as (1,0), (-1,0), (0,1) and so on) for x and y and simple values for θ (such as 0° or 90°), it can be easily seen that the transformation T corresponds to a rotation, rather than a reflection or transformation. A value of θ of 90°, along with the point (1,0), results in a transformed point (0,1), indicating that the rotation is counterclockwise.

53. **Which of the following is always composite if *x* is odd, *y* is even, and both *x* and *y* are greater than or equal to 2?**
    (Average Rigor) (Skill 3.1)

    A) $x+y$
    B) $3x+2y$
    C) $5xy$
    D) $5x+3y$

    Answer: C

    A composite number is a number which is not prime. The prime number sequence begins 2,3,5,7,11,13,17,.... To determine which of the expressions is <u>always</u> composite, experiment with different values of x and y, such as x=3 and y=2, or x=5 and y=2. It turns out that 5xy will always be an even number, and therefore, composite, if y=2.

MATHEMATICS

TEACHER CERTIFICATION STUDY GUIDE

54. What is the smallest number that is divisible by 3 and 5 and leaves a remainder of 3 when divided by 7?
    (Average Rigor) (Skill 3.1)

A) 15
B) 18
C) 25
D) 45

Answer: D

To be divisible by both 3 and 5, the number must be divisible by 15. Inspecting the first few multiples of 15, you will find that 45 is the first of the sequence that is 3 greater than a multiple of 7.

55. Find the LCM of 27, 90 and 84.
    (Easy) (Skill 3.1)

A) 90
B) 3780
C) 204120
D) 1260

Answer: B

To find the LCM of the above numbers, factor each into its prime factors and multiply each common factor the maximum number of times it occurs. Thus 27=3x3x3; 90=2x3x3x5; 84=2x2x3x7; LCM = 2x2x3x3x3x5x7=3780.

56. How many ways are there to choose a potato and two green vegetables from a choice of three potatoes and seven green vegetables?
    (Average Rigor) (Skill 4.1)

A) 126
B) 63
C) 21
D) 252

Answer: A

There are 3 slots to fill. There are 3 choices for the first, 7 for the second, and 6 for the third. Therefore, the total number of choices is 3(7)(6) = 126.

TEACHER CERTIFICATION STUDY GUIDE

57. A jar contains 3 red marbles, 5 white marbles, 1 green marble and 15 blue marbles. If one marble is picked at random from the jar, what is the probability that it will be red?
    (Easy) (Skill 4.1)

    A) 1/3
    B) 1/8
    C) 3/8
    D) 1/24

Answer: B

The total number of marbles is 24 and the number of red marbles is 3. Thus the probability of picking a red marble from the jar is 3/24=1/8.

58. If there are three people in a room, what is the probability that at least two of them will share a birthday? (Assume a year has 365 days)
    (Rigorous) (Skill 4.1)

    A) 0.67
    B) 0.05
    C) 0.008
    D) 0.33

Answer: C

The best way to approach this problem is to use the fact that
the probability of an event + the probability of the event not happening = 1.
First find the probability that no two people will share a birthday and then subtract that from one.
The probability that two of the people will not share a birthday = 364/365 (since the second person's birthday can be one of the 364 days other than the birthday of the first person).
The probability that the third person will also not share either of the first two birthdays = (364/365) * (363/365) = 0.992.
Therefore, the probability that at least two people will share a birthday = 1 – 0.992= 0.008.

MATHEMATICS

TEACHER CERTIFICATION STUDY GUIDE

59. Compute the median for the following data set:
    (Easy) (Skill 4.2)

    {12, 19, 13, 16, 17, 14}

    A) 14.5
    B) 15.17
    C) 15
    D) 16

    Answer: C

    Arrange the data in ascending order: 12,13,14,16,17,19. The median is the middle value in a list with an odd number of entries. When there is an even number of entries, the median is the mean of the two center entries. Here the average of 14 and 16 is 15.

60. Half the students in a class scored 80% on an exam, most of the rest scored 85% except for one student who scored 10%. Which would be the best measure of central tendency for the test scores?
    (Rigorous) (Skill 4.2)

    A) mean
    B) median
    C) mode
    D) either the median or the mode because they are equal

    Answer: B

    In this set of data, the median (see #59) would be the most representative measure of central tendency since the median is independent of extreme values. Because of the 10% outlier, the mean (average) would be disproportionately skewed. In this data set, it is true that the median and the mode (number which occurs most often) are the same, but the median remains the best choice because of its special properties.

TEACHER CERTIFICATION STUDY GUIDE

61. **Compute the standard deviation for the following set of temperatures.**
    (37, 38, 35, 37, 38, 40, 36, 39)
    (Easy) (Skill 4.2)

    A) 37.5
    B) 1.5
    C) 0.5
    D) 2.5

Answer: B

Find the mean: 300/8 = 37.5. Then, using the formula for standard deviation, we get

$$\sqrt{\frac{2(37.5-37)^2 + 2(37.5-38)^2 + (37.5-35)^2 + (37.5-40)^2 + (37.5-36)^2 + (37.5-39)^2}{8}}$$

which has a value of 1.5.

62. **Determine the rectangular coordinates of the point with polar coordinates (5, 60°).**
    (Average Rigor) (Skill 5.1)

    A) (0.5, 0.87)
    B) (-0.5, 0.87)
    C) (2.5, 4.33)
    D) (25, 150°)

Answer: C

Given the polar point (r, θ) = (5, 60), we can find the rectangular coordinates this way: (x,y) = $(r\cos\theta, r\sin\theta) = (5\cos 60, 5\sin 60) = (2.5, 4.33)$.

63. **Which expression is equivalent to $1 - \sin^2 x$?**
    (Rigorous) (Skill 5.1)

    A) $1 - \cos^2 x$
    B) $1 + \cos^2 x$
    C) $1/\sec x$
    D) $1/\sec^2 x$

Answer: D

Using the Pythagorean Identity, we know $\sin^2 x + \cos^2 x = 1$. Thus $1 - \sin^2 x = \cos^2 x$, which by definition is equal to $1/\sec^2 x$.

MATHEMATICS

64. Which expression is not equal to sinx?
    (Average Rigor) (Skill 5.1)

A) $\sqrt{1 - \cos^2 x}$
B) $\tan x \cos x$
C) $1/\csc x$
D) $1/\sec x$

Answer: D

Using the basic definitions of the trigonometric functions and the Pythagorean identity, we see that the first three options are all identical to sinx.
secx= 1/cosx is not the same as sinx.

65. For an acute angle x, sinx = 3/5. What is cotx?
    (Rigorous) (Skill 5.1)

A) 5/3
B) 3/4
C) 1.33
D) 1

Answer: B

Using the Pythagorean Identity, we know $\sin^2 x + \cos^2 x = 1$. Thus

$$\cos x = \sqrt{1 - \frac{9}{25}} = \frac{4}{5}; \cot x = \frac{\cos x}{\sin x} = \frac{4}{3}.$$

66. Find the following limit: $\lim_{x \to 2} \dfrac{x^2 - 4}{x - 2}$
    (Average Rigor) (Skill 5.2)

A) 0
B) Infinity
C) 2
D) 4

Answer: D

First factor the numerator and cancel the common factor to get the limit.

$$\lim_{x \to 2} \frac{x^2 - 4}{x - 2} = \lim_{x \to 2} \frac{(x - 2)(x + 2)}{(x - 2)} = \lim_{x \to 2}(x + 2) = 4$$

67. Find the following limit: $\lim_{x \to 0} \dfrac{\sin 2x}{5x}$

    (Rigorous) (Skill 5.2)

A) Infinity
B) 0
C) 1.4
D) 1

Answer: C

Since substituting x=0 will give an undefined answer, we can use L'Hospital's rule and take derivatives of both the numerator and denominator to find the limit.

$\lim_{x \to 0} \dfrac{\sin 2x}{5x} = \lim_{x \to 0} \dfrac{2\cos 2x}{5} = \dfrac{2}{5} = 1.4$

68. Find the first derivative of the function: $f(x) = x^3 - 6x^2 + 5x + 4$
    (Rigorous) (Skill 5.3)

A) $3x^3 - 12x^2 + 5x = f'(x)$
B) $3x^2 - 12x - 5 = f'(x)$
C) $3x^2 - 12x + 9 = f'(x)$
D) $3x^2 - 12x + 5 = f'(x)$

Answer: D

Use the Power Rule for polynomial differentiation: if y = ax^n, then y'=nax^{n-1}.

69. Differentiate: $y = e^{3x+2}$
    (Rigorous) (Skill 5.3)

A) $3e^{3x+2} = y'$
B) $3e^{3x} = y'$
C) $6e^3 = y'$
D) $(3x+2)e^{3x+1} = y'$

Answer: A

Use the Exponential Rule for derivatives of functions of e: if y = ae$^{f(x)}$, then y' = f'(x)ae$^{f(x)}$.

70. If the velocity of a body is given by v = 16 - t², find the distance traveled from t = 0 until the body comes to a complete stop.
    (Average Rigor) (Skill 5.3)

    A) 16
    B) 43
    C) 48
    D) 64

Answer: B

Recall that the derivative of the distance function is the velocity function. In reverse, the integral of the velocity function is the distance function. To find the time needed for the body to come to a stop when v=0, solve for t: v = 16 – t² = 0. Result: t = 4 seconds. The distance function is s = 16t - $\frac{t^3}{3}$. At t=4, s= 64 – 64/3 or approximately 43 units.

71. Find the slope of the line tangent to $y = 3x(\cos x)$ at $(\pi/2, \pi/2)$.
    (Rigorous) (Skill 5.3)

    A) $-3\pi/2$
    B) $3\pi/2$
    C) $\pi/2$
    D) $-\pi/2$

Answer: A

To find the slope of the tangent line, find the derivative, and then evaluate it at x = $\frac{\pi}{2}$. y' = 3x(-sinx)+3cosx. At the given value of x,
y' = $3(\frac{\pi}{2})(-\sin\frac{\pi}{2}) + 3\cos\frac{\pi}{2} = \frac{-3\pi}{2}$.

MATHEMATICS

TEACHER CERTIFICATION STUDY GUIDE

72. **Find the equation of the line tangent to** $y = 3x^2 - 5x$ **at** $(1, -2)$.
    (Rigorous) (Skill 5.3)

    A) $y = x - 3$
    B) $y = 1$
    C) $y = x + 2$
    D) $y = x$

Answer: A

To find the slope of the tangent line, find the derivative, and then evaluate it at x=1.

y'=6x-5=6(1)-5=1. Then using point-slope form of the equation of a line, we get y+2=1(x-1) or y = x-3.

73. **The acceleration of a particle is dv/dt = 6 m/s². Find the velocity at t=10 given an initial velocity of 15 m/s.**
    (Average Rigor) (Skill 5.3)

    A) 60 m/s
    B) 150 m/s
    C) 75 m/s
    D) 90 m/s

Answer: C

Recall that the derivative of the velocity function is the acceleration function. In reverse, the integral of the acceleration function is the velocity function. Therefore, if a=6, then v=6t+C. Given that at t=0, v=15, we get v = 6t+15. At t=10, v=60+15=75m/s.

MATHEMATICS

TEACHER CERTIFICATION STUDY GUIDE

74. How does the function $y = x^3 + x^2 + 4$ behave from $x = 1$ to $x = 3$?
    (Average Rigor) (Skill 5.3)

    A) increasing, then decreasing
    B) increasing
    C) decreasing
    D) neither increasing nor decreasing

Answer: B

To find critical points, take the derivative, set it equal to 0, and solve for x.
f'(x) = 3x² + 2x = x(3x+2)=0. CP at x=0 and x=-2/3. Neither of these CP is on the interval from x=1 to x=3. Testing the endpoints: at x=1, y=6 and at x=3, y=38. Since the derivative is positive for all values of x from x=1 to x=3, the curve is increasing on the entire interval.

75. Find the absolute maximum obtained by the function $y = 2x^2 + 3x$ on the interval $x = 0$ to $x = 3$.
    (Rigorous) (Skill 5.3)

    A) –3/4
    B) –4/3
    C) 0
    D) 27

Answer: D

Find CP at x=-.75 as done in #74. Since the CP is not in the interval from x=0 to x=3, just find the values of the functions at the endpoints. When x=0, y=0, and when x=3, y = 27. Therefore 27 is the absolute maximum on the given interval.

TEACHER CERTIFICATION STUDY GUIDE

76. **L'Hospital's rule provides a method to evaluate which of the following?**
    (Easy) (Skill 5.3)

A) Limit of a function
B) Derivative of a function
C) Sum of an arithmetic series
D) Sum of a geometric series

Answer: A

L'Hospital's rule is used to find the limit of a function by taking the derivatives of the numerator and denominator. Since the primary purpose of the rule is to find the limit, A is the correct answer.

77. **Find the antiderivative for $4x^3 - 2x + 6 = y$.**
    (Rigorous) (Skill 5.4)

A) $x^4 - x^2 + 6x + C$
B) $x^4 - 2/3x^3 + 6x + C$
C) $12x^2 - 2 + C$
D) $4/3x^4 - x^2 + 6x + C$

Answer: A

Use the rule for polynomial integration: given ax^n, the antiderivative is $\dfrac{ax^{n+1}}{n+1}$.

78. **Find the antiderivative for the function $y = e^{3x}$.**
    (Rigorous) (Skill 5.4)

A) $3x(e^{3x}) + C$
B) $3(e^{3x}) + C$
C) $1/3(e^x) + C$
D) $1/3(e^{3x}) + C$

Answer: D

Use the rule for integration of functions of e: $\int e^x dx = e^x + C$.

TEACHER CERTIFICATION STUDY GUIDE

79. **Evaluate:** $\int (x^3 + 4x - 5)dx$
    (Rigorous) (Skill 5.4)

A) $3x^2 + 4 + C$
B) $\frac{1}{4}x^4 - 2/3x^3 + 6x + C$
C) $x^{4/3} + 4x - 5x + C$
D) $x^3 + 4x^2 - 5x + C$

Answer: B

Integrate as described in #77.

80. **Evaluate** $\int_0^2 (x^2 + x - 1)dx$
    (Rigorous) (Skill 5.4)

A) 11/3
B) 8/3
C) -8/3
D) -11/3

Answer: B

Use the fundamental theorem of calculus to find the definite integral: given a continuous function f on an interval [a,b], then $\int_a^b f(x)dx = F(b) - F(a)$, where F is an antiderivative of f.

$\int_0^2 (x^2 + x - 1)dx = (\frac{x^3}{3} + \frac{x^2}{2} - x)$ Evaluate the expression at x=2, at x=0, and then subtract to get 8/3 + 4/2 – 2-0 = 8/3.

MATHEMATICS

TEACHER CERTIFICATION STUDY GUIDE

81. Find the area under the function $y = x^2 + 4$ from $x = 3$ to $x = 6$.
    (Average Rigor) (Skill 5.4)

A) 75
B) 21
C) 96
D) 57

Answer: A

To find the area set up the definite integral: $\int_{3}^{6}(x^2 + 4)dx = (\frac{x^3}{3} + 4x)$. Evaluate the expression at x=6, at x=3, and then subtract to get (72+24)-(9+12)=75.

82. Find the sum of the first one hundred terms in the progression.
    (-6, -2, 2 . . .)
    (Rigorous) (Skill 5.5)

A) 19,200
B) 19,400
C) -604
D) 604

Answer: A

To find the 100th term: t_{100} = -6 + 99(4) = 390. To find the sum of the first 100 terms: S = $\frac{100}{2}(-6 + 390) = 19200$.

TEACHER CERTIFICATION STUDY GUIDE

83. What is the sum of the first 20 terms of the geometric sequence (2,4,8,16,32,…)?
    (Average Rigor) (Skill 5.5)

    A) 2097150
    B) 1048575
    C) 524288
    D) 1048576

Answer: A

For a geometric sequence $a, ar, ar^2, ..., ar^n$, the sum of the first n terms is given by $\frac{a(r^n - 1)}{r - 1}$. In this case a=2 and r=2. Thus the sum of the first 20 terms of the sequence is given by $\frac{2(2^{20} - 1)}{2 - 1} = 2097150$.

84. Which mathematician is best known for his work in developing non-Euclidean geometry?
    (Easy) (Skill 6.1)

    A) Descartes
    B) Riemann
    C) Pascal
    D) Pythagoras

Answer: B

In the mid-nineteenth century, Reimann and other mathematicians developed elliptic geometry.

MATHEMATICS

85. **Which of the following mathematicians is known for his work in developing calculus?**
    (Easy) (Skill 6.1)

    A) Blaise Pascal
    B) Isaac Newton
    C) René Descartes
    D) Abraham de Moivre

Answer: B

Isaac Newton (along with Gottfried Leibniz, who worked independently) is largely credited with having developed calculus. Newton first published his theory of calculus in 1704 in his book *Opticks*.

XAMonline, INC. 21 Orient Ave. Melrose, MA 02176

Toll Free number 800-509-4128

TO ORDER Fax 781-662-9268 OR www.XAMonline.com

CALIFORNIA SUBJECT EXAMINATIONS – CSET – 2008

PO#   Store/School:

Address 1:

Address 2 (Ship to other):

City, State Zip

Credit card number_____-_____-_____-_____   expiration_____

EMAIL _____

PHONE   **FAX**

ISBN	TITLE	Qty	Retail	Total
978-1-58197-595-6	RICA Reading Instruction Competence Assessment			
978-1-58197-596-3	CBEST CA Basic Educational Skills			
978-1-58197-398-3	CSET French Sample Test 149, 150			
978-1-58197-622-9	CSET Spanish 145, 146, 147			
978-1-58197-803-2	CSET MSAT Multiple Subject 101, 102, 103			
978-1-58197-261-0	CSET English 105, 106, 107			
978-1-58197-049-4	CSET Foundational-Level Mathematics 110, 111			
978-1-58197-285-6	CSET Mathematics 110, 111, 112			
978-1-58197-340-2	CSET Social Science 114, 115			
978-1-58197-342-6	CSET General Science 118, 119			
978-1-58197-585-7	CSET Biology-Life Science 120, 124			
978-1-58197-395-2	CSET Chemistry 121, 125			
978-1-58197-399-0	CSET Earth and Planetary Science 122, 126			
978-1-58197-224-5	CSET Physics 123, 127			
978-1-58197-299-3	CSET Physical Education, 129, 130, 131			
978-1-58197-397-6	CSET Art Sample Subtest 140			
			SUBTOTAL	
			Ship	$8.70
			TOTAL	

www.ingramcontent.com/pod-product-compliance
Lightning Source LLC
Chambersburg PA
CBHW080541230426
43663CB00015B/2665